Flash Cinematic Techniques

Enhancing Animated Shorts and Interactive Storytelling

Chris Jackson

ELSEVIER

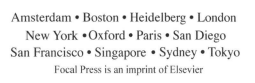
Amsterdam • Boston • Heidelberg • London
New York • Oxford • Paris • San Diego
San Francisco • Singapore • Sydney • Tokyo
Focal Press is an imprint of Elsevier

Focal Press

Focal Press is an imprint of Elsevier
30 Corporate Drive, Suite 400, Burlington, MA 01803, USA
The Boulevard, Langford Lane, Kidlington, Oxford, OX5 1GB, UK

Notices

Knowledge and best practice in this field are constantly changing. As new research and
experience broaden our understanding, changes in research methods, professional
practices, or medical treatment may become necessary.

Practitioners and researchers must always rely on their own experience and knowledge
in evaluating and using any information, methods, compounds, or experiments
described herein. In using such information or methods they should be mindful of their
own safety and the safety of others, including parties for whom they have a professional
responsibility.

To the fullest extent of the law, neither the Publisher nor the authors, contributors, or
editors, assume any liability for any injury and/or damage to persons or property as a
matter of products liability, negligence or otherwise, or from any use or operation of
any methods, products, instructions, or ideas contained in the material herein.

Library of Congress Cataloging-in-Publication Data
Application submitted

British Library Cataloguing-in-Publication Data
A catalogue record for this book is available from the British Library.

ISBN: 978-0-240-81261-8

For information on all Focal Press publications
visit our website at www.elsevierdirect.com

10 11 12 13 5 4 3 2 1

Printed in the United States of America

Contents

Chapter 4: Direct My Eye

Chapter 5: Don't Lose Me

Chapter 6: Move the Camera

Chapter 7: Light My World

Introduction

This book focuses on the visual design of a Flash movie using cinematic techniques: camera placement, composition, motion, lighting, editing, and sound. These tools not only illustrate what's going on in a scene, but also advance the story and elevate its emotional impact for the audience.

What Is This Book About?

Flash Cinematic Techniques maximizes Flash's animation and production power to create web-based animated short stories, interactive graphic novels and online commercials. From major film studios to independent animators, Flash is employed to entertain, educate, and promote stories to their audiences easily and effectively. Written for Flash artists and designers, this book provides valuable insights, timesaving practical tips, and hands-on techniques that illustrate how to produce and deploy great visual stories using Flash.

Flash Cinematic Techniques focuses primarily on enhancing a visual story from storyboards to the final project. The first chapter lays the foundation to defining a good story and how to visualize its structure. Each chapter that follows examines visual design components and translates cinematography techniques used in traditional filmmaking into the Flash environment. Using Flash as the authoring tool and the exercises outlined in this book, a reader will be able to produce animated and interactive cinematic stories, such as online graphic novels and webisodes.

The book is designed to walk the reader through project-based exercises that effectively use Flash to enhance their visual storytelling skills. The first section explores visual components used in stories. Topics include how space, line, color, and movement can be framed on the Flash Stage to communicate emotion and meaning. The second part of the book applies cinematography techniques such as camera movement, lighting, and editing into the Flash workspace.

In addition to animation techniques, **Flash Cinematic Techniques** also discusses adding interactivity using ActionScript to enhance audience participation. The last section of this book discusses optimization and publishing tips and tricks. Chapter exercises consist of practical applications as well as experimental projects. Each exercise provides step-by-step instructions and tips for the reader to use in conceptualizing and visualizing creative solutions to their own Flash projects.

Who Is This Book For?

The book explores animation and interactive concepts and techniques for designing great visual stories in Flash. The technical focus of this book is on the art direction and use of traditional cinematography techniques when building animated and interactive short stories in Flash. Although the book covers the basics in developing a story, it is assumed that the reader already has a good story in mind to "show." The visual storytelling techniques discussed can be applied to entertainment, advertising (branding), and educational applications.

The primary audience for this book is Flash animators and designers. These Flash users can be professionals in the workforce, students, or anyone interested in creatively enhancing their animated stories or interactive projects. This book assumes that readers have some prior Flash experience. They should have a working knowledge of the Flash workspace and basic animation concepts. The chapter exercises teach readers how to think creatively and get excited about animation and interactivity in enhancing visual stories using Flash.

Book Structure and Layout Conventions

Flash Cinematic Techniques is designed to walk the reader through project-based exercises that effectively apply traditional cinematography techniques in Flash to enhance animated and interactive visual stories. To use this book, you need to install Flash CS4 or higher on either your Macintosh or Windows computer. If you do not have a licensed copy, you can download fully functional time-limited trial versions from Adobe's website *(www.adobe.com)*.

Chapter exercises consist of practical applications as well as experimental projects. Each exercise provides step-by-step instructions and tips for the reader to use in conceptualizing and visualizing creative solutions to their own Flash projects. Videos used have been created in the NTSC format.

To help you get the most out of this book, let's look at the layout conventions used in the chapters.

▸ **Words in bold** refer to names of files, folders, layers, or compositions

▸ Menu selections are presented like this: **Modify > Break Apart**

▸ Code blocks in Flash are separated from the text like this:

```
// import Flash class packages
import fl.video.*;
import fl.controls.ProgressBarMode;
```

▸ Icons are used throughout the book. Here is a brief explanation of what they are and what they mean.

 CD: Reference to files on the accompanying CD-ROM

 Note: Supplemental information to the text that sheds a light on a procedure or offers miscellaneous options available to you

 Caution: Warnings that you need to read

All of the footage, source code, and files are provided on the accompanying CD-ROM found in the back of the book. Each chapter has its own folder. Inside each folder you will find the material needed to complete each exercise. Completed versions for every exercise are provided in a **Completed** folder in each chapter folder. As you work through the chapter's exercises, you can choose to manually build the project or review the finished example.

All of the material inside this book and on the CD-ROM is copyright protected. They are included only for your learning and experimentation. Please respect the copyrights. I encourage you to use your own artwork and experiment with each exercise. This is not an exact science. The specific values given in this book are suggestions. The ActionScript is used to provide a solution. If you know of a different method, by all means, use it. There are many ways to perform the same task for both applications.

About the Author

Chris Jackson is a computer graphics designer and tenured professor at Rochester Institute of Technology (RIT). He teaches a variety of graduate-level courses including 2D Computer Animation, 3D Computer Graphics, Instructional Multimedia, and Motion Graphics. Before joining the RIT faculty, Chris was a new media designer with Eastman KODAK Company, creating and delivering online instructional training via the web and CD-ROM.

Chris' professional work has received over 25 distinguished national and international awards for online communication. His areas of research include user's experience design, 2D character animation, digital storytelling, and interactive design for children. Chris continues to publish and present his research and professional work at Adobe MAX, ACM SIGGRAPH and the Society for Technical Communication (STC).

Chris is author of *Flash + After Effects* (Focal Press, February, 2008) and co-author of *Flash 3D: Animation, Interactivity and Games* (Focal Press, October 2006). His books have been translated into foreign languages.

He continues to be a Flash animator, designer, developer, and consultant for worldwide corporations and nonprofit organizations. He lectures and conducts workshops relating to interactive design and Flash animation.

Acknowledgements

This book is dedicated to my graduate students, past and present, in the Computer Graphics Design MFA program at the Rochester Institute of Technology. Thank you for your hard work, dedication, and inspiration.

This book is for my wife, Justine. Thank you for all your unconditional love, constant support, and voice talent.

This book is for my parents, Roger and Glenda. Thank you for all your love and encouragement to become an artist.

This book has taken many months to write with a lot of time and effort put into making the examples. I owe a debt of gratitude to all at Focal Press, but especially Paul Temme, Anais Wheeler, and Anne McGee. Thank you for all your support and advice in enabling me to bring this book to print.

Special thanks goes to two of my Computer Graphics Design students at RIT, Brian Kowalczyk and Karli Tucker. Thank you for graciously agreeing to let me reproduce some of your work with permission in this book. Use of their work is limited strictly to the published SWF examples provided on the CD-ROM.

Credits

The following stock images from *iStockphoto.com* were incorporated into chapter artwork to illustrate cinematic techniques:

- **Cityscape at Night**, illustration courtesy of iStockphoto, Stay Media Productions, Image #1564950
- **Cowboy in the dusk**, illustration courtesy of iStockphoto, Belkarus, Image #9481995
- **Exhaustion**, illustration courtesy of iStockphoto, id-work, Image #10507830
- **Forest Fire**, illustration courtesy of iStockphoto, Steven Foley, Image #5211596
- **Hard Cop**, illustration courtesy of iStockphoto, Bruno Cullen, Image #7839117
- **Light through a door**, illustration courtesy of iStockphoto, ALXR, Image #8685748
- **Metropolis**, illustration courtesy of iStockphoto, 4x6, Image #9207032
- **Railroad Track**, illustration courtesy of iStockphoto, Adini & Malibu Barbie, Image #8235904

For Instructors

Flash Cinematic Techniques provides hands-on exercises that demonstrate core features in Flash. As an instructor, I know you appreciate the hard work and effort that goes into creating lessons and examples for your courses. I hope you find the information and exercises useful and can adapt them for your own classes.

All that I ask is for your help and cooperation in protecting the copyrights of this book. If an instructor or student distributes copies of the source files to anyone who has not purchased the book, that violates the copyright protection. Reproducing pages from this book or duplicating any part of the CD-ROM is also a copyright infringement. If you own the book, you can adapt the exercises using your own footage and artwork without infringing copyright.

Thank you for your cooperation!

CHAPTER 1

....

Show, Don't Tell Me a Story

Animation is all about showing, not telling a story, but what makes a story good? A good story needs a compelling plot that involves appealing characters living in a believable world. Understanding the story structure and how to visualize it using Flash is the topic of this first chapter.

Anatomy of a Story

Stories always start with an idea. Ideas can come from all around you—from your imagination, personal observations, life experiences, to your dreams and nightmares. These random thoughts or observations are recorded as events. Events are then woven together to formulate the story's plot.

The plot is not the story itself; it is all of the action that takes place during the story. How the action affects the characters physically and emotionally builds a good story. The fundamental components to any story involve a character or characters in a setting, a conflict that causes change, and a resolution that depicts the consequences of the character's actions.

Take a look at the following nursery rhyme:

> *Humpty Dumpty sat on a wall;*
> *Humpty Dumpty had a great fall.*
> *All the King's horses and all the King's Men*
> *Couldn't put Humpty together again.*

Figure 1.1: *Stories involve a character in a setting, a conflict that causes change, and a resolution.*

Deceptively simplistic in nature, this nursery rhyme contains all of the necessary building blocks to tell a story (Figure 1.1). The first line establishes the main character in a setting. The second line introduces conflict by having the character fall. A change occurs with all the King's horses and men coming to Humpty's aid. The last line is the resolution; the main character remains injured as a result of his actions. The story is simple, but is it compelling? Perhaps not.

Humpty Dumpty is a one-dimensional character. He exhibits very few characteristics that an audience can relate to. Let's add some element of interest to the rhyme. What if Humpty Dumpty was warned by his mother not to sit on

Chapter 1: Show, Don't Tell Me a Story

Figure 1.2: *Adding interest to your story triggers this emotional response.*

the wall, but disobeyed? What if Humpty Dumpty was depressed and deliberately jumped? What if all the King's Horses and all the King's Men secretly conspired to get rid of Humpty (Figure 1.2)? Now the story takes on more meaning for the audience. Their curiosity is piqued as they seek out answers from the storyline.

A good story is judged by the emotional impact it has on its audience. Adding interest to your story triggers this emotional response. Audiences want to be able to relate to the characters. Once bonded, audience members experience the turmoil the characters go through by projecting themselves into the story. Audiences also anticipate the dramatic tension created by the conflict and want to know what is going to happen next. Without any emotional involvement, a story is reduced to a series of events.

Storytellers typically employ a dramatic story structure to determine when certain events will happen to achieve the greatest emotional response from the audience. This structure can be applied to a three-hour movie or to a 30-second commercial. Developed by the Greek philosopher Aristotle, it has become the narrative standard in Hollywood. Audiences are quite familiar with it and even come to expect it.

The Story Structure

The dramatic structure consists of a beginning, middle, and an end (Figure 1.3). Each act applies just the right amount of dramatic tension at the right time and in the right place. Act One is called exposition and it gives the audience information in order to understand a story. It introduces the setting, the characters, their goals, and the conflicting situation that the story is about.

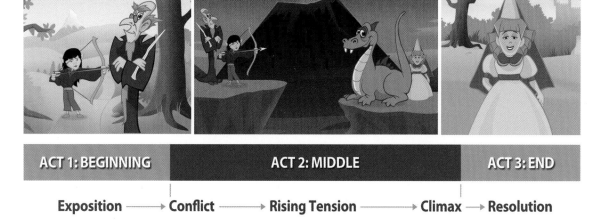

Figure 1.3: *The dramatic story structure determines when events will happen in a story.*

The setting is where and when the story takes place. When developing your story ask yourself where is the story set: on another planet? in a car? underwater? Does the story occur in the past, present, or future? With the setting in place, you next need to populate your world with characters. It is important to note that the world, its timeline and occupants, all need to be believable to the audience. That doesn't mean it has to be realistic. Walt Disney summed it up best with the term "plausible impossible." It means that it is something impossible in reality but still can be convincingly portrayed to the audience.

There are often two types of characters in a story: the hero (protagonist) and the villain (antagonist). The hero is the main character and has a strong goal that he must achieve without compromise. The villain will stop at nothing to prevent the hero from succeeding. Audiences typically root for the hero as he faces a series of ever-increasing obstacles created by the villain. The opposing goals of the hero and villain create the story's conflict.

Chapter 1: Show, Don't Tell Me a Story

Act Two focuses on the conflict. Conflict is the most important element in a story. The problems faced by the characters make the story exciting. The key to creating good conflict is to make the villain stronger than the hero at the beginning. Usually the villain is another person, but can be an animal, nature, society, a machine, or even the hero himself battling an inner conflict. Throughout the story, the villain needs to pursue his own goal as actively as the hero. Audiences love a great villain who is as complex and interesting as the hero.

If the hero can easily beat the villain, you don't have a good story. In order to engage the audience emotionally, they must empathize with the hero. The hero should be someone the audience can feel something in common with, or at least care about. Empathy links the hero's challenges and experiences to the audience. One way to do this is to give the hero certain weaknesses at the beginning of the story that can be exploited by the villain. These weaknesses drive the conflict and raise the audience's emotional connection or bond to the hero. As the character wrestles with the conflict, the audience wrestles with him and cares about the outcome (Figure 1.4).

Figure 1.4: *Empathy links the hero's challenges and experiences to the audience.*

Act Two drives the story forward raising the tension. The villain constantly creates new obstacles causing the hero to struggle towards his goal. The tension reaches a high point at the end of Act Two. This is also referred to as the climax or turning point, when the plot changes for better or for worse for the hero. During this moment, the hero takes action and brings the story to a conclusion.

Act Three is the resolution and end of the story. It resolves the conflicts that have arisen. Act Three ties together the loose ends of the story and allows the audience to learn what happened to the characters after the conflict is resolved. This is often referred to as closure. Storytellers often start developing stories by figuring out the climax or the conclusion of the story and then work their way backwards.

 *A story structure worksheet is provided in the **Chapter_01** folder for you to use when developing your story.*

This dramatic structure provides a framework for a story. Stories created in Flash tend to be less complex than feature films or even television shows. Usually these are short stories that focus on only one incident, have a single plot, a single setting, a couple of characters, and cover a short period of time.

As you begin developing your story in Flash, decide what the audience needs to know and when to add the dramatic tension. Start by showing a path for the audience to follow. Give them visual clues to what is going on in the opening scene. With the compressed format in Flash, it makes cutting to the chase all the more essential.

Make Every Scene Count

Understanding story and its structure is important, but you are working in a visual medium. As a visual storyteller, you can enhance a story's emotional experience by showing how a story unfolds through a sequence of images. However, creating beautiful imagery is not enough if the visuals do not reinforce the story's narrative or meet the audience's expectations.

For each scene in your story, you need to visually answer the following three questions that audience members ask. They are:

1. **What is going on?**

2. **Who is involved?**

3. **How should I feel?**

Most stories created in Flash range from 30 seconds to two minutes in duration. That is not a lot of time to divulge a complex plot. You need to make every scene count by either advancing the story or developing the characters. It is best to throw the audience into the action after the title scene and create enough tension to start the audience worrying about the characters. Director Alfred Hitchcock strongly believed in giving his audience just the right amount of information to get them involved with the story. Hitchcock's "bomb theory" is widely referenced as a good visual storytelling technique in building suspense (Figure 1.5).

Chapter 1: Show, Don't Tell Me a Story

Figure 1.5: *Alfred Hitchcock's applied his "Bomb Theory" to his films to add suspense.*

The theory illustrates the difference between suspense and surprise. An audience would view two people having a conversation seated in a café as an ordinary scene, nothing special. The scene doesn't offer much to the audience in terms of involvement or participation. Then all of a sudden, "Boom!" There is an explosion. The audience is in shock for about 15 seconds. They had no prior warning about a bomb, but what if they did?

Rewind the scene back to the two people talking in the café. This time show the audience that there is a bomb underneath the table. Show the audience that it will explode at one o'clock. Show a clock on the wall behind the two people; the time is five minutes to one. What happens to the audience?

Figure 1.6: *Knowing more information than the characters is a way to get the audience closer to your story.*

The audience's involvement in the scene becomes much greater than before. They know more information than the characters and want to warn them. The scene's sequence of images (bomb, the timer, and the clock on the wall) serves as a visual tool to draw the audience closer into the story (Figure 1.6). Hitchcock wasn't called the Master of Suspense for no reason.

Show, Don't Tell

The best rule to follow when visualizing a story is to always show, don't tell. At the beginning of your story, it is important that the audience knows some information in order to understand the story. In Act One, the exposition will often have information about events that happened before the story began. Exposition gets the audience up to speed on the setting and the characters.

An inherent problem with exposition is that you could have too much and potentially bog down your story before you ever get to the action. This is where visual storytelling can truly shine. Let's take a look at another Hitchcock example. In his film *Rear Window* (1954), the protagonist spies on his neighbors through his apartment window and becomes involved in a murder mystery. The opening scene is a masterful example of using visuals to "show" the story without saying a word to the audience (Figure 1.7).

Hitchcock starts the scene by showing the New York apartment building where the protagonist lives. The audience sees the cast of characters in each of their apartments going about their daily routine. The camera travels inside the protagonist's apartment to show him asleep in his wheelchair and the thermometer at 90°. The camera moves down his left leg to show that it is in a full cast. His

Figure 1.7: *Exposition gets the audience up to speed on the settings and the characters.*

name, L.B. Jefferies (played by actor Jimmy Stewart), is on the cast. The camera moves around Jefferies' apartment to show his smashed camera, the amazing shot that broke both the camera and his leg, and finally a positive and negative photograph of a female model on the cover of a glamour magazine.

The dialogue-free exposition sets the audience up for all of the events that occur later in the film. It is the camera's movement in composing the scene that shows the protagonist, his profession as a photographer, his physical weakness that leads to his voyeurism, the neighbors that he spies on, and a hint about his love life played by actress Grace Kelly. In visual storytelling, this is often referred to as planting information that the audience absorbs without even being aware of doing so. When the information gives meaning to events later in the story it is referred to as payoffs.

Another good example of a plant and payoff occurs in the movie *Raiders of the Lost Ark* (1981). The hero, Indiana Jones, physically shows the audience he has a fear of snakes in the beginning of the film. The audience finds the scene humorous because the hero just survived an entire tribe of warriors trying to kill him only to wimp out over a snake on a plane. The payoff comes later in the film when Indy's quest leads him to a tomb filled with thousands of snakes. He must make a decision to face his fears in order to achieve his goal of retrieving the Ark of the Covenant. Of course it's also a great suspense builder making the descent into the tomb scarier because the audience feels and sees Indy's revulsion.

Sometimes there is just too much exposition to show and you need to tell it to the audience using text or voice-over narration (Figure 1.8). *Star Wars* (1977) is a great example of using text to tell the audience all the background information on the characters and setting at the beginning of the story. The episode starts with scrolling paragraphs of text explaining the entire back story that has led to this moment. Then the action begins.

Figure 1.8: *Sometimes you need to tell the exposition to the audience using text.*

Voice-over narration is effectively used in *The Shawshank Redemption* (1994). The story is narrated by an inmate named Red (played by actor Morgan Freeman) set in a fictional penitentiary in Maine. His narration throughout the film provides the emotional connection between the audience and the protagonist, Andy Dufresne (played by actor Tim Robbins).

In addition to exposition, visual elements can also enhance transitions between acts in the story. In *The Wizard of Oz* (1939), the protagonist, Dorothy (played by actress Judy Garland), is introduced as a farm girl who lives in Kansas with

Figure 1.9: *Color has become an effective tool to draw the audience into the story.*

Chapter 1: Show, Don't Tell Me a Story

her aunt and uncle. Kansas is shown in a sepia tone. The color symbolizes the drabness of the setting. After a tornado whisks Dorothy away, over the rainbow, to the Land of Oz she tells the audience, "We're not in Kansas anymore." Color is used to reinforce that plot point. The color transitions from sepia tones used in Act One to full Technicolor glory at the beginning of Act Two.

Over the years, the use of color has become an effective visual tool to draw the audience into the story. Steven Spielberg's film *Schindler's List* (1993) is primarily in black and white. However, in one scene a little girl is shown wearing a red coat. Through contrast in color, the audience's attention is immediately drawn to her as she wanders alone amid the horrors of World War II.

The red symbolizes the protagonist's (played by actor Liam Neeson) awareness to the cruelty being committing against the Jews. Audiences visually and emotionally connect with the girl and search for her red coat in scenes that follow (Figure 1.9). Will she be saved? Sadly, the sight of her red-tinted coat among the dead becomes one of the film's most harrowing images.

Based on these examples, you can see that movies are an excellent resource for learning more about visual storytelling. Before you start designing your story in Flash, watch some of your favorite movies. Mute the audio so you can focus exclusively on the story's imagery. If you can, pause the movie on a frame that you find visually appealing.

Study its composition, use of color, and camera placement. Subsequent chapters in this book will discuss these cinematic tools in depth. For now, sketch out the visual structure you find effective in "showing" the story you are watching.

Figure 1.10: *Sketch out the composition of scenes you find appealing in movies.*

Remember, one of the goals in creating your Flash story is to have people watch it. Once you have a good story you need to show as much as possible to your audience rather than tell them. Each scene must clearly illustrate to the audience what is going on, who is involved, and how they should feel about what they are seeing. Meeting the audience's emotional expectations is achieved through your creativity and art direction. So what visual style works well in Flash?

Find Your Artistic Direction in Flash

Animation captivates its audience through the magic of making things move from static images. It is a very dynamic art form with varying artistic styles. Animation can be achieved through traditional (hand-drawn) animation, stop-motion, and 2D and 3D computer animation. Flash was originally designed to create 2D computer-generated animation for the web.

2D animation techniques and tools have changed considerably over time. The early pioneers in animation drew a sequence of images and then photographed them in order to create the motion. Today, Adobe Flash is packaged with automated computerized versions of traditional animation techniques such as tweening, morphing, and onion skinning. Its format and workspace allows you to save a considerable amount of time and therefore reduce a project's budget.

Figure 1.11: *Vector art uses math to store and create an image making it resolution-independent.*

Flash is well known for its inherent visual look which is vector-based. Vector art uses math to store and create an image. This makes the artwork resolution-independent. It can be scaled without losing any detail. As a result, vector-based artwork produces rather small file sizes that are ideal for web delivery. The only drawback to using vectors is that the artwork becomes less photorealistic and more mechanical, potentially losing the organic feel of traditional hand-drawn animation.

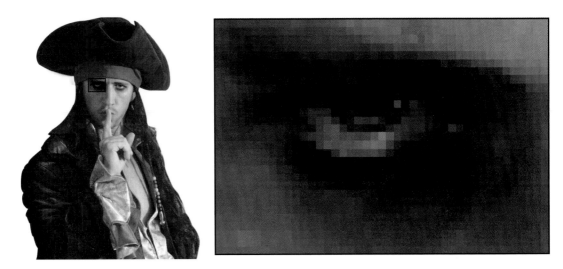

Figure 1.12: *Raster graphics are made up of tiny units called pixels.*

Raster graphics, also called bitmaps, are made up of tiny units called pixels. Pixels are grouped together in a grid that forms the image. The resulting image can be photorealistic but larger in file size.

Another drawback to raster images is scalability. If a raster graphic is scaled too large, the pixel grid will become noticeable, creating a pixellated image (Figure 1.12). If the raster image is optimized properly, Flash can produce outstanding photo-collage animation, often referred to as cutout animation (Figure 1.13).

Figure 1.13: *Paper, fabric, and photographs can be used to create characters.*

Figure 1.14: *Limited animation uses a non-realistic style that depicts caricatures rather than lifelike representations.*

Cutout animation is a technique for creating collaged characters and backgrounds from materials such as paper, fabric, or photographs that were scanned into the computer. The animated TV series *South Park* and *JibJab Media (www. jibjab.com)* online are two great examples of computerized cutout animation. When viewing this style of animation you will notice that the movements of the collaged parts are never as fluid as in traditional animation. This is sometimes called "limited animation."

In the 1950s TV animators began experimenting with a new artistic style that focused more on design than realism. United Productions of America, better known as UPA, was one of the first American animation studios to abandon the realistic approach perfected by Walt Disney in favor of stylized design. The first UPA animation, *Gerald McBoing-Boing* (1951), was visually like nothing audiences had seen before. The theatrical cartoon won an Academy Award for Best Animated Short and was a major step in the development of limited animation.

The visual style uses abstract art, symbolism, and limited movement to achieve the same storytelling effect of high-end animation but with lower production costs (Figure 1.14). Though cost-cutting measures abused the art form in later years, *Gerald McBoing-Boing* and other UPA animated shorts were meant as an artistic exercise rather than a quick way of producing cheap cartoons.

The process of limited animation reduces the overall number of drawings. Static and sequences of images are used over and over again. For example, animators only have to draw a character walking once. Characters are split up into different parts on separate layers. Only portions of a character, such as the mouth or an arm, animate at a time. If you watch any cartoons from the 1960s and '70s produced by Hanna-Barbera (*Scooby-Doo, Yogi Bear*) you will see clever choices in camera angles, editing, and the use of camera techniques such as panning to suggest movement.

Flash, with its reusable symbols, tweening features, and the need to reduce file size for the web, is the perfect application for producing limited animation. The word "limited" doesn't mean inferior in terms of animation. It is important to understand the concept of limited animation because it dictates how you design your characters, props, and backgrounds for it.

Whichever visual style you choose for your story, there are many ways to make the artwork in Flash rich with spontaneity and life. The next chapter examines different techniques that can help you to design characters in Flash that are dynamic and appealing to your audience.

Summary

Today, Flash has revolutionized the animation production process by building on the limited animation techniques used in the past. It has become a professional tool for developing high-quality animation for the web and broadcast. A typical production pipeline for a Flash animation is shown in Figure 1.15.

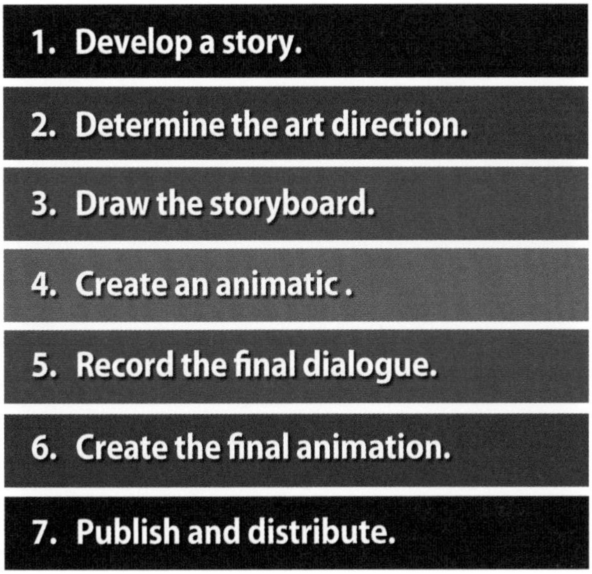

1. **Develop a story.**

2. **Determine the art direction.**

3. **Draw the storyboard.**

4. **Create an animatic .**

5. **Record the final dialogue.**

6. **Create the final animation.**

7. **Publish and distribute.**

Figure 1.15: *The production pipeline for a typical Flash animation*

This completes the chapter on story, its structure, and how to begin to "show," not tell, it to your audience. A good story is judged by the emotional impact it has on its audience. Understanding its structure is a key factor in making your stories great. Most animation begins with the development of a story.

Once your story is developed, the next step is to determine the "look," or art direction of your Flash story. The best thing about Flash is that it allows artists to show their stories in any style they can imagine. Will your characters be hand-drawn and scanned into Flash? Created from stock photography? Self created directly in Flash? The next chapter explores each of these techniques to help you decide which artistic vision best illustrates your story.

CHAPTER 2

....

Get into Character

The key to an effective story is the appeal of its characters. Characters come in all shapes and sizes. Creating a unique and compelling character often begins with a distinct look. This chapter explores character design and how to effectively incorporate different visual styles in Flash.

What is your character going to look like? The answer is completely up to you. Character design is an art form unto itself. As you read in Chapter 1, there are different artistic directions that can be used in Flash. This chapter is not going to promote one specific direction to follow over another. Instead, let's look at some basic guidelines that, if used, will improve your character designs in Flash.

Casting the Characters

During the pre-production stage in film, the producer, director and writer determine the type of actor they need to cast for each character's role. You must perform a similar casting by creating a mental image of each character that visualizes its unique physical characteristics.

Before you start sketching out your characters, reread the story you have chosen to animate or make interactive. Answer the following questions that your audience will want to know:

- What is the character's physical body makeup?
- Two arms and two legs? Four legs? Eight tentacles?
- Does the character resemble a person, an animal, a plant, an object, or something no one has ever seen before?
- Is the character's body thin, overweight, muscular, or soft?
- Is the character tall, short, or hunched over?
- Is the character male, female, or something else?
- Does the character walk, slither, fly, or swim?
- What colors identify the character?
- What type of clothes does the character wear, if any?

After picturing the visual look, think about the character in regards to the animation capabilities and limitations in Flash. When casting your character for the Flash Stage, ask yourself:

- Is the character the center of interest or merely a prop?
- How big is the character in relation to the other characters? The background? The props?
- Does the character animate? How much does the character move?
- Will the audience see the character from different angles?
- Does the character speak?

The goal is to design an appealing character for the audience plus have the design be conducive to Flash. To do this, compare the visual look to the technical capabilities in Flash. If the character is seen from multiple angles, you need to create these additional views, which takes time. Knowing if a character animates or speaks will impact the complexity of the design. The simpler the design, the easier it is to animate.

Flash cartoon characters are often composed of several layers. It is good practice to create a different layer for each body part. The benefit you gain is more flexibility in adjusting or changing your character. If you plan to animate, the layers provide you the ability to fine-tune each part's movement. The number of layers is up to you.

The best advice when working in Flash is to simplify when possible. That doesn't mean create stick figures; no offense to stick figures. The word "simplify" means design clarity. There should always be a minimum amount of detail, no more than you need to recognize the character clearly.

Remember the old saying, "The devil is in the details." The audience will be able to identify each character based on their general look and not by the number of hairs on their head or freckles on their face. So, where do you start?

Figure 2.1: *Simplify your design. The simpler the design, the easier to animate in Flash.*

Shaping Up

Simplify the design by building your characters out of basic shapes. Look at the world around you; you should be able to distinguish squares, rectangles, circles, ovals, and triangles present in almost everything you see. These basic shapes become the building blocks for your character's design.

These shapes can also help the audience understand what type of character it is. Each shape subliminally conveys a different personality trait. The shapes you choose become the underlying structure for your character's makeup and personality. Let's take a look at some character designs using basic shapes.

Squares and Rectangles

Characters built primarily out of rectangles tend to be big, muscular jocks, superheroes, bullies, and military characters. Square and rectangular shapes suggest strength, dependability and also unintelligent, as in the phrase "blockhead." Figure 2.2 illustrates how the tough guy was built using cubes.

Figure 2.2: *Rectangular shapes suggest strength.*

Circles and Ovals

Circular shapes are used for characters with small bodies, for example, children. Familiar cartoon characters such as Charlie Brown and the Power Puff Girls have heads made out of one big circle. A character constructed out of circular, round shapes appears soft, cuddly and non-threatening (Figure 2.3).

Figure 2.3: *Rounded shapes suggest cute, cuddly and non-threatening.*

Transforming a circular shape can create different meanings for the audience. If a circle is stretched, the oval shape could be considered for a character that is goofy or thin. If the circle is squashed, it could suggest that the character is jolly and/or overweight.

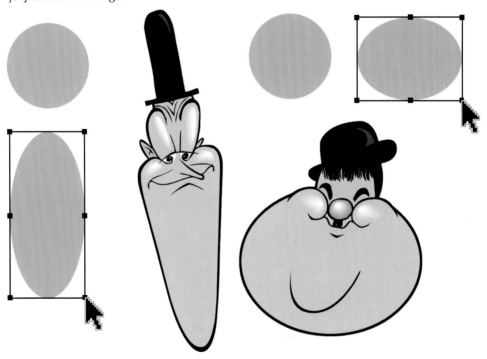

Figure 2.4: *Transforming the sphere shape can imply different personality traits.*

Triangular Shapes

Similar to rectangles, triangluar shapes can be used for strong characters that have a chiseled jawbone structure or a really large neck. If the triangle is turned upside down, the resulting shape can be used for female characters (Figure 2.5) or nerdy characters that lack self-confidence.

Figure 2.5: *Triangular shapes can suggest strong characters or just the opposite.*

These shapes are by no means your limit in character design. Use them as a starting point. Remember, you can stretch, squash, poke, pull, and combine these shapes together to build your character. Two spheres can create a bean or pear shape that is a common design used in animation. A cone can be morphed into a teardrop shape.

Start sketching your characters to determine which shapes best suits them. The possibilities are endless (Figure 2.6). Don't worry about making mistakes. Accidents can become interesting facets of your character's design. Look over your sketches and note which aspects of the character's design you would like to keep and which you can ignore.

Creating Model Sheets

Once you have decided on a basic design for your character, practice drawing its body and several poses. Personality is expressed through the character's posture and movement. As you assemble your character, create a model sheet. Character model sheets detail the visual design of a character from a variety

Figure 2.6: *Experiment with the basic shapes to determine which shape best suits your character design.*

of angles and poses. Think about who your character is and what actions they perform in the story. Then sketch out a series of action poses (Figure 2.7).

Figure 2.7: *The line of action defines the character's posture and movement.*

Figure 2.8: *A character turnaround illustrates its construction and proportion.*

Similar to a gestural drawing, sketch a line of action for each pose. This is an imaginary line that travels through the entire figure from the top of the head, down the spine, and out through the hands and feet. Its curvature defines the character's posture and movement.

The line of action should always be sweeping curves or diagonal lines that are active. Avoid drawing vertical lines as they stiffen the character and make it uninteresting to the audience. The more curved the line of action is, the more dynamic the character's pose will be. Chapter 8 explores Flash character animation techniques and staging in more detail.

For now, keep your sketch loose to capture the action of the pose. Once the line of action is established, add your basic shapes to it. Use three dimensional forms with axis lines. Axis lines act like a wire frame to help you see the dimension.

Connect the forms using simple lines to build the body structure. Attach the legs and hips to the bottom of the body. Draw cylindrical shapes for the arms that end in spheres at the shoulder. The neck is added on the front side of the body not centered. The details, such as clothes, are the last elements you add to a character design.

A model sheet typically contains a number of rough sketches that bring your character to life. In addition to the poses, draw the character from all views:

front, back, three-quarter, and profile. This is also referred to as a character turnaround or character rotation. These views help you understand the character's construction and proportion (Figure 2.8).

Keep in mind the subliminal connotations associated with each shape. If your character is soft and delicate, build its body out of round shapes. The more hard edges and angles in the design, the more the character will be seen as active, aggressive, dominant, and sometimes evil. Villains are often angular in design. Study the classic Disney villains such as Cruella De Vil from *101 Dalmatians* (1961), Jafar from *Aladdin* (1992), and Hades from *Hercules* (1997).

This is not to say that you have to make a stereotypical character. We all carry mental pictures of what different types of characters should look like. Theses stereotypes have been ingrained in us through the constant bombardment of television, movies, books, and the web. Be aware of these preconceptions before you design your characters. They can, in fact, work to your advantage.

Adopting Stereotypes

If you were shown an image of a young man in a ten-gallon hat, wearing chaps and jingling spurs you would recognize the character as a cowboy. The class nerd wears glasses held together with tape, has a pocket protector in his plaid shirt, and wears pants hiked up past his belly button. Not all scientists have a bald head, a mustache, and wear a white lab coat but this image is a generally accepted stereotype (Figure 2.9).

Figure 2.9: *Generally accepted stereotype for a cowboy and a mad scientist.*

These stereotypes are caricatures that audiences associate with. A caricature exaggerates or distorts distinguishing features of a person or thing to create an easily identifiable likeness. It captures the essence of the character by accenting only the details that are visually defining. So what goes into making a stereo-typical character?

Think about the character's body. In addition to its face, the character's posture often suggests its demeanor. A happy-go-lucky character can be portrayed as round, openly expressive with an upright stance. An irritable, down-right nasty character can be shown crouched over with shriveled features and a defiant posture (Figure 2.10).

Figure 2.10: *The character's posture suggests its demeanor.*

Clothes also make the character. In general, the happier the character is, the lighter, brighter, and more colorful its clothes usually are. Conversely, a gloomy character is often drawn in dark, ill-fitting clothes that stick to its body. Cloth-ing can indentify the character's occupation such as a police officer, chef, doctor, fireman, and so on. Clothing also places characters in their historical context.

Don't just copy a stereotype, expand on it. Sometimes it is good to break all the rules and go against the accepted stereotype. For example, the character Sulley from *Monsters Inc.* (2001) is a huge, furry monster with sharp teeth, but his personality is that of a gentle giant that wouldn't harm a fly.

Remember to think about these attributes when designing your characters. Since stories animated in Flash tend to be short in duration, you would do your-

Figure 2.11: *Clothing can establish the character's occupation and the historical timeline they live in.*

self a favor in considering adopting these "types." Your audience will accept the storyline more quickly when the characters are familiar and easily identifiable.

Visually, each character in your story should be unique with distinct physical details. Watch any cartoon or animated film. Do the characters look like real humans or animals? No. There is some degree of caricature present to make each character stand out. Exaggeration is the key to individuality.

Exaggerating Personality

Just like there are different types of people, there are different types of characters. Exaggerating the defining features of your character helps the audience to identify its type. Character types include the following:

- ▸ Cute as a Button
- ▸ The Girl Next Door
- ▸ Tough Guy
- ▸ The Average Joe or Jane
- ▸ Mad Scientist
- ▸ Grumpy Old Man
- ▸ The Nerd
- ▸ The Rebel
- ▸ The Comic Relief

Your character should always look the part. For example, if you are designing a cute character, it typically is constructed out of round shapes with the proportions of a baby. They have chubby arms and legs. The proportion of the head is often larger than the overall height of the body.

Tough guys have an overly expanded chest, huge shoulders, and bulging biceps. Their heads sit low on the body with no neck visible. Small legs draw attention to the massive upper body. The exaggeration in correct human body proportions is an important concept to understand when creating exaggerated caricatures.

Basic Character Proportions

The average human adult is about six to eight heads tall. What does that mean? Take a look a Figure 2.12. Use the character's head as a unit of measurement; stack a bunch of heads on top of each other. An adult human character would be six to eight of those heads tall including the head of the character.

Figure 2.12: *Use the character's head as a unit of measurement.*

The age and gender of your character determines how many heads tall the character should be. The unit of measurement doesn't change; it's always based on the height of your character's head. A child has a much smaller head ratio of about two to three. A mother is about five to seven heads tall.

Remember that this is a general rule for characters that mimic human proportions. If you are creating more of a caricature, you do not need to fit the character exactly within these dimensions but it does give you a starting point that you can use.

Contrasting Characters

If you are building more than one character, keep in mind that they all need to live together in the same environment. In order to get along, all characters should share a fairly similar visual style. A good way to see this is to line them all up next to one another. Make a size comparison chart that show's each character's size relative to the other characters in the story. The end result looks something like a police line-up (Figure 2.13).

Figure 2.13: *Create a character size comparison chart to make sure they all share the same visual style.*

Having a similar visual style does not mean that you have to forego contrast. There is truth in the saying, "Opposites attract." If all your characters shared the same physical build with the only difference in design being clothes, who would you focus on more? Audiences need to be intrigued by your character's individuality and contrast is a good method to use.

Two characters that contrast well against each other are always more interesting than two characters who are exactly the same. As you read in Chapter 1, stories have a least two characters, or two sides to a character. Think about popular cartoon duos: Tom and Jerry, Yogi Bear and Boo Boo, Snoopy and Woodstock. Both characters differed in physical height, build and color.

Using Color

Let's focus on color. Certain colors communicate information about a character. It is generally accepted that red can be passionate and sometimes dangerous. Blue is cold and masculine, while a lighter shade can be perceived as feminine. Yellow conveys a sense of being cheerful, bright, and it is eye catching.

Figure 2.14: *What does each character's color communicate?*

The color green symbolizes healthy and alive. Purple is associated with royalty. Orange is warm and inviting. Neutral grays are rather dark and mysterious. The color brown is considered earthy and old. Be aware of these color connotations in designing your characters because the audience will pick up on their meanings subconsciously. What about black?

To make sure your character stands out in the crowd fill in its outline using black. Only using positive and negative space removes all detail except the defining outline of the character. A memorable character can be reduced to a silhouette, and still be immediately recognizable (Figure 2.15).

Figure 2.15: *A memorable character can be immediately recognized through its silhouette.*

German filmmaker Lotte Reiniger is a pioneer in silhouette animation. Her 65-minute film *Die Abenteuer des Prinzen Achmed* (*The Adventures of Prince Achmed*) is widely considered to be the world's first animated feature. Her method of animation was simple.

Lotte cut out a character's body parts from black paper and joined the parts together using wire hinges. The figure was then arranged on a horizontal glass table lit from below. A camera directly overhead exposed one frame of film at a time. After a slight modification in the position of the figure, another frame was exposed. Her visual style was an expressive use of shape, form, and positive and negative space.

Going Graphic

The artistic style of the United Productions of America (UPA) cartoons in the 1950s favored a more graphical design approach than a realistic one. Their cartoons revolutionized a whole new approach in visual storytelling. Popular cartoons shown today (*Cow and Chicken, Edd 'n Eddy, Dexter's Laboratory, The Grim Adventures of Billy & Mandy*) on the Cartoon Network and Nickelodeon push the graphic boundaries established by UPA to the extreme.

Instead of building the characters out of various primitive objects, this style focuses more on using interesting shapes that define the character's outline (Figure 2.16). The outlines are created using thick, bold strokes with thinner lines used for detail. Detail is optimized to keep only what is necessary to identify the character.

Figure 2.16: *Focus on using interesting shapes that define your character.*

Even though these thick outlines create rather flat imagery, attention is given to contrasting straight and curved lines. This gives the character a more dynamic look. Flash designers have adopted this graphic style because its simplicity in design lends itself well to Flash's built in tools and animating capabilities.

Assembling the Cast in Flash

From your various sketches, model sheets, and turnarounds, it is time to assemble the character in Flash. There are many ways to do this. The following exercises provide some tips and techniques in building your characters to use in animation, interactive projects, or as mascots for branding design.

As mentioned in the introduction, this book assumes that you have a working knowledge of Flash, its workspace and drawing tools. Feel free to substitute your own artwork in place of what is provided on the CD-ROM. Let's get started.

*Locate the **Chapter_02** folder on the CD-ROM. Copy this folder to your hard drive. The folder contains all the files needed to complete the chapter exercises.*

Exercise 1: From Paper to Pixels to Vectors

In traditional hand-drawn animation, a character's outlines were inked and then filled with color and shading. It was a tedious and time-consuming job with thousands of hand painted cels. Flash has simplified the process digitally through its easy-to-use Pencil, Brush, and Paint Bucket Tool. The ability to create reusable symbols also helps reduce production time and costs.

Figure 2.17 illustrates the process used in creating the character used in this exercise. First, a rough pencil sketch was drawn to define the basic shapes. The outlines were then cleaned up using a black pen. The outlined character was scanned into Photoshop at 300 dpi to retain as much detail as possible.

Figure 2.17: *Evolution of a Flash cartoon character*

In Photoshop, the Brightness and Contrast controls were adjusted to create a high-contrast image. The image size was changed to a resolution of 72 dots-per-inch (dpi). Why? That is the resolution displayed by the computer monitor, television set, and video recorder.

The scan was then saved as a JPEG image at maximum quality. That takes care of the paper-to-pixels portion. Now you will finish the character in Flash.

01_ImportCharacter

1. Locate and open **01_ImportCharacter.fla** located in the **Chapter_02** folder that you copied from the CD-ROM. It contains one, empty layer labeled scan.

2. Select **File > Import > Import to Stage** to open the Import dialog box.

3. Locate the **01_CharacterScan.jpg** file in the **Assets** folder in **Chapter_02**. Click **Open**. The scanned bitmap image appears on the Stage.

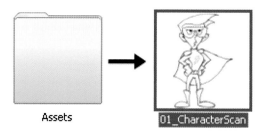

Assets   01_CharacterScan

Figure 2.18: *Import the scanned artwork to the Flash Stage.*

4. Lock the **scan** layer. Click the dot directly under the padlock symbol. Get into the habit of locking the layer that holds your scanned artwork. This prevents you from accidentally moving or drawing on the wrong layer.

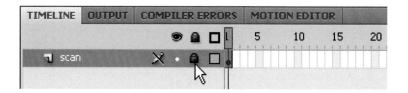

Figure 2.19: *Lock the layer that holds the scanned JPEG image.*

5. Now that you have successfully imported the original artwork you can begin the process of tracing it.

   ▶ Create a new layer directly above the original artwork layer by clicking on the **New Layer** icon at the base of the Timeline panel.

   ▶ This will be the base layer to start your drawing. Double-click on the layer name and rename it to **head**.

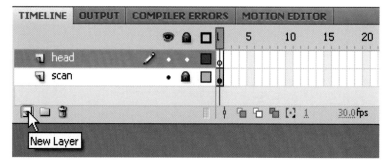

Figure 2.20: *Create a new layer to start tracing the character in Flash.*

6. Go to the Tools panel. Set the **Stroke Color** to a medium pink color (**#CC6666**) and set the Fill color to no fill.

7. Select the Pencil Tool. The keyboard shortcut is **Y**. At the bottom of the Tools panel, click on **Smooth** from the Pencil Mode options. This option automatically smoothes your strokes while retaining the basic shape you intended to create.

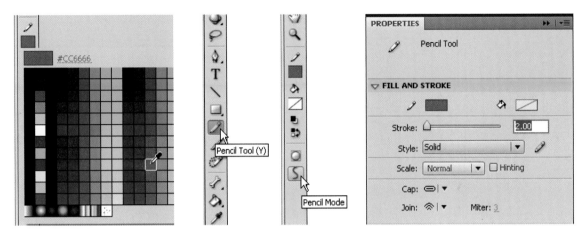

Figure 2.21: *Settings for the Pencil Tool.*

8. Go to the Properties panel. Set the **Stroke** value to **2**.

9. With the Pencil Tool still selected, carefully trace around the outline of the head. Make sure you are drawing on the **head** layer. Don't worry about accuracy and staying on the lines.

Figure 2.22: *Trace around the head using the Pencil Tool. Don't worry too much about staying on the line; you will correct that in the following steps.*

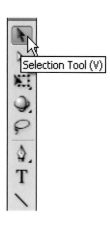

Selection Tool (V)

10. Select the Selection Tool (**V**). Hover the cursor over the stroke and you will notice the cursor change and have a curved line next to it.

   ▶ Click and drag the stroke by pressing and holding the left mouse button.

   ▶ Adjust the stroke to match the outline of the scanned character as best as possible (Figure 2.23).

Figure 2.23: *Use the Selection Tool to adjust the curves of the stroke.*

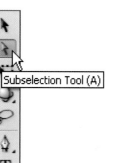

Subselection Tool (A)

11. Select the Subselection Tool (**A**). Click on the stroke to see the points that make up the shape. The more points an object contains, the bigger the file size of the project. Flash always seems to over compensate the number points needed. You can easily reduce the number of points and still maintain the shape you desire.

   ▶ Remove points by clicking and deleting them. Use the Bezier handles to adjust the stroke's shape as necessary (Figure 2.24).

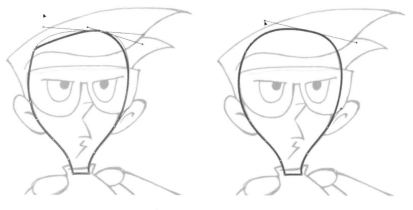

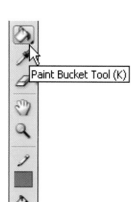

Paint Bucket Tool (K)

Figure 2.24: *Use the Subselection Tool to delete unwanted points and to adjust the stroke's curve.*

12. Go to the Tools panel and change the **Fill Color** to a pale pink color (**#FFCDCD**).

13. Select the Paint Bucket Tool (**K**). Click inside the stroke outline to fill it with your chosen skin tone. *Note:* If you have problems with the fill, first check whether you have the head layer as your active layer by clicking on its name on the Timeline. Then check also to see if the entire stroke is connected from end to end.

Chapter 2: Get into Character

14. Once you have completed the shape, select both the fill and stroke by double-clicking anywhere in the head's pink fill color.

15. Select **Modify > Convert to Symbol**. This opens the **Convert to Symbol** dialog box.

   ‣ Enter **Boy_Front_Head** as the symbol's name.
   ‣ Select **Graphic** as the symbol type.
   ‣ Click on the center square for the registration point.
   ‣ Click **OK**.

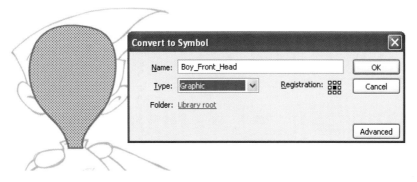

Figure 2.25: *Convert the head shape into a graphic symbol.*

Why convert the shape into a graphic symbol? Symbols allow shapes and objects to be reusable without impacting the overall file size. Graphic symbols also enable you to see its nested animation play when you scrub the playhead back and forth on the Timeline. Contents in a movie clip symbols do not play beyond Frame 1 unless you test your movie or publish it as an SWF file. Flash animators often place an entire animation inside a graphic symbol's Timeline.

16. Once you have converted the head shape into a graphic symbol, lock the layer. Create a new layer above it to draw the character's eyes. Double-click on the layer name and rename it **eyes**.

17. Notice the **head** layer obscures the original scanned artwork. One way to hide the layer is to click on the colored square next to the lock symbol dot. This is the **Layer Outline** toggle that switches the head layer to an outlined shape, allowing you to see the artwork underneath.

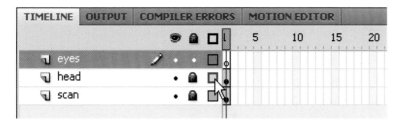

Figure 2.26: *Turn on the **Layer Outline** for the **head** layer in the Timeline.*

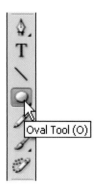

18. Now that the head shape layer is an outline, go to the Tools panel and change the **Fill Color** to white (**#FFFFFF**). Leave the **Stroke Color** set to medium pink.

19. Select the Oval Tool (**O**). Make sure the eyes layer is selected in the Timeline.

   ▶ Position the cursor at the bottom left corner of the right eye in the scanned image.

   ▶ Click and drag up and to the left with the mouse to create the eye shape.

Figure 2.27: Draw an oval for the character's right eye.

20. Select the Line Tool (**N**). Position the cursor over the right eye lid and draw a diagonal line across the top of the oval shape. Delete the top part of the oval.

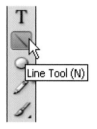

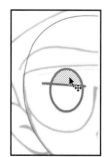

Figure 2.28: Use the Line Tool to create the top of the character's eye lid.

21. Select both the shape's fill and stroke of the eye. Select **Modify > Convert to Symbol**. The **Convert to Symbol** dialog box opens.

   ▶ Enter **Boy_Front_Eye** as the symbol's name.

   ▶ Select **Graphic** as the symbol type.

   ▶ Click on the center square for the registration point.

   ▶ Click **OK**.

22. While the eye symbol is still selected on the Stage, hold down the **Option (Mac)/Alt (Windows)** key and click and drag it to create a duplicate copy.

23. With the duplicate copy selected, select **Modify > Transform > Flip Horizontally**. Position the duplicate eye over the left eye in the scan. Lock the **eyes** layer.

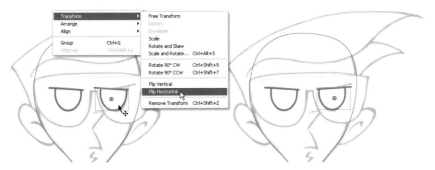

Figure 2.29: *Duplicate the eye symbol. Flip the duplicate horizontally.*

24. Create a new layer above the **eyes** layer. Double-click on the layer name and rename it **pupils**.

25. Go to the Tools panel and change the **Fill Color** to a light blue (**#6699CC**). Set the **Stroke Color** to no stroke.

26. Select the Oval Tool (**O**). Make sure the **pupils** layer is selected in the Timeline. Position the cursor at the center of the right eye graphic you created. Hold down **Option/Alt + Shift** as you drag a circle from the center of the eye.

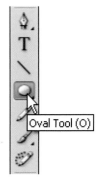

27. Go to the Tools panel and change the **Fill Color** to a black (**#000000**).

28. Select the Brush Tool (**B**). At the bottom of the Tools panel, set the **Brush Mode** to **Paint Normal** and select a medium size brush. Position the cursor over the center of the blue circle and single-click to add the black pupil. If you want to add a highlight to the eye, change the **Fill Color** to white, reduce the brush size and draw a small circle in the top left corner of the pupil.

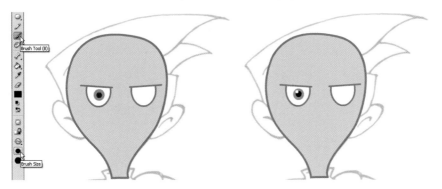

Figure 2.30: *Use the Brush Tool to create the pupil and highlight for the eye.*

29. With all of the pupil layer's shapes highlighted, select **Modify > Convert to Symbol**. The **Convert to Symbol** dialog box opens.

  ▸ Enter **Boy_Front_Pupil** as the symbol's name.

  ▸ Select **Graphic** as the symbol type.

  ▸ Click on the center square for the registration point.

  ▸ Click **OK**.

30. While the pupil graphic symbol is still selected on the Stage, hold down the **Option/Alt** key and click and drag it to create a duplicate copy. Move the duplicate pupil over to the left eye. Lock the **pupils** layer.

Figure 2.31: *Copy the pupil graphic symbol and position it over the left eye.*

These basic vector tools: the pencil, brush, oval, and line are what most designers use to create a character in Flash. Continue to trace the character's remaining parts:

  ▸ The nose, mouth, body, gloves, belt, cape, and hair are drawn using the Pencil Tool similar to the technique used to trace the head.

  ▸ Each of these character elements should be created on separate layers labeled respectively: **nose**, **mouth**, and so on.

  ▸ To see a completed version, open **01_ImportScan_Complete.fla** in the **Completed** folder inside the **Chapter_02** folder.

Let's pause a moment to discuss two important steps you should always perform when assembling your Flash character. First, all of the character's parts should be on separate layers in the Timeline. When it is time to animate them, they should be independent of the other objects (Figure 2.32).

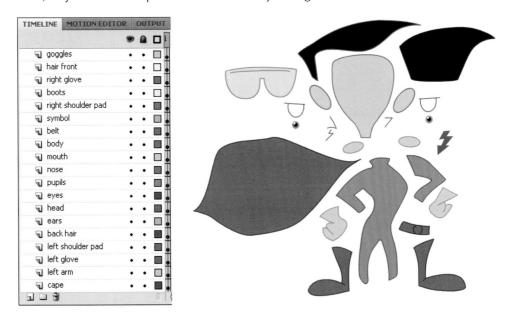

Figure 2.32: *Separate body parts on separate layers in the Timeline.*

Secondly, define a good naming convention for all of your symbols. The more complex the character, the more symbols you will have in the Flash library. Using a consistent naming convention will allow you to easily search the library to find what you are looking for. In this exercise, each symbol's naming structure consists of the character's name, the position, and the body part.

Figure 2.33: *Determine a naming convention for your symbol library in Flash.*

Exercise 2: Adjusting the Line Thickness

A drawn shape in Flash consists of two elements: a stroke (line) and a fill. The stroke is set to a consistent line weight around the fill and is a dead giveaway that the art originated in Flash. As you saw in the first exercise, the uniform line thickness looks very mechanical and not hand-drawn.

As you sketch your character use lines of varying weight to establish strength and weakness (Figure 2.34). Obviously, thick lines create a bolder emphasis while thin lines are used for a more subtle emphasis. Varying the thickness of a line in Flash can have a dynamic impact on your drawings.

Original Sketch   *Flash Strokes = uniform thickness*   *Flash Fills = varying thickness*

Figure 2.34: *Use varying line thickness to add emphasis to your character's design.*

Many artists prefer to draw in Flash because the vector graphics are easily scalable, but sometimes have trouble using the mouse. Investing in a graphics tablet is a good option if you plan on using the drawing tools in Flash. Wacom Technology offers a number of pressure sensitive tablets to choose from. Flash can recognize pressure sensitivity if you have a tablet, which makes drawing a bit easier and allows for lines of varying thickness.

Figure 2.35: *Flash can recognize pressure sensitivity when drawing on a graphics tablet.*

Chapter 2: Get into Character

Before you open Flash, plug your graphics tablet into your computer and install any necessary software. Open Flash and select the Brush Tool. While you can use the tablet just as you would use your mouse to draw with any tool, only the Brush Tool has pressure sensitivity options. At the bottom of the Tools panel you'll see the options for the Brush Tool and a new button called **Use Pressure**.

Click the **Use Pressure** button (Figure 2.35). With this button on, Flash will recognize the pressure sensitivity on the tablet. This allows you to paint using fills in lines of varying thicknesses depending on how hard you press on the tablet pen. To make Flash stop recognizing the tablet's pressure sensitivity, click **Use Pressure** again to turn it off.

Even if you choose not to invest in a graphics tablet, you can still achieve the same effect in Flash. It is a little more time consuming to do, but delivers the same results. Let's experiment with the line thickness.

1. Open the file **02_LineThickness.fla** in the **Chapter_02** folder you copied to your hard drive. The detective's head on the Stage was traced from a scanned image similar to the first exercise.

02_LineThickness

2. Double-click on the detective's head to select both the fill and stroke.

3. Select **Modify > Shape > Convert Lines to Fills**. The stroke now becomes a filled shape and gives you more anchor points to manipulate.

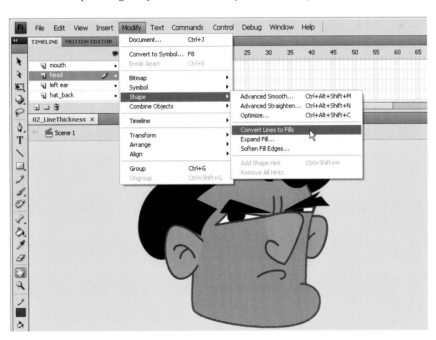

Figure 2.36: *Convert the stroke lines of the face to fills.*

4. Select the Selection Tool (**V**) and hover it near the bottom edge of the detective's chin. The cursor will change to indicate a curve. Click and drag to get a varied line as if the artwork was drawn by hand.

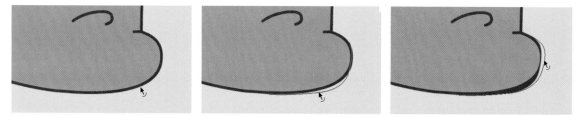

Figure 2.37: *Use the Selection Tool and alter the fill's shape to create a varied line.*

5. Double-click on the detective's nose to select both the fill and stroke.

6. Select **Modify > Shape > Convert Lines to Fills**.

7. Use the Magnify Tool (**M**) to zoom in to the end cap at the top of the nostril. It is made up of five points.

8. Use the Subselection Tool (**A**) to delete the two points on either side of the center point. Adjust the path of the line to give it a more tapered look.

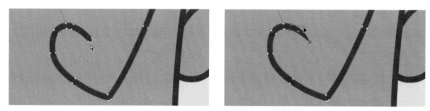

Figure 2.38: *Use the Subselection Tool to delete points and alter the fill's shape.*

9. Repeat these steps with the remaining layers to give the detective a more hand-drawn look and feel. To see a completed version, open **02_LineThickness_Complete.fla** in the **Completed** folder inside the **Chapter_02** folder.

Figure 2.39: *The image on the left is the starting point; the image on the right is the final result using fills instead of strokes.*

Exercise 3: From Illustrator to Flash

The art of character animation requires a lot of patience and practice. Adobe Illustrator provides many great tools for designing 2D characters. Once imported into Flash, these static characters become virtual puppets that can walk, run, and jump.

Let's start by deconstructing the Adobe Illustrator file you will be using in this exercise:

1. Locate and open the file **03_Vector_Character.ai** file in the **Assets** folder in **Chapter_02**.

   ▸ The character has already been designed and assembled for you.

   ▸ Notice that each body part is on its own individual layer.

   ▸ Each layer has been labeled to correctly identify the part.

03_Vector_Character

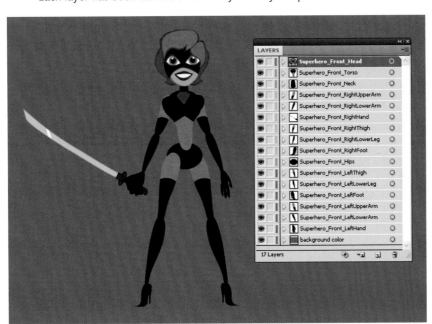

Figure 2.40: *The 2D character is made up of separate layers in Adobe Illustrator.*

You are now ready to import the Illustrator artwork into Flash.

2. Open the file **03_IllustratorCharacter.fla** in the **Chapter_02** folder you copied to your hard drive. It contains one, empty layer labeled **vectorArt**.

3. Select **File > Import > Import to Stage** to open the Import dialog box.

4. Locate the **03_Vector_Character.ai** file in the **Assets** folder in **Chapter_02**. Click **Open**. The Importer Wizard automatically launches. It provides a thumbnail preview of each Illustrator layer and the ability to deactivate any layer by clicking on the checkmark to the left of the thumbnail image.

03_IllustratorCharacter

5. Make sure the **Convert layers to** option is set to **Flash Layers**. This option places all selected layers on their own layer. Each layer is labeled with the name of the layer in the Illustrator file. The layers in Illustrator are imported as vector art.

6. Make sure the check box for the **Place layers at original position** option is checked. The contents of the Illustrator file retain their exact position.

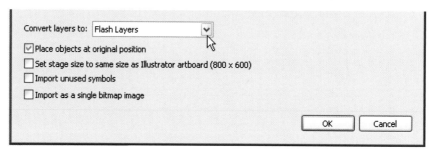

Figure 2.41: *Convert each Illustrator layer into a Flash layer.*

7. Select the **Superhero_Front_Head** layer. Individual import options specifically for that layer appear on the left of the thumbnail images.

   ▸ Check the box for **Create movie clip** for this layer.

   ▸ Click on the center square for the registration point.

Figure 2.42: *Convert each Illustrator layer into a movie clip with center registration.*

8. Repeat these steps with the remaining Illustrator layers. Create movie clips for every layer with a center registration point.

9. Uncheck the checkmark to the left of the **background color** thumbnail image.

Figure 2.43: *Do not import the **background color** layer.*

10. When you are done, click **OK**. The layered character appears assembled on the Flash Stage. Each layer in the Illustrator document was converted into a separate Flash layer. The Library holds all of the movie clips that you created in the Import Wizard (Figure 2.44).

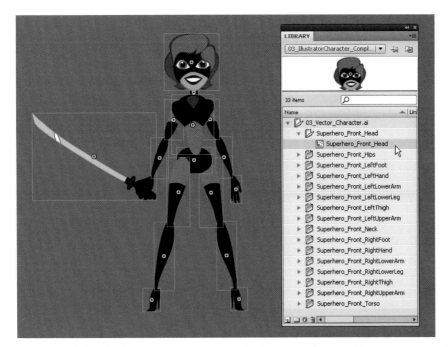

Figure 2.44: *The imported Illustrator file retains its separate layers in Flash.*

11. Before you start creating keyframes to animate the character, you need to adjust the registration point's position for each movie clip. This is the pivot point that will "hinge" the individual body parts together. It doesn't link the layers together, but allows you to animate each layer more effectively.

   ▸ Select the Free Transform Tool (**Q**).

   ▸ Click on a movie clip. The registration point is the solid white circle in the center.

   ▸ Using the Free Transform Tool, click and drag the white circle to its proper "hinge" position for the body. For example, the head's registration point should be moved to the bottom center of the character's chin.

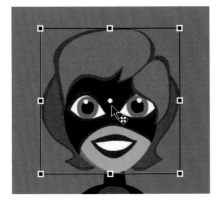 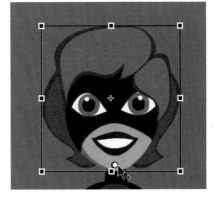

Figure 2.45: *Reposition the registration points to properly "hinge" the body.*

Once all of the individual movie clip's registration points have been positioned properly, you are ready to animate your character. To see an animated example of this exercise, open **03_IllustratorCharacter_Complete** in the **Completed** folder inside the **Chapter_02** folder.

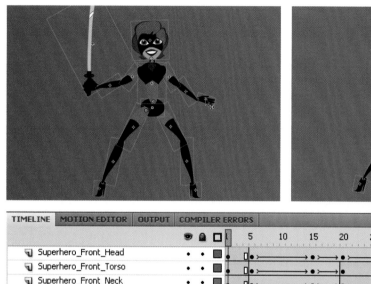
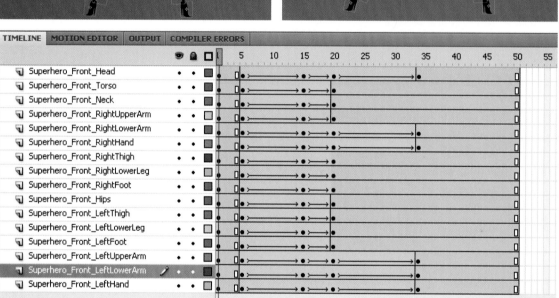

Figure 2.46: *Each layer's art was repositioned on the Stage on different frames.*

Keyframes were set for each layer on frames 15 and 20. Each body part was repositioned on the Stage for both frames. A Classic Tween was applied to complete the animation (Figure 2.46). The Easing property was also used to ease in and out of the different poses (Figure 2.47).

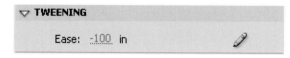

Figure 2.47: *Easing was applied to the tweens for a more natural motion.*

Exercise 4: From Photoshop to Flash

In addition to vector-based art, Flash is a great tool for building characters cut out of bitmap images. JibJab Media is an animation studio *(www.jibjab.com)* that has produced a number of hilarious animated shorts that have a distinct visual style. This next exercise is designed to show you an alternative method for assembling characters in Flash using photo collage.

Sketch out all the poses that your character will perform in the animation or interactive project. Yes, even though you will be using photos, you still need to draw. Use these sketches as a check list for the various photos you will need to take. When you are ready for your photo shoot, find a location that is evenly lit with little to no shadows. Using a digital camera, take a variety of photos of your model to capture as much detail and different facial expressions as possible.

Figure 2.48: *Anatomy of a photo collage character.*

Transfer the digital images to Adobe Photoshop. Prepare your images by cutting and pasting the photo(s) onto different layers. Figure 2.48 illustrates an exploded view of the cutout character you will use for this exercise. Notice how the arms and legs were rounded at each end.

Hiding how a character is joined together is a trademark in limited animation. Hanna-Barbera layered characters using one cell on top of another. This technique reduced the number of drawing that had to be made for an animation.

04_Raster_Character

Study the character design of Yogi Bear. His green necktie is a unique visual identifier for the audience but also serves to help the animator. The necktie hides how the head is connected to the body so the animators do not have to draw the body again.

Label each Photoshop layer. The name should clearly identify the body part. Refer to the naming convention used in the first exercise. These layer names will be transferred into Flash. When you are all done, assemble the character by positioning all the body parts in their proper locations. Save the file as a Photoshop (PSD) file.

You are now ready to import the photo collage into Flash.

04_PhotoshopCharacter

1. Open the file **04_PhotoshopCharacter.fla** in the **Chapter_02** folder you copied to your hard drive. It contains one, empty layer labeled **cutout**.

2. Select **File > Import > Import to Stage** to open the Import dialog box.

3. Locate the **04_Raster_Character.psd** file in the **Assets** folder in **Chapter_02**. Click **Open**. The PSD Importer Wizard automatically launches. It provides a thumbnail preview of each Photoshop layer and the ability to deactivate any layer by clicking on the checkmark to the left of the thumbnail image.

4. Make sure the **Convert layers to** option is set to **Flash Layers**. This option places all selected layers on their own layer. Each layer is labeled with the name of the layer in the Photoshop file. The layers in Photoshop are imported as bitmap objects and the layer name is the object's name in the Library panel in Flash.

5. Make sure the check box for the **Place layers at original position** option is checked. The contents of the PSD file retain the exact position that they had in Photoshop.

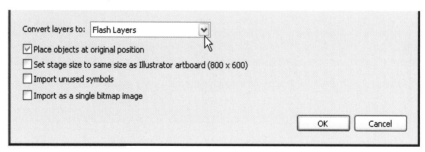

Figure 2.49: *Convert each Photoshop layer into a Flash layer.*

6. Select the **head** layer. Individual import options specifically for that layer appear on the left of the thumbnail images.

   ▸ Select **Flattened Bitmap Image**. This option rasterizes the bitmap image preserving its appearance in Photoshop.

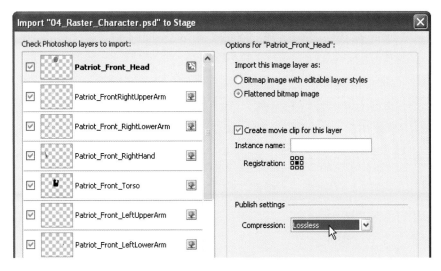

Figure 2.50: *Convert each Photoshop layer into a movie clip with center registration.*

- ▸ Check the box for **Create movie clip** for this layer. Click on the center square for the registration point. This automatically converts the bitmap object into a movie clip symbol when imported into Flash and is a production time saver.

- ▸ Under the **Publish settings** options, select **Lossless** as the compression setting. Lossy compresses the image in JPEG format and is generally good for rectangular bitmap images. Since the character is made up of irregular shaped bitmaps use Lossless to compresses the image in PNG file format.

7. Repeat these steps with the remaining Photoshop layers. Create movie clips for every layer and use lossless compression. When you are done, click **OK** to import the character.

8. Go to the Library panel. Locate the imported bitmap objects in the **Asset** folder that was created.

- ▸ Double-click on the bitmap icon to open the **Bitmap Properties** dialog box.
- ▸ Check the box for the **Allow smoothing** option. This applies anti-aliasing to the bitmap. Anti-aliasing maintains the image's clean edges and prevents pixilation that occurs as the pixels are rotated.
- ▸ Repeat these steps for all imported bitmap images.

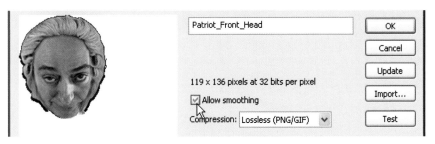

Figure 2.51: *Activate the **Allow smoothing** option for all bitmap library items.*

Now that your character is imported, let's "rig" it together using the Bone Tool. "Rigging" is a term used by 3D modelers and animators. Like in our own bodies, our 2D characters are given bones that act as a controlling skeleton structure.

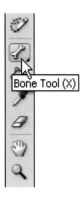

Bone Tool (X)

9. Select the Bone Tool (**X**). This tool only works with graphic or movie clip symbols. To create a bone, you simply drag from one symbol to another to link them.

10. The first bone you create is the root or sometimes called the parent bone of the armature. Click on the upper chest of the character and drag down to the hips movie clip. You have now linked these two movie clips together.

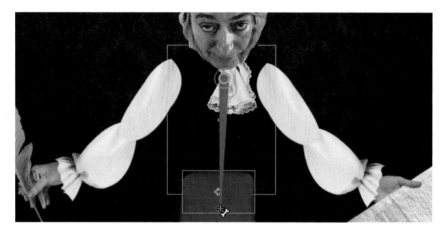

Figure 2.52: *Create the root bone that connects the torso to the hips.*

11. To add another bone, drag from the tail of the first bone to the next symbol instance you want to add to the armature.

   ▸ From the hips' bone, click and drag to each of the character's thighs.
   ▸ Each thigh needs to be connected to its lower leg.

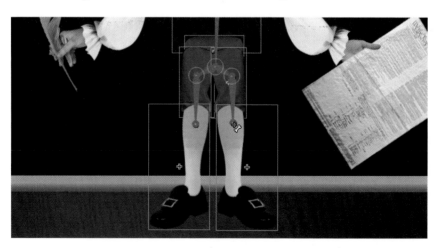

Figure 2.53: *Create the bones that connect the hips to each leg.*

Chapter 2: Get into Character

12. To create a branched armature, click the head of the root bone and drag to create the first bone of the new branch. You will do this to create a branch for each arm and the head movie clip.

   ▶ Go back to the root bone and connect the arms, forearms, and hands similar to the technique you used for the legs.
   ▶ Connect the root bone to the head movie clip.

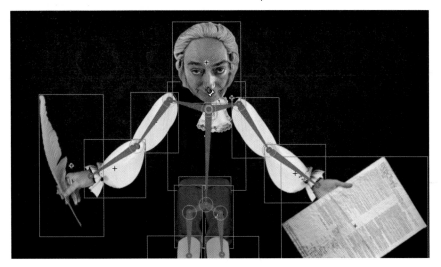

Figure 2.54: *Create branching bones that connect the torso to each arm and head.*

When using the Bone Tool, a new pose layer **(Armature_1)** is automatically generated in the Timeline. As you add more bones, Flash moves the symbol instance into this pose layer. Think of the armature as a skeletal structure.

13. As a result of how you add your bones, you may need to adjust the stacking order of each layer. To do this, select the object on the Stage and right-click. Select **Arrange** and the stacking order you desire.

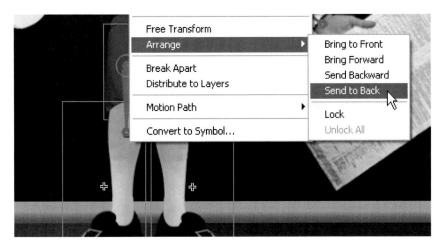

Figure 2.55: *Adjust the stacking order for each bone.*

14. To adjust the position for the bone's end points select the Free Transform Tool. Click and drag the registration point to a new position. This will also change the position of the bone that is attached to it.

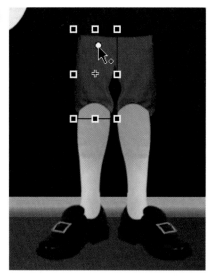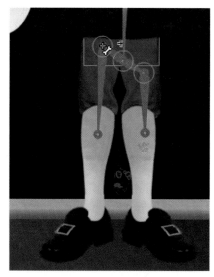

Figure 2.56: *Adjust the bone's end points by changing the registration point.*

15. You can constrain the rotation for each bone by clicking on it and then checking the **Constrain** boxes in the **Properties** panel. The constrained angle is visually displayed at the bone's end points (Figure 2.57).

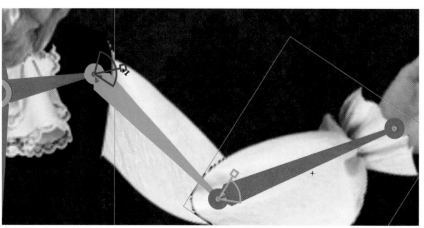

Figure 2.57: *Constrain the joint rotation in the* **Properties** *panel.*

16. With the armature in place, click and drag any of the bones to manipulate your character. The **Armature_1** layer is automatically set up with a motion tween. Move the playhead to a different frame and pose your character to create a new keyframe.

Chapter 2: Get into Character

17. Continue to reposition the playhead on different frames and adjust the character's pose. Test the movie to see the animation created from pose to pose.

To see a basic animated version of this exercise, open **04_Photoshop Character_Complete.fla** in the **Completed** folder inside the **Chapter_02** folder.

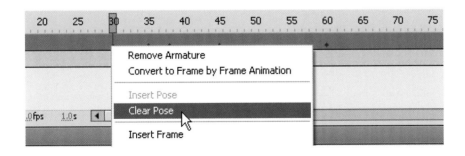

Figure 2.58: *The **Armature** layer is automatically set up with a motion tween.*

Each keyframe holds a specific pose that you create. To reposition a keyframe, hold down the **Control** key to select it. Once the keyframe is selected, click and drag it to a new frame. To delete a keyframe, right-click on it and select **Clear Pose** (Figure 2.59).

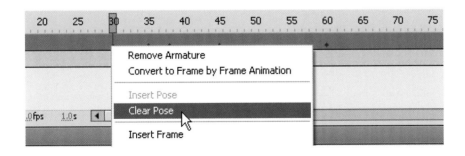

Figure 2.59: *To remove a keyframe, right-click on it and select **Clear Pose**.*

Exercise 5: Using Bitmaps as Textures

Flash is a great tool for designing vector and raster-based characters. Vector characters successfully capture the cartoon look and feel. Cutouts can be used to create humorous photo realistic characters. What if you wanted the best of both worlds: a cartoon character with photo realistic textures? That is no problem with Flash. In this last exercise, you will create a cartoon character using bitmap textures.

Where do you find these textures? The answer is all around you. A digital camera can be your best friend in creating a database of textures. A scanner is another good device that can be utilized to scan various paper stocks or fabrics. Always scan or capture your original digital images at the highest resolution possible for the detail.

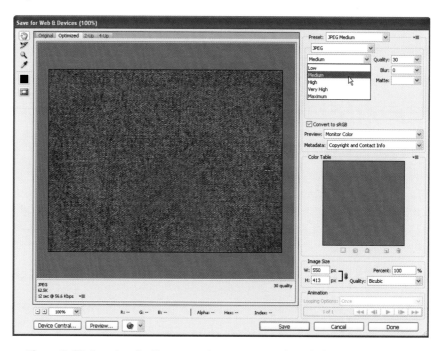

Figure 2.60: *Experiment with compression settings to reduce the bitmap image to the smallest size possible while still maintaining image quality.*

Prior to importing the bitmaps into Flash, use Photoshop for any color correction and reduce the pixel resolution to 72 dpi. Save the retouched bitmap as a JPEG copy into your project folder leaving the original bitmap intact. Use the **Save for Web** feature in Photoshop to preview the JPEG compression. For textures that are busy with detail, you can compress quite a bit without noticing the artifacts.

Let's create some bitmap textures in Flash.

1. Open the file **05_BitmapTexture.fla** in the **Chapter_02** folder you copied to your hard drive. The file contains all the vector artwork you need to complete this exercise. The cartoon character on the Stage is made up of vector shapes.

05_BitmapTexture

2. Make sure the blank keyframe on the **texture** layer is highlighted. Select **File > Import > Import to Stage** to open the Import dialog box.

3. Locate the **05_Denim.jpg** file in the **Assets** folder in **Chapter_02**. Click **Open**.

4. With the JPEG image highlighted on the Stage, select **Modify > Break Apart**.

5. Select the Eyedropper Tool (**I**) and click on the texture. It is added to the Color panel as a new swatch.

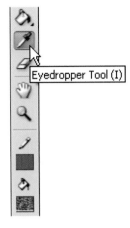

6. Select the Paint Bucket Tool (**K**) and single-click on the character's pants. The shape color fills with the denim texture.

Figure 2.61: *Use the Paint Bucket Tool to fill in a shape with a photo texture. The Gradient Transform Tool allows you to scale the texture.*

7. To scale the texture, use the Gradient Transform Tool (**F**). The tools that surround the texture's bounding box allow you to stretch, rotate, skew, and scale the texture.

8. Experiment with creating your own textures to finish the character. To see a completed version of this exercise, open **05_BitmapTexture_Complete.fla** in the **Completed** folder inside the **Chapter_02** folder.

Summary

This completes the chapter on character design. Some key concepts to remember include:

- Simplify the design. There should always be a minimum amount of detail, no more than you need to recognize the character clearly.
- A memorable character can be reduced to a silhouette, and still be immediately recognizable.
- Character model sheets detail the visual design of a character from a variety of angles and poses.
- Personality is expressed through the character's posture and movement.
- Exaggerating the defining features of your character helps the audience to identify its type.
- Think about accepted character stereotypes. Audiences will accept the storyline more quickly when the characters are familiar and identifiable.
- Flash cartoon characters are often composed of several layers. Create a different layer for each body part.
- Hiding how a character is joined together is a trademark in limited animation.

A character needs a personality; it is not merely a combination of shapes and colors. Chapter 8 builds on the design concepts discussed in this chapter to enrich your character designs with personality. Before you jump to that chapter, you first need to understand how to set up your visual story in Flash. The next chapter focuses on "setting the stage" for your story.

CHAPTER 3

Give Me Space

Proper planning is essential in producing Flash movies. This chapter "sets the stage" for your Flash story and analyzes two important film concepts involved in visual storytelling, the frame and the shot. At the end of this chapter, you will apply these cinematic tools to design a storyboard and animatic in Flash.

Defining the Space

Whether your story is intended for the web or broadcast, the technical requirements and limitations in Flash can't be ignored. Before you start any Flash project, you first need to determine the dimensions of the document's Stage. This is crucial because it defines the space in which you compose your story elements.

As a web designer, a good place to start is with the three standard monitor settings: 640 x 480, 800 x 600, and 1024 x 768 pixels. You can also design smaller for a compact layout, but keep in mind that the screen real-estate also shrinks. This can cause a potential readability problem if you have a lot of information crammed into such a small space.

If you choose a larger format, you run the risk of having your audience with smaller monitors scroll to see everything. The goal is to design something that will fit comfortably within a browser. It can also be viewed at least on a standard monitor size, and won't look so cramped on larger monitors. For the web, a browser-safe resolution to design to is 800 x 600 pixels which is a Stage size of about 750 x 500 after you factor in the web browser's interface (Figure 3.1).

Figure 3.1: *The goal is to design your Flash file at a Stage size that fits comfortably within a web browser.*

In video, the dimensions are referred to as the **frame aspect ratio**. It is the relationship between the width and height of an image. Standard computer monitors and television have a 4:3 frame aspect ratio. Where did this ratio come from?

Motion pictures through the early 1950s had roughly the same aspect ratio. This became known as Academy Standard: an aspect ratio of 1.37:1. Television adopted the Academy Standard to a 1.33:1 aspect ratio. This is the recognized video standard commonly referred to as a 4:3 frame aspect ratio.

Figure 3.2: *For every four units of width, there are three units of height.*

In 1953 Hollywood introduced the widescreen format for motion pictures in an effort to pry audiences away from their television sets. Today, widescreen film has two standardized ratios: Academy Flat (1.85:1) and Anamorphic Scope (2.35:1). High-definition (HD) television adopted Academy Flat and has an aspect ratio of 1.78:1. This is referred to as a 16:9 aspect ratio (Figure 3.3).

Figure 3.3: *for every sixteen units of width, there are nine units of height.*

There are three popular video format standards used throughout the world. NTSC, which stands for National Television Standards Committee, is the video format used in the United States, Canada, Japan, and the Philippines. Phase Alternating Line, or PAL, is the format of choice in most European countries. France uses SECAM, which stands for Séquential Couleur Avec Memoire. All three standard video formats use a 4:3 frame aspect ratio.

As previously mentioned, HDTV displays a 16:9 frame aspect ratio. It is a digital television broadcasting system that provides higher resolution than the standard video formats—NTSC, PAL, and SECAM. How does all this affect Flash and its Stage size when Flash movies can be resolution independent?

If you use only vector art, the published Flash movie can be scaled as big or small as you want without any loss in quality. Even though the movie size may not be important, designing for the correct aspect ratio is. If you don't, image distortion will occur going from Flash to video or DVD.

Square versus Non-square Pixels

If you are developing your story for video, you need to be aware of the **pixel aspect ratio**. This refers to the width and height of each pixel that makes up an image. Computer screens display square pixels. Every pixel has an aspect ratio of 1:1. Video uses non-square rectangular pixels, actually scan lines.

To make matters even more complicated, the pixel aspect ratio is not consistent between video formats. NTSC video uses a non-square pixel that is taller than it is wide. It has a pixel aspect ratio of 1:0.906. PAL is just the opposite. Its pixels are wider than they are tall with a pixel aspect ratio of 1:1.06 (Figure 3.4).

Computer Screen	**NTSC DV or D1**	**PAL DV or D1**
(square pixels)	(non-square pixels)	(non-square pixels)

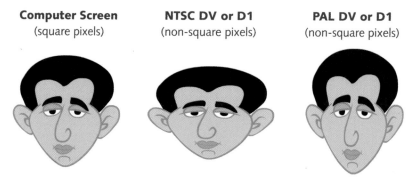

Figure 3.4: *The pixel aspect ratio can produce undesirable image distortion if you do not compensate for the difference between square and non-square pixels.*

Flash only works in square pixels on your computer screen. As the Flash file migrates to video, the pixel aspect ratio changes from square to non-square. The end result will produce a slightly stretched image on your television screen.

On NTSC, round objects will appear flattened. PAL stretches objects making them appear skinny. The solution is to adjust the dimensions of the Flash Stage.

Table 3.1: *Flash Stage size settings for different video formats*

Video Format	Frame Ratio	Pixel Ratio	Video Size	Flash Stage
NTSC DV	4:3	non-square	720 x 480	720 x 534
NTSC D1	4:3	non-square	720 x 486	720 x 540
PAL DV/D1	4:3	non-square	720 x 576	768 x 576
NTSC DV	16:9	non-square	720 x 480	864 x 480
NTSC D1	16:9	non-square	720 x 486	864 x 486
PAL	16:9	non-square	720 x 576	1024 x 576
HDTV 720p	16:9	square	1280 x 720	1280 x 720
HDTV 1080i	16:9	square	1920 x 1080	1920 x 1080

A common Flash Stage size used for NTSC video is 720 x 540 which is slightly taller than its video size of 720 x 486 (D1). For PAL, set the Stage size to 768 x 576. This is wider than its video size of 720 x 576. The published movie can be rescaled in video editing applications, such as Adobe After Effects, to fit the correct dimensions. Even though the image may look distorted on the computer screen, it will appear correct on video. Table 3.1 shows the correct Stage size needed for each video format.

There is some good news with high-definition (HD) television. HD uses square pixels. This means that depending on the HD format you choose, either 720p or 1080i, your Flash Stage dimensions are the same as the video size. We'll discuss other methods of adapting a 720 x 540 Stage size to HDTV's wider aspect ratio later in the chapter. Let's focus next on setting the proper frame rate.

Frame Rates

Flash's Timeline consists of a sequence of frames. Frame rate is the speed at which Flash plays back its frames. The smoothness of an animation is affected by its frame rate and how complex the animation is. Early versions of Flash had a default frame rate of 12 frames-per-second (fps). Starting with Flash CS4, the default frame rate was increased to 24 fps. This is the standard frame rate for a theatrical film.

For web development, a frame rate of 12 fps is the minimum for acceptable smooth animation. It is used most often in Flash banner advertisement. This frame rate frees up the computer's processor cycles for the rest of the web page's content. A low frame rate of 12 or 15 fps is also a good setting if you know your audience will most likely have older computer processors. For newer computers, you can use a higher frame rate of 24 or 30 fps.

If you choose a lower frame rate, select a rate that is a multiple of your original frame rate. For example, if the standard frame rate for film is 24 fps, compress your Flash frame rate to 12 fps. The best advice is to test your animations on a variety of computers to determine optimum frame rates. What about video and translating its frame rate to Flash?

NTSC video has a frame rate of 29.97 fps. Why not 30 fps? When black and white television became popular in the early 1950s, the broadcasts ran at 30 fps. When the color signal was added to the broadcast, the video frame rate had to be slowed to 29.97 due to technical issues. Video engineers were forced to allocate a certain amount of time each second for the transmission of the color information. PAL and SECAM operate at 25 fps.

Flash movies cannot be set to 29.97 fps. If your Flash movie is intended for NTSC video, use a frame rate of either 15 or 30 fps. Adobe Premiere or After Effects can convert the different frame rate to match 29.97 fps. Just remember that lower frame rates will not play back smoothly after being converted. If your Flash movie is migrating to PAL or SECAM video, use 25 fps.

Interlaced versus Progressive Video

Have you ever gotten really close to your television screen? Each frame of video is split into two sets of scan lines. Interlaced video draws each set of scan lines in an alternating fashion. The scan lines are held in two fields: the odd field consists of the odd-numbered lines and the even field consists of the even-numbered lines. Two fields equal one frame of image (Figure 3.5).

Field 1	Field 2	Interlaced Frame

Figure 3.5: *Interlaced video is made up of two sets of scan lines, or fields.*

In the United States, interlaced video refreshes the screen 60 times per second in order to create 30 frames of images per second. First the even lines appear on the screen, then the odd lines appear. All analog televisions use an interlaced display. High-definition video can be either interlaced or progressively scanned.

Your computer screen uses progressive video. The video is scanned from side to side, top to bottom to create a frame. Every pixel on the screen is refreshed in order. The result is a higher perceived resolution and a lack of "jitters" that can make the edges in your artwork or patterns appear to move or shimmer.

Your artwork in Flash can be severely impacted by the alternating scan lines used in interlaced video. Avoid using thin lines or small text in your Flash file. A horizontal line 1 point thick or less will flicker on video. It is visible when the first set of scan lines appear, then disappears as the second field is displayed.

To have your Flash artwork and text display properly on video, a general rule is to set all horizontal lines to 2 points thick or greater. All screen text should be at least 18 points in size. Use bold san serif typefaces. Avoid typefaces with very thin lines or serifs. These will tend to flicker on a television screen.

Title Safe and Action Safe Areas

If you look at the edge of your computer screen, you see every pixel in the displayed image. Television screens do not show the entire video picture. This problem is known as overscan. An average of 10% of the image around the edges of the screen is not visible to the viewer. This percentage can be smaller or larger and varies due to the television's make and model.

Figure 3.6: *Title Safe and Action Safe areas solve broadcast overscan.*

To solve this problem, television producers defined the Title Safe and Action Safe areas. The Title Safe area is a space, roughly 20% in from the edges of the screen, where text will not be cut off when broadcast. The Action Safe area is a larger area that represents where a typical TV set cuts the image off.

 *Title Safe and Action Safe templates are provided in the **Chapter_03** folder for you to use in your projects. Simply copy the frame and paste it into your file.*

What about high-definition? HDTV also overscans the image so that older programming will be framed as intended to be viewed. Some broadcasters crop, magnify, or stretch the original video based on the picture's aspect ratios.

You can easily adapt your 720 x 540 Flash file to accommodate the wider HDTV aspect ratio. One method is to keep the Stage height at 540 pixels. The Stage width needs to be increased to 961 pixels. Where did that number come from? HDTV has an aspect ratio of 1.78:1. Multiply the height (540) by 1.78 and the result is 961. This size is smaller than the HDTV dimensions so you will need to increase the resolution of the QuickTime movie when you export the Flash file.

Figure 3.7: *Two possible solutions for creating an HDTV Flash Template*

If you want to maintain a 4:3 Stage size but have a widescreen image, you need to set up a new layer that masks, or letterboxes, the HDTV aspect ratio (Figure 3.7). Increase the resolution of the QuickTime movie when you export your file from Flash (Figure 3.8). Adobe Premiere or After Effects allows you to resize or crop your published Flash movie to the proper HDTV dimensions.

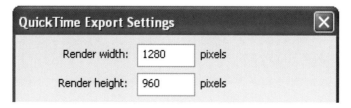

Figure 3.8: *Export your Flash animation at a higher resolution.*

Chapter 3: Give Me Space

Color Issues

Computer screens display RGB colors. Video uses a YUV color space. While computers provide millions of colors to choose from, video has a limited range of colors it can display. So it is possible to use RGB colors on a computer monitor that cannot be reproduced on a television screen.

NTSC video makes life even more complicated. It uses the YIQ color space, which has an even smaller color range than YUV. NTSC is not as consistent at reproducing colors as PAL. If Flash designers are not careful with their color choices, their movie will not display properly on NTSC video.

This results in the colors bleeding, or spilling into neighboring colors. It produces a visible muddiness to the overall image. Warm, saturated colors such as red tend to bleed the most, making them a bad choice for fine detail or text. Blues translate quite well from RGB to video and make good background colors.

The best way to avoid any color shifts or bleeding is to create original art using only broadcast-safe colors. The full range of RGB color values is represented numerically from 0 to 255. The color value for black is 0-0-0 (red, green, blue). The color value for white is 255-255-255. To create safe broadcast colors, limit the R, G, and B values between 16 and 235.

In Flash, go to the Color panel and select the black swatch. Make sure you are using the RGB color mixer. Change the R, G, and B values to 16. Add the color to the swatches. Next, select the white swatch. Change the R, G, and B values to 235 and add the swatch. A general rule to follow is that all colors should have a saturation value lower than 236, especially the color red (Figure 3.9).

Figure 3.9: *Limit the RGB color values between 16 and 235 for broadcast video.*

You can also replace the default color palette in Flash by importing an existing color palette or even a GIF file. Warren Fuller at *www.animonger.com* provides a NTSC color palette that you can download for free.

As you can see, there are a lot of technical issues surrounding setting up your Flash file for different outputs. You need to be aware of these before you begin creating your Flash movie. Once you have defined the space, you next need to picture how the individual frames will visualize the story. This is the job of a cinematographer in the motion picture industry.

Showing the Space

Cinematography is the art and technology of motion picture photography. It is the cinematographer's artistic vision and imagination that helps frame a scene viewed through a camera lens and bring that image to the screen. In film, the art of cinematography includes:

- ▸ Visualizing the script with what the Director wants to show
- ▸ Composing the actors and props within a scene
- ▸ Establishing a visual "look" and "mood" for the story
- ▸ Lighting the scene and actors

The cinematographer, also known as the director of photography, creates the cinematic look of the film and is involved from pre-production to the final post-production of the film. In Flash, you are the cinematographer. There is no camera in Flash to look through so you must illustrate each scene in such a way that best serves your story. What makes up a scene?

The Frame

Figure 3.10: *A Hollywood movie is made up of frames, shots, scenes, and sequences.*

What are a Frame, a Shot, and a Scene?

A **frame** is a single still image. In film, a frame equals one twenty-fourth of a second. The illusion of movement occurs when frames are shown in rapid succession. This is often referred to as **persistence of vision**.

This phenomenon takes place in the eye where a frame's afterimage is thought to persist for approximately one twenty-fifth of a second on the retina. This afterimage is overlapped by the next frame's image and we interpret it as continuous movement.

Figure 3.11: *Persistence of vision is an optical illusion of movement.*

A **shot** is whatever the camera is looking at, at a particular moment in time. It is a continuous view filmed by one camera without interruption. When a camera begins filming, the shot begins. When the camera stops, the shot is over. Since the camera doesn't have to remain static, it can move to view the setting or action from another viewpoint. Once the camera shows another viewpoint, it is considered another shot.

Multiple shots in a given location make up a scene. A **scene** defines the place or setting where the action takes place. A scene may consist of one shot, or a series of shots. A sequence is a series of scenes or shots complete in itself. A sequence may occur in one or more settings. A series of sequences makes up the whole picture (Figure 3.10).

During the development stage of a movie, a director meets with a storyboard artist who illustrates the shots that tell the story. As you begin visualizing your story, break up the narrative into workable shots. Shots can be defined by the area of space they cover and the angle in which they capture the images. Carefully planned camera shots and angles can greatly impact the emotional reaction from your audience.

Camera Shots

A cinematographer looks though the camera viewfinder to frame a shot. The three most common camera shots used are the long shot, medium shot, and close-up. Of course, films are not made up of these three camera shots alone.

The long shot and close-up can also have extremes that can visually heighten the drama and tension in a story. Keep in mind that these shots do not refer to the actual distance between the camera and the subject, but to the relative size of the subject in the viewfinder.

An **extreme long shot** (ELS) shows the vastness of an area or setting. It is typically used to frame the setting at the beginning or ending of a story. Think of all the movies that begin with a city skyline, such as Tim Burton's Batman (1999). That shot orients the audience to Gotham City, the time of day, and the dark, brooding atmosphere of the story.

Figure 3.12: *An extreme long shot can not only show the setting for your story, but provide an emotional response from the audience.*

Any characters shown in an extreme long shot would appear quite small (Figure 3.12). This can be an effective visual tool in generating an emotional response from your audience. For example, if a character is lost in the desert, an extreme long shot would not only amplify the desert's grand scale but the character's isolation from civilization to the audience.

With the setting established, a **long shot** (LS) is used to frame the action. This shot shows the place, the characters, and the action. Examples of a long shot include action that takes place in a room, on a street, outside a house, or under a tree. A character is shown complete from head to toe, occupying about one third of the height of the frame. A long shot also provides enough space for the characters to move around in (Figure 3.13).

Figure 3.13: *A long shot frames the action in the story.*

A **medium shot** (MS) frames the characters from the waist or knees up. The character's gestures and facial expressions are shown with just enough background to establish the setting. It is the most common shot used in film and television. It draws the audience in closer, making the story more personal for them. Often this shot is used when characters are speaking to one another. This is also referred to as a two-shot.

If the characters in a two-shot are framed from the same basic position, keeping the same distance from the audience, the result is a pretty boring scene. Remember a shot is a change in the camera framing or viewpoint. To keep your audience engaged long enough to connect with your characters and become involved with your story, use close-ups to push your narrative forward.

Figure 3.14: *A medium shot frames the characters from the waist or knees up. A common medium shot is called a two-shot.*

In a **close-up** (CU), a character's head and shoulders are shown (Figure 3.15). This shot invites the audience to become a participant in the story by visually coming face-to-face with the characters. They can see and hopefully feel the emotions of the character. Watch a soap opera dialogue scene. Notice how the camera cuts back and forth between characters to show each person talking.

Figure 3.15: *A close-up shot reveals the character's emotional state and is used for dialogue.*

Chapter 3: Give Me Space

Sometimes an **over the shoulder shot** (OSS) is used to frame the characters' conversation. In this shot, the camera is positioned behind the shoulder of one of the characters. The shot looks from behind a character at the subject. It is often combined with close-ups to show each character physically reacting to the dialogue (Figure 3.16).

Figure 3.16: *When animating characters talking to one another, use reaction shots.*

For more dramatic effect, use an **extreme close-up** (ECU). This shot focuses the audience's attention on whatever is significant in the shot or facial reaction of a character. A close-up or extreme close-up doesn't always have to frame emotion. Close-ups can also reveal private information to the audience or emphasize symbols within the shot. For example, a letter being read, a door handle being turned, or a quick glance at a wrist watch creates visual impact for the audience while reinforcing the story's narrative (Figure 3.17).

 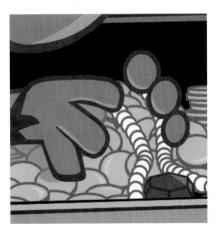

Figure 3.17: *Extreme close-up shots add dramatic effect by either framing emotion or emphasizing an action.*

Like a painter, the way in which you frame the space has a direct effect on your audience. Always try to introduce variety by using different types of camera shots. The goal is to move from one shot to another without the audience becoming confused or lost. Figure 3.18 illustrates a popular scenario.

Long Shot

Long Shot

Long Shot

Long Shot – frame the setting

Medium Shot – frame the action

Close-up – frame the emotion

Figure 3.18: *Introduce variety into your visual storytelling by using different types of camera shots.*

The top three images show a scene between two characters shot from the same relative distance throughout. Each image is a long shot that doesn't draw attention to any particular character or action. This scene is not as dynamic as the bottom scene that uses the three basic camera shots. The scene starts with a long shot to establish the setting. Next, a medium shot introduces the characters and the action. This shot is followed by a close-up that brings out the emotional detail in the main character.

Do you always have to see these basic camera shots in this particular order? No. First select a camera shot appropriate for the action. Then determine the order of the shots that best serves the dramatic needs of your story.

Camera shots play an important role in visual storytelling. Each shot provides a visual step closer for the audience to take and become fully involved with the story. Equally important to the relative size of the subject in the shot is the camera's point of view or angle. Not all shots are taken at eye-level.

Camera Angles

A carefully chosen camera angle can heighten the drama of the story. It is the camera angle that makes a shot dynamic. Positioning the camera determines the point of view from which the audience will see the shot. Each time the camera is moved, it transports the audience to a new point of view. That's why every change in camera angle should be carefully planned.

Figure 3.19 illustrates three different types of camera angles used in film. Changing the camera's height and angle, with respect to the subject, affects the emotional impact of the shot. It is a film technique that is used to create specific effects or moods. Let's look at each camera angle in more detail.

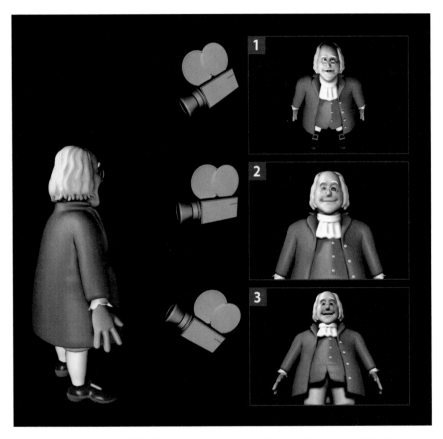

Figure 3.19: *A carefully chosen camera angle can heighten the drama of the story.*

Camera 1 is a **high angle shot**. The camera is placed above the horizon line tilted down to view the subject. This camera angle can be used in conjunction with an extreme long shot to frame an aesthetically pleasing landscape. If combined with a medium shot, the high angle can create a sense of insignificance or vulnerability in the character shown. The character appears weak and defenseless.

Camera 2 is an **eye-level shot**. The camera is at the eye-level of an observer of average height. This angle creates a fairly neutral shot. The audience sees the scene as they would in the real world. This camera angle looks directly into the character's eyes. As a result, the audience indentifies with the character as an equal.

Camera 3 is a **low angle shot**. The camera is tilted up to view the subject. This camera angle creates a sense of awe and superiority. Strong characters shown from a low angle seem to have more power as they dominate the frame. Monsters and villains will appear more menacing from this camera angle.

Cinematographers sometime choose to tilt the camera slightly. This is referred to as a **Dutch angle shot**. In this shot the vertical axis of the camera is at an angle to the vertical axis of the subject. It creates a sense of being off balanced or insecure. Often evil characters or characters in dangerous situations are shown through a tilted angle.

Figure 3.20: *A Dutch angle shot creates a sense of being off balanced or insecure.*

A **bird's-eye view** takes the high angle shot to the extreme. The camera is positioned directly overhead the action. Examples of the bird's-eye view in film include looking down on buildings in a city or following a car driving on a road. The opening scene in Stanley Kubrick's film adaptation of *The Shining* (1980) and the crop dusting scene in Alfred Hitchcock's *North by Northwest* (1959) effectively use this camera angle to enhance the storytelling and drive the narrative forward.

Figure 3.21: *A bird's-eye view is an extreme high-angle shot used often to show landscapes.*

The opposite of a bird's-eye view is a **worms-eye view**. The camera is placed low on the ground and titled upward. A worms-eye view is used to make the audience look up to something or to make an object look tall, strong and mighty. Slasher movies, such as *Halloween* (1978) or *A Nightmare on Elm Street* (1984), incorporate worms-eye views to emphasize the antagonist's menacing stature.

Figure 3.22: *A worm's-eye view is an extreme low-angle shot used often to emphasize a character's strength or domination in the scene.*

Camera Movements

Shots can also be defined by the movement of the camera. Camera movements are used to focus the audience's attention and involve them in the scene they are watching. Let's discuss some common camera movements used in film. Chapter 6 explores how to achieve these camera movements in Flash.

A **pan** (P) shot rotates the camera horizontally from left to right or right to left, similar to moving your head from side to side. Pans are used for establishing shots, where the camera pans across the horizon of a landscape. A pan can also give the feeling of searching for something within in a shot. This type of movement should be used sparingly. Too much panning becomes unsettling to watch. You also run the risk of having the audience notice the camera movement more than what's going on in the shot.

Figure 3.23: *A panning shot is typically used to establish a location or setting for the story.*

A **tilt** (T) is a pan in the vertical direction, up or down. It is most commonly used to reveal a tall building or a person. It can be a very effective visual storytelling technique if used properly. For example, tilting up from a character's feet to their head creates added tension as the audience anticipates what the character's face will look like.

Figure 3.24: *A tilt is a pan in the vertical direction.*

Cameras can also travel from one place to another within a single shot. This is called a **tracking shot** (TS). The camera tracks or follows along with the subject. In some tracking shots, both the camera and the character move. For example, the camera can follow a character from behind or travel alongside them as they move across the shot.

A tracking shot can also be applied when the subject matter stays in one place and the camera moves in relation to it. The camera can move forward, called a truck in, or backward, called a truck out. This type of tracking movement adds depth to the shot. Don't confuse tracking with zooming.

Figure 3.25: *Tracking adds depth to a shot while a zoom magnifies the foreground and background equally.*

When a camera trucks in or out it is moving through space. The shot's perspective is constantly changing as a result of the camera's movement. Zooming is an optical effect that magnifies the image. Perspective is not affected because the foreground and background are magnified equally. Even though there is no camera in Flash, all of these camera techniques can still be used to effectively tell your story.

Illustrating the Space

As a visual storyteller, you do not write a script, you draw it. Start applying the camera techniques you just learned by drawing rough thumbnail sketches. On a sheet of paper, sketch out camera shots that you think would be effective in illustrating your story. You don't have to draw well to create a thumbnail board so don't spend a lot of time fine-tuning your art (Figure 3.26).

Figure 3.26: *When visualizing your story, start with a series of rough thumbnail sketches.*

The purpose of a thumbnail board is to quickly determine the layout of your shots, not highlight your illustration skills. Even though the artwork is rough, the thumbnails should still clearly define which characters are in a shot, the camera's position, and the direction of motion, if any. List details underneath each sketch as notes to clarify what you envision. This can include anything from sound effects to special effects. Creating rough thumbnails first help you organize your animation layout and provide a visual format to build your storyboard.

A storyboard is a production tool that illustrates a story shot-by-shot using a series of sequential images. In film, it allows the director to plan the camera shots, the camera angles, and the camera movement to produce a cohesive and entertaining story to the audience. When finished, your storyboard will become a blueprint for all the important shots that will be in the final animation. In visual form it looks like a comic strip (Figure 3.27).

Figure 3.27: *Storyboards illustrate a story shot-by-shot.*

The Walt Disney Studios developed the storyboarding process in the 1930s for its animated films. Storyboarding is still used in Hollywood today as a visual tool to lay out a movie, one sketch for each shot or scene. These sketches show the layout of the shot and provide information about what is happening and how the shot fits in the movie. A storyboard should visually answer the following questions:

- ▶ Which characters are in the frame, and how are they moving?
- ▶ What are the characters saying to each other, if anything?
- ▶ Where is the "camera" positioned? Is the camera moving?

Let's apply the cinematic techniques discussed so far to design a storyboard for the popular nursery rhyme, Little Miss Muffet. The rhyme contains all the necessary storytelling ingredients. Little Miss Muffet is the protagonist who's goal is to eat her curds and whey. The villain, or antagonist, is the spider. The climax occurs when the spider drops in to visit our heroine. This action results in scaring Miss Muffet away—the resolution to the story.

Chapter 3: Give Me Space

Each line in the nursery rhyme can be conveniently broken down into a manageable shot. There are a lot of ways to visually show this story. For this example, let's follow a traditional cinematic approach that many filmmakers might use. Table 3.2 outlines one possible treatment using a variety of camera shots.

Table 3.2: *Storytelling treatment for Little Miss Muffet*

Line	Camera Shot	Rationale
Little Miss Muffet	ELS	Establishing shot
Sat on a tuffet,	Track in / LS	Frame the action
Eating her curds and whey;	MS	Frame the protagonist
Along came a spider,	Tilt / MS	Frame the antagonist
Who sat down beside her	CU	Bring the audience face-to-face
And frightened...	ECU	Frame the emotion
... Miss Muffet away	ELS	Re-establish the setting

The opening shot establishes the setting for where the story takes place using an extreme long shot (ELS). This shot clearly outlines for the audience the setting, the tree on the hill, and the main character of Miss Muffet sitting underneath the tree. This can be referred to as an establishing shot, or if the story takes place in only one location as this one does, a master shot.

Figure 3.28: *The opening shot establishing the setting for where the story takes place.*

To draw the audience in slowly, the camera tracks in to a long shot that frames the action of Miss Muffet sitting on her tuffet. When storyboarding the camera movements, use arrows to indicate direction (Figure 3.29). Arrows can drastically save time by indicating a single movement without you having to drawing multiple frames. In this sketch the inner rectangle represents the stopping point for the camera's tracking motion.

Figure 3.29: *Use arrows to indicate camera movements in your storyboards.*

The next shot is a medium shot that shows Miss Muffet from the waist up. This shot provides enough space to capture her physical body gestures and her facial reactions as she enjoys eating her food. The audience sees how the main character feels at that particular moment in the story.

Figure 3.30: *The medium shot frames the character's body gestures and expressions.*

Chapter 3: Give Me Space

This medium shot of Miss Muffet continues until the camera's point of view changes. The camera tilts up vertically and tracks in to reveal the spider slowly descending down toward Miss Muffet's head. The camera angle used is a low angle shot to make the spider appear more menacing.

Arrows are used to indicate the vertical tilt in camera direction, the movement of the spider, and the minor camera tracking used to focus the audiences' attention on the spider (Figure 3.31).

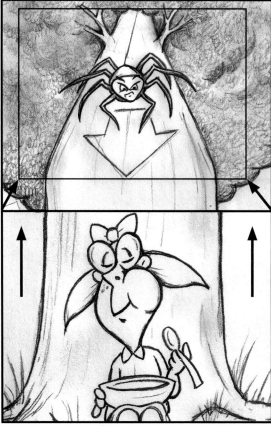

Figure 3.31: *The camera tilts up to reveal the story's anatagonist.*

After the spider moves out of the frame, a close-up shot is used to show the spider's body and its proximity to Miss Muffet's face. The close-up primarily focuses on the main character's face. The camera angle is at eye-level, putting the audience face-to-face with the villain and equal to Miss Muffet's point of view.

Figure 3.32: *The close-up shot and camera angle put the audience face-to-face with the antagonist of the story and equal to Miss Muffet's point of view.*

When our heroine becomes aware of her little friend, an extreme close-up highlights the terror. Many horror films make use of extreme close-ups, especially zeroing in on a character's eyes to convey fear. This type of shot is great for adding a dramatic punch, or emphasis to the action in the story.

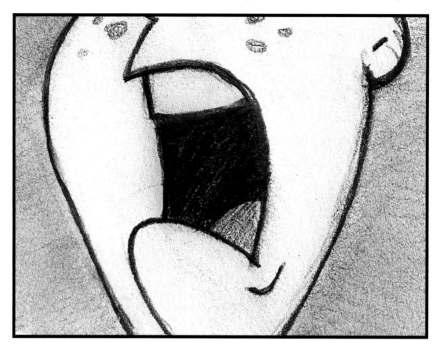

Figure 3.33: *The extreme close-up highlight's Miss Muffet's fright.*

The last shot provides closure by reestablishing the extreme long shot shown at the beginning. This shot also clearly illustrates how the setting has been altered by the events of the story with our heroine running away. This is one way to show this story. Experiment with different camera shots in a different order to see how it affects the narrative.

The Opening Shot   **The Closing Shot**

Figure 3.34: *The last camera shot provides closure to the story.*

Drawing a Storyboard

The previous storyboard panels were created using a good old pencil and paper. Drawing on paper is still an effective way to build storyboards. As you can see, each drawn panel shows the basic shot layout, character gestures, and camera placement.

It is always good practice to draw your storyboard panels at the same dimensions as your final Flash file. That is why it is so important for you to determine your Flash Stage size from the beginning. For this example, the final Stage dimensions will be set to 720 x 540 pixels. As discussed in the first part of this chapter, this is a common setting used for NTSC video.

7.5"

10"

Figure 3.35: Draw your storyboard panels at the same dimensions as your Flash Stage.

At 72 pixels per inch, this dimension creates a rectangular box that is 10 x 7.5 inches and fits nicely on a letter size sheet of paper. To conserve paper you could reduce the dimensions by 50% creating two 5 x 3.75 inch boxes. You can also use 3 x 5 plain white index cards to rough out your storyboard. Pin each card up so that you can see the story's visual flow. This technique makes early editing a breeze as you can simply remove a card from, or add a card to, the pinned-up sequence.

 *Storyboard worksheets are provided in the **Chapter_03** folder for you to use when building your storyboards.*

Digital Storyboards in Flash

Drawing storyboards directly into Flash has its advantages for those who like to dive in and start animating. Flash's drawing tools and Timeline provide an excellent workspace to construct a storyboard. *Toon Boom Storyboard (www.toonboom.com/products/storyboard/)* is an application that is worth taking a look it. This is a storyboarding application specifically built for visual storytelling.

If you choose to create your storyboards digitally, invest some money in a pressure-sensitive tablet, such as a Wacom graphics tablet. As mentioned in Chapter 2, this device allows you to draw naturally using a pen-like stylus. It is ideal for artists who started off with hand-drawn sketching as they find it quicker to draw with a Wacom pen rather than learn how to use a mouse to create their cartoons.

When using a pressure-sensitive tablet in Flash, extra options appear in the Tools panel when the Brush Tool is selected. The Use Pressure toggle varies the thickness of each brush stroke based on the amount of pressure you use when drawing with the pen. This captures the rough sketch quality of a traditional hand-drawn storyboard.

Use Pressure

Locate the **Chapter_03** *folder on the CD-ROM. Copy this folder to your hard drive. The folder contains all the files needed to complete the chapter exercises.*

digitalStoryboard

Locate and open the Flash file, **digitalStoryBoard.fla**, in the **Chapter_03** folder you copied to your hard drive. Let's compare a digital storyboard version of Little Miss Muffet to the hand-drawn version deconstructed earlier. Once the file has opened in Flash, scrub through the Timeline to see each shot. For the most part, it looks similar to the hand-drawn version. The difference is not in the visuals but in the setup.

Figure 3.36: *The ability to reuse graphics in Flash helps reduce the storyboard production time.*

One big time-saving advantage to creating a storyboard in Flash is the ability to reuse symbols. Backgrounds, props, and even the characters can be converted into graphic or movie clip symbols and reused without you having to redraw them from shot to shot. Using the layers in the Timeline provides easy adjustments to the overall layout. Each element in the shot can be on its own individual layer and can move separately from the background.

	👁 🔒 ☐	55	60	65	70	75	80
labels	• • ☐		sat on her tuffet				
Miss Muffet	• • ☐						
tree	• • ☐						
foreground hill	• • ☐						
background hill	• • ☐						
sky	• • ☐						

131   30.0 fps   4.3 s

Figure 3.37: *Layers provide easy adjustments to the overall storyboard layout.*

Building an Animatic in Flash

Once each element is constructed in Flash, the Timeline allows you to sequence out each shot over time. If you add background music and/or sound effects you create an **animatic**. An animatic consists of the storyboard images synchronized to a soundtrack. This allows you to work out any timing issues that may exist with the current storyboard. Let's build an animatic using scanned images from the Little Miss Muffet storyboard.

The files you will use for the following exercise have been organized into two folders in the **Chapter_03** folder. The folder labeled **Images** contains digital files of all of the storyboard images. If you have drawn multiple images on one storyboard panel, scan in each drawing as a separate digital file. These smaller images will allow for much smoother playback in Flash when testing the animatic (Figure 3.38).

Images

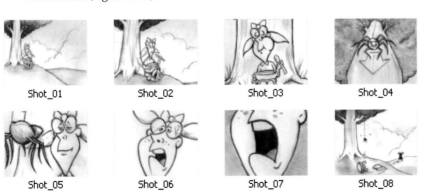

Shot_01   Shot_02   Shot_03   Shot_04

Shot_05   Shot_06   Shot_07   Shot_08

Figure 3.38: *Scan each storyboard image into the computer as a separate file to allow for smoother playback in Flash.*

Each image was scanned into Photoshop at 300 dpi. After the image was adjusted for brightness and contrast, a copy of it was saved as a 72 dpi JPEG file. It is a good idea to save the original higher resolution scan as a backup.

Audio

The folder labeled **Audio** contains one MP3 audio file. Animatics often use a "scratch" audio track which is a rough version of the soundtrack or dialogue. For this example, the audio file will be used as background narration in the animation. With all the files ready to import, open Adobe Flash.

Exercise 1: Setting up an Animatic

1. Create a new **Flash File (ActionScript 3.0)**.

2. Go to the **Properties** panel and click on the **Edit** button next the default Stage size. Change the width to **720** pixels and the height to **540** pixels. Keep the background color set to **white** and the frame rate at **24** frames per second. Click **OK**.

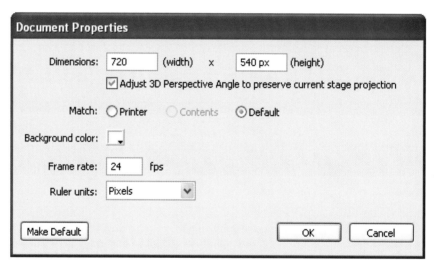

Figure 3.39: *Set the Stage dimensions to match NTSC digital video settings.*

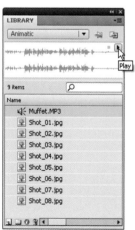

3. Select **File > Import > Import to Library** to open the Import dialog box. Locate and select all the JPEG files in the **Images** folder. Click **Open**. Go to the Library panel. There is a bitmap icon for each image in the sequence. Click on each image to see a thumbnail preview at the top of the Library panel.

4. Select **File > Import > Import to Library.** Locate and select **Muffet.mp3** in the **Audio** folder. Click **Open**. Go to the Library to see that the MP3 file has been added. Click on the **Play** arrow in the thumbnail preview area to listen to the audio.

Chapter 3: Give Me Space

5. Now that all the elements have been imported into Flash, let's organize the Library. Even though this is a very simple story, get into the habit of organizing your Library using folders. More complex Flash files tend to have hundreds of library items, so being organized helps you locate the assets quicker and more efficiently. To organize the Library panel:

    ▶ Click on the **New Folder** icon at the bottom of the Library panel.

    ▶ Double-click on the folder name and rename it **Imported_Images**.

    ▶ Click and drag all of the bitmap assets into the folder. To see the folder's contents in the Library, simply double-click on the folder icon.

    ▶ Click on the **New Folder** icon again. Rename the new folder **Audio_Files**.

    ▶ Click and drag the audio library item into the **Audio_Files** folder.

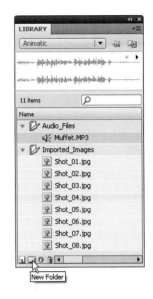

6. Since an animatic consists of storyboard images synchronized to a soundtrack, let's start by adding the audio to the Timeline. Go to the Timeline and double-click on the **Layer 1** name and rename it **audio**.

7. Click and drag **Muffet.mp3** from the Library panel to the Stage. The audio is added to the **audio** layer. To see the entire waveform in the Timeline, click on the empy cell on frame **350**. Select **Insert > Timeline > Frame (F5)** to extend the audio to frame 350.

8. To magnify the waveform, right-click on the **audio** layer name and select **Properties**. In the Layers Properties dialog box, change the layer height to **300%**. Click **OK**.

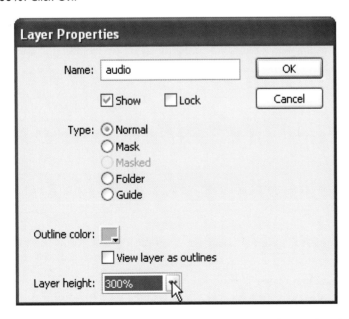

Figure 3.40: *Increase the layer height from 100 to 300% to see the waveform better.*

9. Go to the Properties panel and set the Sync property to **Stream**. Flash supports four different types of sync: **event**, **start**, **stop**, and **stream**. An event sync allows you to play multiple tracks at the same time. A start sync allows only one track to play at a time. A stop sync stops tracks. A stream sync breaks the audio into frame-sized chunks of sound that play back-to-back seamlessly. If you scrub through the Timeline with the sync set to stream, you will hear the audio.

10. Create a new layer directly above the **audio** layer by clicking on the **New Layer** icon at the base of the Timeline panel. Rename the layer to **labels**. You will use this layer to mark the frames that each storyboard image should start on. Lock the **labels** and **audio** layers by clicking on the dot under the padlock symbol.

11. Select the empty keyframe on frame **1** of the **labels** layer. Go to the Properties panel and enter **title** in the **Name** text entry box.

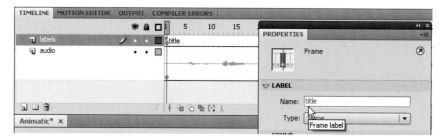

Figure 3.41: *Label the frames using the* **Name** *property in the Properties panel.*

12. Scrub through the Timeline to frame 85. This is where the narration begins in the audio. Click on the empty cell on frame **85** of the **labels** layer. Select **Insert > Timeline > Blank Keyframe** (the keyboard shortcut is F7). Go to the Properties panel and enter **Little Miss Muffet** in the **Name** text entry box.

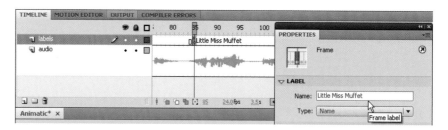

Figure 3.42: *Label the frames using the* **Name** *property in the Properties panel.*

13. Repeat this step to set labels for the remaining storyboard images. To do this, add these frame labels on the following frames:

   ▸ On frame **118** add a frame label named **sat on a tuffet**.
   ▸ On frame **145** add a frame label named **eating her curds and whey**.
   ▸ On frame **218** add a frame label named **along came a spider**.

- On frame **250** add a frame label named **sat down beside her**.
- On frame **283** add a frame label named **frightened Miss Muffet**.
- On frame **314** add a frame label named **away**.

14. Create a new layer by clicking on the **New Layer** icon at the base of the Timeline panel. Rename it **shot_01**. Click and drag **shot_01.jpg** from the Library to the Stage. Center the bitmap image on the Stage.

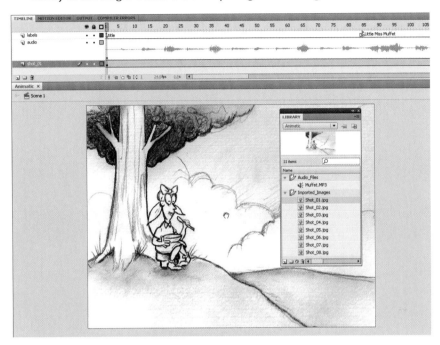

Figure 3.43: *Add the first storyboard image on frame 1 in the Timeline.*

15. Create a new layer above the **shot_01** layer. Rename it **shot_02**.

16. Click on the empty cell on frame **85** of the **shot_02** layer. Select **Insert > Timeline > Blank Keyframe** (the keyboard shortcut is F7). Click and drag **shot_02.jpg** from the Library to the Stage. Center it on the Stage.

Figure 3.44: *Add the second storyboard image on frame 85 in the Timeline. Use the frame labels to help you determine which frame to add the next storyboard image.*

17. Create a new layer above the **shot_02** layer. Rename it **shot_03**.

18. Click on the empty cell on frame **145** of the **shot_03** layer. Select **Insert > Timeline > Blank Keyframe** (the keyboard shortcut is F7). Click and drag **shot_03.jpg** from the Library to the Stage. Center it on the Stage.

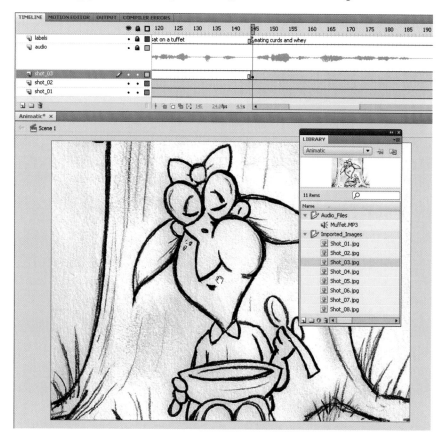

Figure 3.45: *Add the third storyboard image on frame 145 in the Timeline.*

19. Create a new layer above the **shot_03** layer. Rename it **shot_04**.

20. Click on the empty cell on frame **218** of the **shot_04** layer. Select **Insert > Timeline > Blank Keyframe**. Click and drag **shot_04.jpg** from the Library to the Stage. Center it on the Stage.

21. Create a new layer above the **shot_04** layer. Rename it **shot_05**.

22. Click on the empty cell on frame **250** of the **shot_05** layer. Select **Insert > Timeline > Blank Keyframe**. Click and drag **shot_05.jpg** from the Library to the Stage. Center it on the Stage.

23. Create a new layer above the **shot_05** layer. Rename it **shot_06**.

24. Click on the empty cell on frame **283** of the **shot_06** layer. Select **Insert >
    Timeline > Blank Keyframe**. Click and drag **shot_06.jpg** from the Library
    to the Stage. Center it on the Stage.

25. Create a new layer above the **shot_06** layer. Rename it **shot_07**. Click on
    the empty cell on frame **295** of the **shot_07** layer. Select **Insert > Timeline >
    Blank Keyframe**. Click and drag **shot_07.jpg** to the Stage.

26. Create a new layer above the **shot_07** layer. Rename it **shot_08**. Click on
    the empty cell on frame **314** of the **shot_08** layer. Select **Insert > Timeline >
    Blank Keyframe**. Click and drag **shot_08.jpg** to the Stage.

27. When you are done, save and test your movie to see the animatic. To see
    a completed version, open **Animatic_Complete.fla** in the **Completed** folder
    inside the **Chapter_03** folder (Figure 3.46). The Title and Action Safe area
    was added as a new layer.

Animatic_Complete

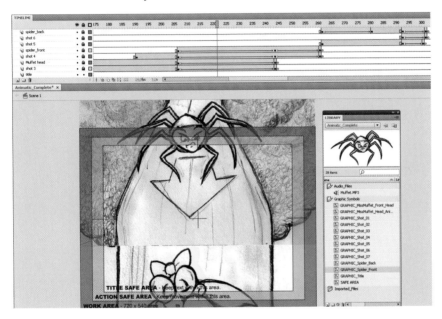

Figure 3.46: *Camera movements are achieved in Flash using motion tweens.*

The completed animatic adds motion tweens to mimic the tracking camera in
the second and fourth shot. Each bitmap image was converted into a graphic
symbol. Keyframes were added in the Timeline and the graphic symbols were
scaled and repositioned on the Stage to achieve the track in shots. A Classic
Tween was applied to each layer to create the animation.

Notice that the image for the tilt camera shot is two images stacked one on top
of the other. The images animates in a downward movement to achieve the tilt.

The cinematography techniques of camera panning and tracking are achieved in Flash using tweens. When panning a shot using a real camera, the image moves across the field of view of the camera lens. In Flash there is no camera. To simulate the camera movements, the position of each layer is tweened across the Stage which acts as the field of view for the audience.

Summary

This completes the chapter. Before your start designing in Flash you need to be aware of the technical requirements and limitations for web and broadcast design. Some key concepts to remember include:

- ▸ Frame aspect ratio is the relationship between the width and height of an image. There are two common video aspect ratios: 4:3 and 16:9.
- ▸ Computers use square pixels and video does not. To compensate for this, adjust the dimensions of your square pixel art to properly display on video.
- ▸ Frame rate is the speed at which Flash plays back its frames. Film uses a frame rate of 24 fps. NTSC video uses 29.97 fps. PAL and SECAM use 25 fps.
- ▸ Computer screens use a progressive scan while television uses an interlaced scan. The interlaced scan is broken up into two fields of scan lines and can affect the display of thin lines and small text.
- ▸ Title Safe and Action Safe guides solve the problem of television overscan.

Once you have determined your delivery output, the next step in the production process is to develop a storyboard. Storyboards illustrate a story shot-by-shot. A feature-length animation can contain hundreds, if not thousands, of shots. A storyboard becomes the blueprint for all the important shots that produce a cohesive and entertaining story for the audience.

The next step is to create an animatic using the storyboard. An animatic consists of the storyboard images synchronized to a soundtrack. This allows you to work out any timing issues that may exist with the current storyboard.

This chapter analyzed camera shots in terms of distance, angle, and movement. The next chapter focuses on three more aspects of the camera shot: framing, depth, and light. While each of these elements is discussed separately in this book, keep in mind that they all come into play within a single shot.

CHAPTER 4

....

Direct My Eye

Good composition arranges visual elements into a harmonious whole, while concentrating the audience's attention to the most significant area of interest in the shot. This chapter focuses on building good compositions and the arrangement of elements in three-dimensional space.

Composing the Space

The previous chapter introduced an important cinematic component called the shot. Shots are the building blocks to your visual story. Every shot in a film or animation is about something, from two characters talking to revealing an object of significant importance (Figure 4.1).

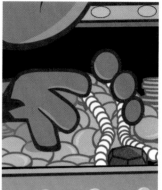

Figure 4.1: *Every shot is about something.*

A cinematographer chooses how to frame a shot using the camera's relative distance from the subject, its angle, and movement. Prior to doing this, it is important to understand how to arrange the elements captured within the frame. When framing a shot, cinematographers position the actors, props, and lights in a way that look aesthetically pleasing to their eye and hopefully to the audience's.

The Rule of Thirds

As a visual storyteller, you must keep the audience visually interested in the scene. How you compose the scene is completely up to you. Some compositions are more effective than others. Building a good composition is not an exact science. Do some research. When you watch a film or animation ask yourself the following questions:

- ► What grabs your attention first in a scene?
- ► What do you notice after that?
- ► What guides your eye around to the most interesting part?

Your imagery should encourage your audience to scan the frame, seeking out what is most important. The **Rule of Thirds** is a compositional guideline that can help. It is a method employed by painters, designers, and photographers to create engaging, dynamic compositions.

The concept behind the Rule of Thirds is to divide the frame horizontally and vertically into thirds (Figure 4.2). The image is divided into nine equal parts by four straight lines, two equally-spaced horizontal lines and two equally-spaced vertical lines. The important compositional element is positioned at the intersection of two lines. Actually any one of the four points of intersection highlighted is a strong place for a point of interest. What about the center?

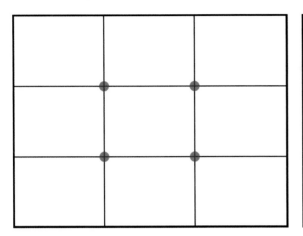 

Figure 4.2: *The Rule of Thirds can help you create engaging, dynamic scenes.*

It is compositionally acceptable to center characters when they directly face the audience. If a character is facing profile, it should be positioned about a third of the way across the shot. The character should look into a space wider than the space behind it (Figure 4.3). This is referred to as **lead room**. If it's not positioned this way, the audience perceives the character as boxed in, with no place to go. No matter how the character faces the audience, make sure you provide enough headroom.

Figure 4.3: *Position the character about a third of the way across the shot with more space in front of it.*

Take a look a Figure 4.4. The left image shows a lack of headroom resulting in an unconformable composition. We feel like the man is going to hit his head on the top of the frame. The middle image provides too much headroom and the character appears to fall out of the frame. The right image illustrates proper headroom by providing just enough open space above the man's head.

Figure 4.4: *Make sure you provide enough headroom for your character in the frame.*

The horizon line, if visible, should never be in the center of the composition where it divides the composition in half. If the frame is split into two equal halves, there is no tension generated. The composition appears weak and uninteresting to the audience. Each half of the frame visually communicates different emotional connotations.

The top half of a composition implies a feeling of freedom, aspiration or accomplishment. Characters placed in the top half of a composition dominate the shot. The bottom half suggests a heavier, oppressed feeling. Characters placed in the lower half of a composition look and feel dominated or constrained (Figure 4.5).

Figure 4.5: *Each half of the frame communicates different emotional connotations.*

Try to balance the elements of the composition. Make sure the top or sides of the shot do not appear visually 'heavier' than the bottom or the opposite side. If you are going to follow any rule regarding composition, the best one to follow is to keep it simple. Clarity is essential. Each composition should clearly focus the audience's attention.

Design elements such as line, shape, color, and value are used together to form a composition. Each element conveys a certain message. When combined together, they evoke an emotional response from the audience. Let's look at these elem ents of visual design in more detail.

Drawing the Line

Lines are a good place to start because they are the most basic element of design. They imply movement and direct the viewer's eye within a frame. Lines can be horizontal, vertical, or diagonal. Each line orientation generates a different psychological and emotional reaction from the audience.

A horizontal line conveys a sense of stability, restfulness, or calm. Most of us associate horizontal lines with the horizon or a floor, something stable that we can walk on without the risk of falling down. When we go to sleep at night, we lie down in a horizontal position.

A composition primarily made up of horizontal lines implies an overall sense of peacefulness to an audience. Figure 4.6 shows a cowboy riding his horse across the flat, open prairie. The horizontal nature of the composition communicates an uneventful journey to the audience with no visible danger lying ahead for the character.

Figure 4.6: *Horizontal lines convey a sense of stability and calm.*

Vertical lines do just the opposite. They convey strength and power. Compared to horizontal lines, vertical lines are more dynamic, active and tend to dominate the scene. If we add a cactus to the previous shot, the viewer's eye would be attracted to its vertical direction. Vertical lines can also represent walls or barriers. The cactus is now perceived as an obstacle in the cowboy's path.

Figure 4.7: *Vertical lines convey a sense of strength and power. They are more dynamic and active.*

Diagonal lines imply motion. Static objects arranged in a diagonal composition appear to move. Tilting a stable horizontal world diagonally evokes a sense of disorientation and instability. Diagonal lines can be effective in adding tension to a scene. Compositions comprised mainly of diagonal lines can cause considerable psychological discomfort in the audience.

Tilting the flat horizon diagonally changes the cowboy's peaceful journey into an uphill adventure (Figure 4.8). Why? Think about gravity and how it affects you when you climb a hill or stairs. The diagonal line ascending from left to right implies a movement that is more physical to follow than a flat, stable line.

Figure 4.8: Diagonal lines evoke a sense of disorientation and instability. They imply a movement that is more physical to follow than a horizontal line.

What if the shot was flipped horizontally? Now the diagonal line is ascending right to left (Figure 4.9). This makes the journey appear even more difficult. In addition to fighting gravity, the implied movement created by the diagonal line goes against how we read from left to right. Our eyes want to travel across the screen comfortably from left to right. Any element or motion that goes against this requires more focus and attention.

Figure 4.9: Implied movement goes against how we read an image from left to right.

Lines provide a visual pathway for the viewer's eye to follow. However, a line in a composition does not have to physically be a line. Implied lines come in all forms. This is often referred to as **leading lines** in scenes. When designing your composition, have something lead into the subject from near a bottom corner, like a road, path, fence, or line of trees to help the eye find the way to the center of interest (Figure 4.10).

Figure 4.10: *Leading lines help the audience find the center of interest.*

Lines can also be connected to form shapes such as a triangle. A triangle is commonly used in compositions to frame action involving characters or objects. The dynamic nature of a triangle allows the audience to follow around the three points to create a sense of unity in the composition.

Figure 4.11: *Triangular compositions communicate the roles of each character.*

A court room scene is a good example of a triangular composition. The judge is positioned at the height of the triangle's apex making him superior to the lawyer and the witness testifying. If the triangle is reversed, with the apex at the bottom, the character positioned there appears much weaker than the other two. An interrogation scene in a crime drama is a good example (Figure 4.12).

Figure 4.12: *Turning the triangle upside down conveys a different emotional response from the audience.*

Lines can be curved to create circular compositions. The circle is a universal symbol signifying completeness, unity, perfection, and eternity. A circular composition draws the audience deeper into the shot. It provides a more intimate space for the audience.

Figure 4.13: *A circular composition draws the audience deeper into the shot.*

No matter how you use lines or shapes, your composition needs to have one and only one center of interest. The audience needs to be attracted to that one point. In the previous examples, note the gaze of each character. They do not look out towards the audience but at the center of interest in the shot. Their gazes carry our eyes to what is important.

Lines are strong design elements that direct the audience's attention and imply dynamic action. However, lines can also be distracting elements in a frame if used incorrectly. For example, if a line passes through the head of a character, it seems to cut into the head (Figure 4.14).

Figure 4.14: *Avoid using lines that pass directly through a character.*

Overlapping lines are OK, but avoid connecting outlines of one form to another. The connection made is called a **tangent** and can be visually confusing to the eye. It joins the two forms as one when they need to be distinguished as two separate elements. To fix this, separate your objects or make sure there is no clear intersection of lines in the shot (Figure 4.15).

Figure 4.15: *Tangent lines can create awkward compositions. Try and separate your objects or make sure there is no clear intersection of lines in the composition.*

Being Dominant

If all the elements in a shot are of equal size or shape, with nothing being clearly dominant, it becomes very difficult for the audience to know what to focus on. Often certain elements within a composition seem to leap off the screen and take visual precedence. Contrasting scale establishes dominance and creates visual harmony in a composition. In Figure 4.16, the middle cow is the dominant figure based on its size in the frame. Audiences naturally seek out the most dominant element in a composition.

Figure 4.16: *Contrasting scale establishes dominance in the frame.*

Color serves as a dominant element. It can separate one object from others to attract the audience's attention. Figure 4.17 illustrates this. In Chapter 1, the film *Schindler List* (1993) was referenced for its use of color in visual storytelling. Steven Spielberg photographed much of the film in black and white. About half way through the film a girl is shown in a red coat. Spielberg costumed her in red to visually reinforce her as a dominant element. The audience immediately focuses its attention due to the contrast in color.

You can also tap into a viewer's psychological interpretation of color. Your audience members will have different reactions to different colors. The color red is a good example; it can be perceived as meaning power, strength, or passion, but it can also be associated with anger, violence, or danger. Each color has distinctive emotions attached to it based on the viewer's personal experiences.

Figure 4.17: *Color establishes dominance in the frame.*

Cultures share common opinions about color, for example:

- **Red** = hot, power, anger, violence, love, fire
- **Yellow** = warm, joyful, sickness
- **Blue** = cold, tranquil, peace, water, sadness
- **Orange** = courage, cheerful, energy
- **Green** = growth, healthy, greed, envy, good luck

Color can be manipulated to reflect the mood of a scene and personality of its occupants. Figure 4.18 shows a woman standing next to an open door. She is holding a letter. Even though we cannot read the letter's content, the use of the color blue establishes a mood of melancholy. We can deduce through the color that the letter did not bring good news.

Figure 4.18: *The color blue helps establish a mood of melancholy in the scene.*

Value refers to the lightness and darkness of a color. Contrast between light and dark can also create compositional dominance in a scene. Every element within the frame has a specific brightness. By increasing the light in one area or on a subject you create an area of dominance within a composition. A bright object or area in a frame gives it extra weight and attracts the viewer's eye.

On the other hand, areas of darkness can also serve as dominant compositional elements. The term **film noir**, French for "black film," refers to Hollywood crime dramas popular in the 1940s and '50s. Cinematographers in the Film Noir genre experimented with shadows in their shots. For them, black was the most important element (Figure 4.19).

Figure 4.19: *The film noir genre experimented with dramatic lighting and shadows.*

Forms can be very effective in telling a visual story. Having a character in shadow forces the audience to focus more on the figure's form, less on the detail. If the character is gesturing, the resulting silhouetted image clearly communicates all the visual information the audience needs to know without losing them to any secondary details (Figure 4.19).

Cinematographers sometimes add forms and shapes to "frame" the focal point in the composition. This framing device can be anything from a rectangular doorway or window, to more organic shapes such as a tree branch that hangs into the shot. Using a frame within the frame breaks up the space in interesting ways. It also allows the audience to focus on two separate events in the same frame.

Figure 4.20: *Add forms or shapes to "frame" the focal point in the composition.*

In order for the frame to read as a frame, you need to provide enough negative space between the frame edge and the subject inside the frame. These frames tend to be positioned in the foreground with the subject matter placed behind it. In addition to adding more interest to the composition, the resulting image illustrates a three-dimensional space within a two-dimensional frame.

Having Some Depth

The world around us has three physical dimensions: height, width, and depth. The images you create in Flash have only two dimensions: height and width. The illusion of depth can be illustrated within a two-dimensional space. How?

The answer is right in front of us. We start with our perception of depth and the visual cues found in the real world. Artists throughout the centuries have relied on their depth perception to vividly construct three-dimensional worlds on two-dimensional surfaces.

Depth Perception

Take a moment to look at the environment around you. What do you see? You see a world in three dimensions. Now focus on an object that is close to you. Your mind tells you how far the object is from you, the space it occupies in front of or behind something else, and its three-dimensional shape. What makes this incredible is that our eyes are producing only two-dimensional images. It is the human brain that assembles each image and extrapolates the depth.

This sense of depth is a result of **stereoscopic vision** (Figure 4.21). Our eyes are spaced apart, which produces a slightly different image on each retina. To demonstrate this, hold this book in front of you. Take turns closing one eye. Notice the difference in what you see from the left eye to the right. Your left eye will see the left side of the book, while the right eye will reveal the right side of the book.

Figure 4.21: *Stereoscopic vision—each eye produces a slightly different image.*

Our brain interprets this retinal difference and then merges the two images into a single three-dimensional image. The resulting image allows us to perceive depth and estimate distance. The difference between each retinal image is a direct result of the depth of the objects that we are looking at—the closer the object, the greater the difference in each retinal image. Distant objects, such as mountains, are so far away that our eyes produce essentially the same image, making depth imperceptible.

Stereoscopic vision isn't the only way our brain interprets depth. Similar to a camera lens, our eyes adjust themselves to bring something into focus. Try the following experiment. Hold your finger in front of you. Position it about six inches from your face and focus on it. What happens to the objects in the distance? They are blurry and out of focus. Our brain uses the eye's focal adjustment to determine the distance of the object from ourselves. We perceive the finger to be closer to us based on the level of detail our eyes adjusted to.

We can take advantage of these visual cues when working in a two-dimensional medium. These include linear perspective, relative image size, interposition, light and shadows, surface shading, and aerial perspective. Let's start with perspective.

Getting into Perspective

Perspective drawings are the most realistic type of representational drawing. Before illustrating perspective, let's look at what goes into a 3D drawing. In order to simulate three dimensions within a 2D world you need four components. They are:

- ▶ A three-dimensional object
- ▶ A picture plane with a horizon line and vanishing point
- ▶ Projection rays to project the object onto the picture plane's surface
- ▶ A viewer to observe the object's image on the picture plane

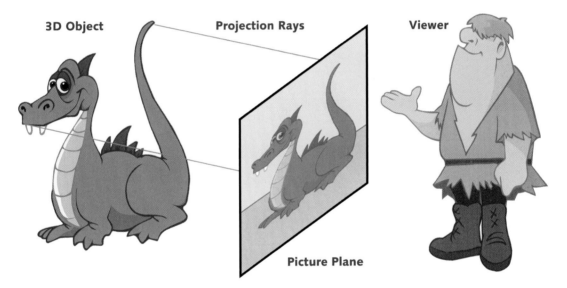

3D Object   **Projection Rays**   **Viewer**

Picture Plane

Figure 4.22: *Three dimensional drawings consist of four components.*

In perspective, parallel lines that recede into the distance appear to get closer together. A common image used to illustrate this is a railroad track. The parallel lines of the track appear to converge at a **vanishing point** on the horizon. There are three types of perspective drawings: one-, two-, and three-point perspective. Let's look at each in more detail to see how you can apply it to your compositions.

If one face of an object is parallel to the picture plane, or its horizontal lines and vertical lines are parallel to the picture plane, the resulting image is a **one-point perspective**. There is only one vanishing point on the horizon line. In animation, one-point perspective is commonly used for roads, railroad tracks, or buildings and props that directly face the audience.

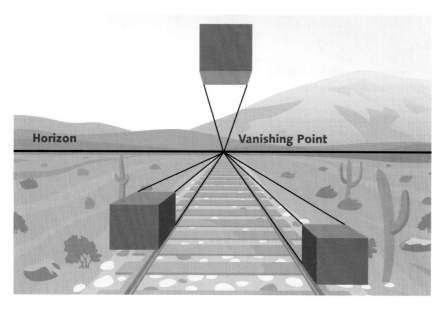

Figure 4.23: *One-point perspective.*

If only vertical lines are parallel to the picture plane and no faces of the object are parallel to the picture plane, the resulting image is a **two-point perspective**. This is the most common perspective used in building basic cityscapes or street scenes in animation.

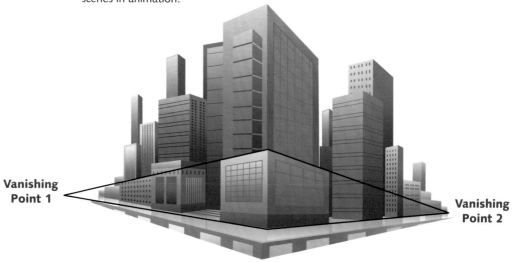

Figure 4.24: *Two-point perspective.*

If no faces or edges of an object are parallel to the picture plane, the resulting image is a three-point perspective. This perspective is commonly used for high or low angle camera shots when the audience is looking at a tall building.

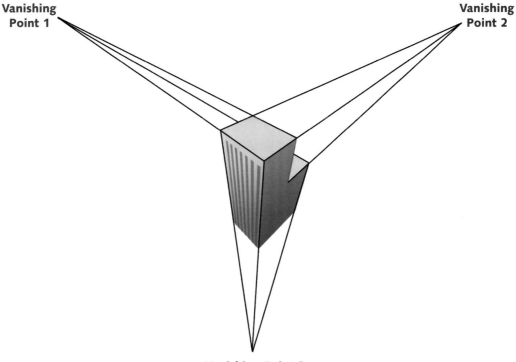

Vanishing Point 1

Vanishing Point 2

Figure 4.25: *Three-point perspective.*   **Vanishing Point 3**

Visual Depth Cues

Perspective is a visual depth cue that can be simulated within a two-dimensional world. What other information in our environment allows us to perceive depth? Another simple visual cue called **relative size** is easy to reproduce.

The size of each object suggests its relative distance to the viewer. Objects larger in scale are perceived to be in closer proximity than smaller scaled objects, as shown in Figure 4.26. Even though this is a flat, two-dimensional image, the soldier on the left appears closer because of his larger size when compared to the other soldiers in the scene.

Dramatic manipulation of scale directs the eye to what is important. It can also help establish the mood in the scene. If a character is small in scale, he may be perceived as insignificant. Larger objects can convey a feeling of menace, especially if they overlap other elements in the shot.

Figure 4.26: *Relative size—which Roman soldier is closer?*

Figure 4.27 demonstrates **interposition**, or overlapping shapes. All of the objects are at the same distance from the screen to your eyes, yet the composition portrays a sense of depth. Overlapping objects assist in creating this illusion. The red ball is partially blocking the view of the man. It appears to be closer to the viewer. The cast shadow also helps establish that the ball's position is in front of the man. Light and shadows are essential in creating the illusion of three-dimensional space.

Figure 4.27: *Interposition—which object is closer?*

Chapter 4: Direct My Eye

Without these two elements, objects would appear flat. Highlights are a result of light illuminating or reflecting off an object. Shadows exist where the light cannot reach. Light and shadows differentiate parts of an object that are at different depths. Figure 4.28 demonstrates how light and shadows affect the perception of depth. Both images are the same. The image on the right has been flipped vertically.

 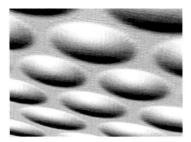

Figure 4.28: *Depth perception based on light and shadow.*

Notice what happens to the highlights and shadows and how depth is perceived. The raised bumps in the left image become recessed pits in the right image. Surface shading defines form by giving an object a three-dimensional feel. In Figure 4.29 the light is coming from the left. The highlights showcase the light's angle and define the blue ball's smooth surface.

The gradient shading across the ball's surface shows the falloff of light around the object. It helps illustrate the object's spherical shape. The illusion of roundness is achieved through the curvature of the shadows near the bottom. The cast shadow underneath the ball also helps establish where the light is coming from.

Figure 4.29: *Light and shadows define the surface of the ball.*

Our atmosphere scatters light, which affects our depth perception. Figure 4.30 simulates this occurrence. Both soldiers are the same size and distance from the viewer. The right image has been blurred, and the overall coloring is blended into the background. With these changes, the man on the right appears slightly farther away than the soldier on the left. This depth change in coloring and clarity is known as **aerial perspective**.

Figure 4.30: *Aerial perspective—which Roman soldier is closer?*

Focusing Attention

In addition to understanding depth cues found in nature, it is important to understand how a camera lens captures depth. **Depth of field** is the area in front of a camera where everything appears sharp and in focus. For example, if a cinematographer focuses on an actor standing ten feet in front of the camera, the depth of field can be anywhere from eight to 15 feet. Objects positioned within this area will be in focus; objects falling outside the area will be soft and out of focus.

When dealing with 35mm film, a 50mm focal length creates an image that most closely approximates human sight. Changes in the focal length can drastically impact the depth perceived in your 3D environment. Wide angle lenses have much shorter focal lengths and tend to exaggerate depth. Figure 4.31 shows a stretched haunted hallway seen through a 20mm focal length.

Figure 4.31: *Wide angle lenses have much shorter focal lengths and tend to exaggerate depth.*

A telephoto lens uses a longer focal length. It does not capture a wide area of the 3D environment. The perceived depth is reduced considerably. Figure 4.32 shows the same 3D environment seen through a 135mm focal length. The hallway now looks like a very small, compressed space.

Figure 4.32: *Telephoto lenses use a longer focal length and tend to compress depth considerably.*

Cinematographers use a technique called **racking focus** to selectively shift the emphasis from one part of the shot to another. For example, the shot may start with only the background in focus. As this technique begins, the background blurs and the foreground comes into focus.

You can employ this cinematic technique to dramatically reveal plot points in your story. Figure 4.33 shows a man sitting in a chair. Based on his posture, he appears to be upset about something. Through the use of racking focus (bottom image) the audience sees what is upsetting the man.

Figure 4.33: *Racking focus can dramatically reveal plot points in your story.*

Simulating Depth in Flash

Let's apply what you have just read about to Flash. Flash provides you with an assortment of tools and programming code to simulate depth. Both of the following exercises focus on developing the illusion of three-dimensional worlds within a two-dimensional environment. Let's begin.

Locate the Chapter_04 folder on the CD-ROM. Copy this folder to your hard drive. The folder contains all the files needed to complete the chapter exercises.

Exercise 1: Perspective Angles and Vanishing Points

Flash CS4 introduced the ability to position and animate objects in three-dimensional space. Prior to that, Flash designers simulated depth through scaling objects. The 3D Rotation Tool and the 3D Translation Tool allow you to maneuver movie clip symbols in 3D space.

These 3D tools only work on movie clips and no other types of symbols. Also, the 3D capabilities of Flash only work in Flash Player 10 and ActionScript 3.0.

Before you begin using these 3D tools you need to understand the 3D coordinate system. Similar to any 3D modeling application, Flash divides its screen coordinate system into three axes (Figure 4.34).

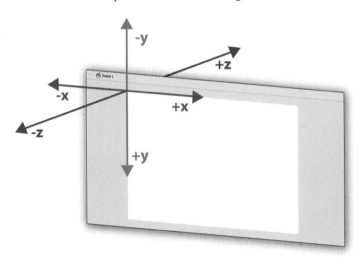

Figure 4.34: *The 3D coordinate system in Flash.*

- ▸ The **x-axis** runs horizontally across the Stage with its origin, or 0-point at the left edge of the Stage.
- ▸ The **y-axis** runs vertically, with its 0-point at the top edge of the Stage.
- ▸ The **z-axis** runs into and out of the plane of the Stage (toward and away from the viewer), with its 0-point at the plane of the Stage.

01_3DPerspective

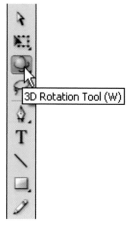

3D Rotation Tool (W)

1. Open the file **01_3DPerspective.fla** in the **Chapter_04** folder you copied to your hard drive. It contains all of the files you need to complete this exercise. There are four layers in the Timeline labeled **character**, **title**, **guides**, and **background**. The title on the Stage is a movie clip instance.

2. Select the 3D Rotation Tool (**W**).

3. Single-click on the title movie clip. A guide for the 3D rotation appears as a multicolored circular target. Each guide line is color coded: the red line rotates the movie clip instance along the x-axis, the green line rotates the instance along the y-axis, and the blue line rotates the instance along the z-axis.

Figure 4.35: *A guide for the 3D rotation appears as a multicolored circular target.*

4. Experiment with the 3D Rotation Tool. Click on one of the guides and drag the mouse in either direction to rotate the title movie clip instance in 3D space. The orange circular guide allows you to freely rotate the instance in all three directions.

Figure 4.36: *The orange circular guide allows you to freely rotate the movie clip.*

5. Reset the rotation of the movie clip instance. Open the Transform panel and click on the **Remove Transform** button in the lower-right corner (Figure 4.37).

Chapter 4: Direct My Eye

Figure 4.37: *Remove the 3D transformation using the Transform panel.*

You can adjust the Perspective Angle and Vanishing Point properties of the Flash file. Adjusting the Perspective Angle is similar to zooming in or out of the Stage. Changing the Vanishing Point position affects the 3D objects' transformations on the Stage. These settings will only affect the appearance of movie clip instances that have a 3D transform applied to them. It is also important to mention that Flash only has one viewpoint, or "camera." Each Flash file has one perspective Angle and Vanishing Point setting.

6. Make sure the title movie clip instance is highlighted on the Stage. Go to the Properties panel. Expand the **3D Position and View** section. The default location of the Vanishing Point is the center of the Stage. The **guides** layer shows where the vanishing point would be in this scene. Adjust the vanishing point to match. In the Properties panel:

   ▸ Click-and-drag the **X** value of the Vanishing Point setting to **-515.0** to move the vanishing point indicated on the Stage by intersecting gray lines.

   ▸ The background image's horizon line is above the horizontal center of the Stage. Click-and-drag the **Y** value of the Vanishing Point setting to **35.0** to change the vertical position of the vanishing point.

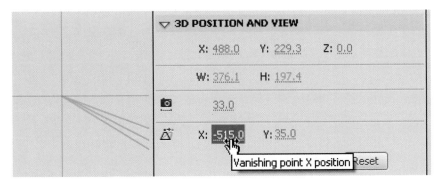

Figure 4.38: *Adjust the vanishing point's X and Y positions to match the guides layer.*

7. Using the 3D Rotation Tool, click on the **y-axis** (green line) and rotate the title to fit comfortably on the brick wall. Notice that by repositioning the vanishing point the title matches the drawn perspective in the scene better.

Figure 4.39: *Rotate the title along the y-axis.*

8. Go to the Properties panel, and change the Perspective Angle to zoom in or out of the Stage.

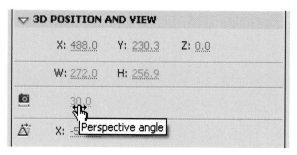

Figure 4.40: *Adjust the perspective angle to zoom in and zoom out.*

9. In the Filters section, click on the **Add Filter** icon at the bottom of the Properties panel. Add a drop shadow to the title movie clip instance. Increase the amount of blur in the drop shadow by changing the Blur X and Y directions to **15 pixels**.

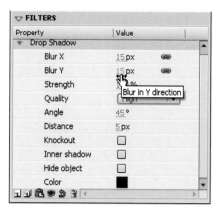

Figure 4.41: *Add a drop shadow to the title.*

Chapter 4: Direct My Eye

10. Save your file. Select **Control > Test Movie** to see the final results. To see a completed version of this exercise, open **01_3DPerspective _Complete.fla** in the **Completed** folder inside the **Chapter_04** folder.

Figure 4.42: *Save and test your movie to see the final results.*

Exercise 2: Racking Focus Using the Blur Filter

This exercise will simulate racking focus using the Blur filter in Flash. To review, cinematographers use racking focus to selectively shift the emphasis from one part of the shot to another. In this exercise, the animation starts with only the background in focus. As the rack focus begins, the background blurs and the foreground comes into focus.

1. Open the file **02_RackFocus.fla** in the **Chapter_04** folder you copied to your hard drive. It contains all of the files you need to complete this exercise. There are two layers in the Timeline labeled **foreground** and **background**. Each object on the Stage is a movie clip instance.

02_RackFocus

2. Select the foreground movie clip instance. Go to the Properties panel.

3. In the Filters section, click on the **Add Filter** icon at the bottom of the Properties panel. Select **Blur** from the drop-down menu. Make sure that the Blur X and Y factors are set to **5**. Set the Quality to **High**.

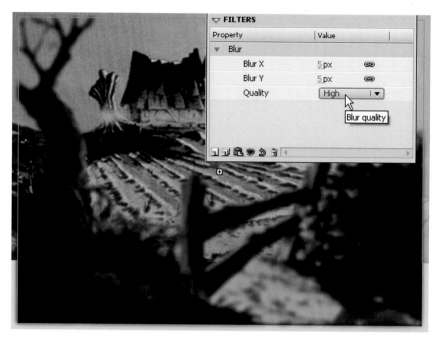

Figure 4.43: *Apply a Blur filter to the foreground movie clip instance.*

4. Click on the empty cell in frame **20** on the **foreground** layer.

5. Select **Insert > Timeline > Keyframe** or press the keyboard shortcut of **F6** to generate a new keyframe.

6. With the foreground still selected on frame **20** go to the Properties panel and reduce the Blur X and Y factors to **0**.

7. Add a tween to the foreground layer by right-clicking on the gray area in between the two keyframes and selecting **Create Classic Tween**.

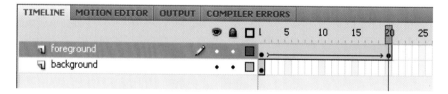

Figure 4.44: *Apply a tween to animate the blur filter.*

8. Save your file. Select **Control > Test Movie** to see the animation. The foreground slowly comes into focus. You are halfway there. Now you need to blur the background.

9. Click on the empty cell in frame **20** on the **background** layer.

10. Select **Insert > Timeline > Keyframe** or press **F6** to generate a new keyframe.

11. With the background movie clip instance still selected on frame **20** go to the Properties panel.

- ▸ In the Filters section, click on the **Add Filter** icon at the bottom of the Properties panel.
- ▸ Select **Blur** from the drop-down menu.
- ▸ Increase the amount of blur by changing the Blur X and Y factors to **7**.
- ▸ Set the Quality to **High**.

Figure 4.45: *Apply a Blur filter to the background movie clip instance.*

12. Add a tween to the background layer by right-clicking on the gray area in between the two keyframes and selecting **Create Classic Tween**.

13. Save your file. Select **Control > Test Movie** to see the animation. To see a completed version of this exercise, open **04_ RackFocus _complete.fla** in the **Completed** folder inside the **Chapter_04** folder.

Figure 4.46: *Save and test your movie to see the final results.*

Summary

This chapter focused on composition. Composition is the structure behind your shot. Its function is to direct the audience's attention to what is happening in the scene. Key points to remember from this chapter include:

- Compositions need to have one and only one center of interest.
- Design elements such as line, shape, color, and value are used together to form a composition.
- Lines direct the audience's attention and imply dynamic action.
- Color can be manipulated to reflect the mood of a scene and personality of its occupants.
- Visual depth cues include linear perspective, relative image size, interposition, light and shadows, and aerial perspective.
- Depth of field is the area in front of a camera where everything appears sharp and in focus.
- Cinematographers use racking focus to selectively shift the emphasis from one part of the shot to another.

Flash provides you with an assortment of tools to simulate depth.

- The 3D Rotation Tool and the 3D Translation Tool allow you to maneuver movie clip symbols in 3D space.
- Adjusting the Perspective Angle is similar to zooming in or out of the Stage.
- Changing the Vanishing Point position affects the 3D objects' transformations on the Stage.
- Flash offers filters that can be applied to symbol instances. These filters include Drop Shadow, Blur, Glow, and Bevel.

Understanding composition works well for individual shots, but you also have to deal with an additional element: time. An animation consists of a sequence of shots that manipulate both space and time. The next chapter focuses on editing shots together into narrative order. The magic of editing is that it can help build on the dramatic tension created from each shot's composition.

CHAPTER 5

Don't Lose Me

In film, an editor stitches together various camera shots to create a seamless sequence of events that appear to take place in a certain space for a certain amount of time. This is a cinematic illusion created by carefully planned camera shots and editing.

Manipulating Time and Space

In Chapters 3 and 4, we studied how cinematographers manipulate the space perceived in a shot. Through clever camera positions, angles, and composition they can create almost any spatial relationship between the elements in the shot. What about time?

Think about it; most movies that you watch take place over the course of a few days, or weeks, or even years. You, as an audience member, see a compressed timeline of the events that transpire. The events shown are essential to drive the narrative forward and condense the actual running time.

So how do you condense time? Figure 5.1 illustrates the first three shots for an animation of a boy painting a fence. Similar to a story's three act structure, a scene can achieve visual continuity using three basic shots: the long shot, the medium shot, and the close-up. Let's deconstruct the sequence of shots as shown in Figure 5.1.

Figure 5.1: *Time can be manipulated using a series of camera shots and editing.*

The opening shot is a long shot that establishes the boy and the fence he has to paint. The next shot is a medium shot showing the boy starting the job. A close-up reveals the boy's determination to finish. The animation contincues with another close-up showing the paintbrush applying the paint, but does not show too much of the fence. Finally, the animation concludes the scene with the same opening long shot, and shows that the painting is almost complete.

A two-hour job has been condensed into a 20-second animation. Had the animation been shown in real time, it would have been about as exciting as watching the paint dry. With that being said, time can also be expanded to add tension or drama to a scene. Locate and open the file **01_ExpandedTime.swf** inside the **Examples** folder in **Chapter_05**.

Figure 5.2: *Editing can expand time to add tension or drama to a scene.*

In this scene, the villain falls off a cliff of a tall mountain. The actual event may only take a few seconds for the character to hit the ground. Clearly this is too short of a time to portray because it cheats the audience in seeing the villain get what he deserves. Instead the animation inserts close-ups of his facial reactions, his clutching hands, his kicking feet, and the background whirling past him as he freefalls (Figure 5.2).

01_ExpandedTime

All of these shots create an expansion in time. The audience doesn't care because they are caught up in the visual storytelling. So, you can see that it is possible to manipulate time through breaking up long scenes into several shots. This makes the story more interesting for the audience. It also allows you to edit the length of each shot too add emphasis to the story where you desire.

Editors achieve this cinematic illusion by editing the movie together after the film has been shot. As a Flash designer, you don't have that luxury. You need to do all of your editing during the storyboard stage. The goal is to establish continuity from shot to shot. Continuity can be achieved by understanding screen direction, applying the 180-degree rule, and the proper use of cuts.

Understanding Screen Direction

Screen direction refers to the direction of movement, or the direction a character is facing within the frame. Too many shots filmed from too many different camera angles can create problems with continuity in screen direction. If a character's position moves forward in one shot and then changes to a move backwards in the next shot, the continuity of the picture is disrupted and the audience is confused (Figure 5.3). Note the skyline in relation to the superhero.

Figure 5.3: *The continuity is disrupted from one shot to the next causing confusion for the audience.*

It is important to understand how a frame transposes our world in two-dimensional space. If a character facing the camera moves to the right, he actually moves toward the left edge of the frame, or screen left. If the character moves to the left, he moves screen right (Figure 5.4). It may seem confusing at first, but the rules of screen direction not only help maintain continuity but also the audience's perception of the space they are viewing.

All screen movement should be mapped out in the storyboard before production begins. If a character's screen movements are not planned out properly, the resulting scenes may be a mix of right-to-left and left-to-right opposing movements, which jeopardizes continuity. What about having two or more people in the shot?

Chapter 5: Don't Lose Me

Figure 5.4: *Screen direction refers to the direction of movement on the Stage.*

Using the 180-Degree Rule

A scene showing two people having dinner in a restaurant might consist of three basic shots: a medium shot showing both of them seated at the table and two close-ups, one for each person. These shots orient the viewer to the space and how the characters occupy it. In order to shoot the scene and edit each shot together effectively it is important to understand the 180-degree rule.

Figure 5.5 illustrates three shots from an animated scene of a conversation between two characters. Notice that something is awkward about the editing of the shots. The second shot of the woman changes in screen direction. She appears to be talking to the back of the man's head. This is called **reversed screen direction**. The line of action has been crossed creating an error in continuity. What is the line of action?

The **line of action** is an imaginary line that determines the direction your characters and objects face when viewed through your virtual Flash "camera." When you cross the line of action, you reverse the screen direction of everything captured through the camera, even though the characters or object have not moved an inch.

Figure 5.5: *The reversed screen direction in Shot 2 causes an error in continuity.*

Top View

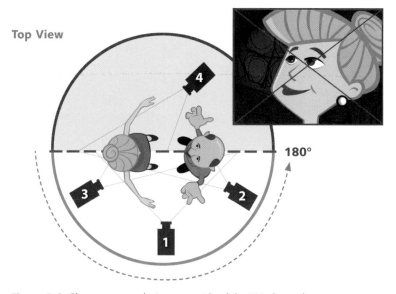

Figure 5.6: *Choose camera shots on one side of the 180-degree line.*

Figure 5.6 illustrates this concept using the two characters seen from an overhead view. The imaginary line runs through both characters' heads. Its direction is based on how each character faces one another. The primary rule is to pick one side of the line and stay on it throughout the scene. This is called the **180-degree rule**.

As long as the camera stays on the front side of the line, the man will be looking screen left and the woman will be looking screen right. If you cross the line, they'll be looking in the opposite directions, although they haven't moved at all. You can choose from a variety of camera shots and angles as long as you stay on one side of the 180-degree line.

Note the matching eye lines (Figure 5.7). When using the line of action, the characters' eye line also needs to match from one shot to another. In this example the man is slightly taller than the woman. His downward glance is matched by her eyes looking up from shot to shot.

Figure 5.7: *Match the eye lines when editing shots of two people interacting with one another.*

Locate and open the file **02_LineofAction.swf** inside the **Examples** folder in **Chapter_05**. Click on the different cameras to see how they frame the characters. A mismatch in continuity is achieved by clicking on **camera 4**. Figure 5.6 illustrates the crossing of the line of action.

02_LineofAction

Is there a way to cross the line and still have continuity? Do you always have to follow this rule? Similar to the Rule of Thirds discussed in Chapter 4, the 180-degree rule is only a guideline for maintaining continuity. There may be circumstances in which you want to cross the line. There are a couple of ways to achieve this without confusing the audience. Let's take a look at how to break the 180-degree rule.

Breaking the Rule

The easiest way to break the 180-degree rule is to have your subject change screen direction on camera, within the frame. For example, Figure 5. 8 shows a character physically turn around to face another character in the opposite direction. As long as the change in screen direction is made on camera, there is no confusion.

Figure 5.8: *You can maintain continuity by changing a character's screen direction.*

Another method is to cross the line using one continuous move with the camera. Figure 5.9 shows a robber trying to break into a safe. The initial camera position blocks his actions. To show the audience what he's doing, the camera moves from his left side, behind his back, to the right side. The camera movement transports the audience to a new angle without any disorientation.

In film, a car chase scene typically breaks the 180-degree rule. Locate and open the file **03_CarChase.mov** inside the **Examples** folder in **Chapter_05**. The chase scene is set up left to right along the line of action. The bank robber's point of view (POV) in the second shot reinforces the left to right line of action. In order to show the police officer's POV, the 180-degree rule must be broken.

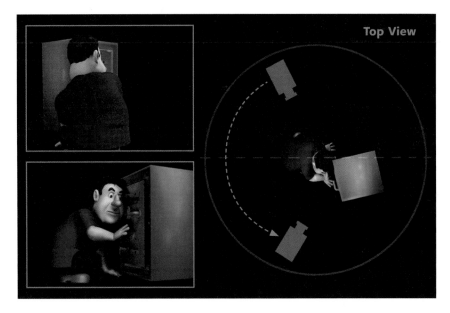

Figure 5.9: *You can maintain continuity by repositioning the camera using one continuous movement.*

A neutral shot of the robber's car is shown in the third shot (Figure 5.10). The camera is placed on the line of action. **Neutral shots** are head-on shots of a subject, with no evident screen direction. By inserting this neutral shot between the robber's POV and the officer's POV taken from the opposite side of the line of action, you can change screen direction and still retain continuity.

03_CarChase

Figure 5.10: *A neutral camera angle allows you to cross the line of action.*

When a shot is completely framed from the character's point of view it is called a **subjective shot**. The camera is perceived to be inside the character's head. The audience sees what the character sees. In the opening scene of John Carpenter's film *Halloween* (1978), the audience looks through the eyes of the killer. This intensifies the audience's fear by participating in the on-screen action.

Subjective shots can be great for establishing not only what a character sees but how it sees. As you read in Chapter 4, applying a simple blur effect creates an out-of-focus shot. When combined with a subjective shot, you can achieve a feeling of a character slipping out of consciousness (Figure 5.11).

Figure 5.11: *Subjective shots establish not only what the character sees but how it sees.*

Building a Sequence

One common mistake used in Flash animation is to contain all of the action to one shot. To convey a story in an interesting manner, you need a series of shots joined together; each shot being continuous like in a stage play. During postproduction on a film, an editor selects, cuts, and arranges various shots into narrative order. An editor must determine:

▸ Which shots to use
▸ What order to put them into
▸ How long each shot will last on screen

Most visual storytelling can be done in animation using a combination of three basic shots. Chapter 3 discussed each shot and what it conveys to the audience. To review, a long shot shows where the action takes place. A medium shot is

Chapter 5: Don't Lose Me

used to focus on a specific character and his or her actions. A close-up is used for character's speaking or showing the action in detail. Choosing the wrong shot can ruin a scene.

Equally important to a shot's image is the order in which it is placed. This is often referred to as **continuity editing**. The action is generally presented in a logical, chronological sequence. Placing shots before or after other shots can create totally different meanings for the audience.

For example, Figure 5.12 shows two images in a sequence. The left image shows a forest fire and the right image shows a man running away. If the sequence is read from left to right, the audience sees that the man escaped from the fire. What if the sequence is reversed? Now the audience thinks that the man running away is responsible for the forest fire (Figure 5.13).

Figure 5.12: *Continuity editing presents each shot in a chronological sequence.*

Figure 5.13: *Reversing the sequence of shots can create a totally different story.*

What about a shot's duration? That depends on the type of story you are telling. The rhythm of a scene is determined by the length and frequency of its shots and the movement within each shot. Watch any chase scene in a movie. These scenes start with a slow build-up with long establishing shots. As the chase reaches its climax, the shots get shorter and shorter in duration. They are presented to the audience in rapid succession to intensify the action.

Horror movies build suspense through skillful editing. A typical horror movie sequence starts with a series of tight close-ups revealing a character's anxiety. This is followed by a long continuous shot of the character walking down a dark path. The deliberately slow pacing heightens the audience's anticipation of what is to come next.

Suddenly a quick cut jolts the audience right out of their seats. Usually it is a shot of a cat jumping out of the shadows. This is followed by slow reaction shots of the character laughing over the situation. The slower pace relaxes the audience allowing them to catch their breath. Just when the audience thinks they are safe, another explosion of quick cuts occurs as the sequence reaches its climax.

Figure 5.14: *Horror movies build suspense through skillful editing.*

In Alfred Hitchcock's film, *Psycho* (1960), a woman is brutally murdered in the shower. Hitchcock used a combination of close-up and extreme close-up shots with short durations. The rapid editing of this sequence implies a more

       Chapter 5: Don't Lose Me

uncontrolled violent death, even though the knife is never shown piercing the body. The subjective camera angles place the audience inside the shower and the rhythmic editing of shots mirrors the killer stabbing the victim.

Building Sequences in Flash

So how do you build a sequence in Flash? One possible solution is to organize your entire animation into separate scenes. Sound familiar? Flash has adopted the filmmaking concept of a scene that allows you to build smaller, more manageable sections of your movie in one document. When you create a new Flash file you are given one scene to work in. **Scene 1** is indicated by the small clapboard icon underneath the Timeline (5.15).

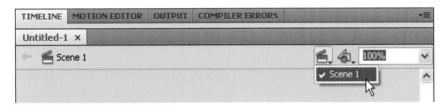

Figure 5.15: *Scenes in Flash allow you to build smaller, more manageable sections for your movie.*

To add a new scene, simply select **Insert > Scene**. Flash creates a new, empty scene labeled **Scene 2**. You can add as many scenes as you want. To manage all of the scenes in a Flash file, open the Scene panel by selecting **Window > Other Panels > Scene** (Figure 5.16). In this panel you can rename each scene by double-clicking on the name.

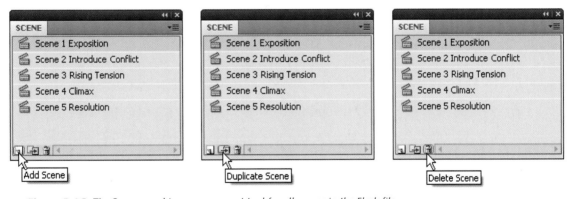

Figure 5.16: *The Scene panel is a management tool for all scenes in the Flash file.*

Flash will play back each scene in order from top to bottom as listed in the Scene panel. Once the playhead reaches the last frame of one scene, it automatically jumps to the first frame in the next scene. To rearrange the scene sequence, click and drag a scene to reposition it in the list. A bright green horizontal line appears to indicate where the scene will be positioned after you release the mouse.

04_TheDuel_Scenes

Locate and open the file **04_TheDuel_Scenes.fla** inside the **Examples** folder in **Chapter_05**. Select **Control > Test Movie** to see the animation. The Flash file is made up of several scenes. To access each scene's separate Timeline single-click on a scene name in the Scene panel or select a scene from the drop-down menu located at the bottom right corner of the Timeline. This technique is great for short animated films under two minutes in duration.

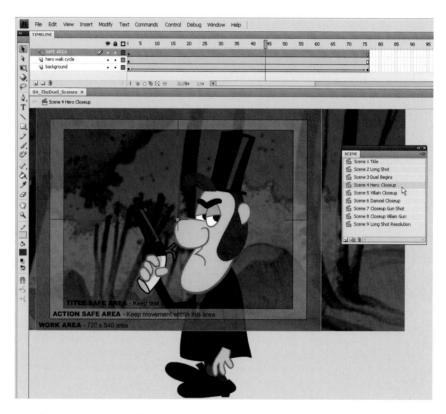

Figure 5.17: *To quickly access each scene's Timeline select a scene from the drop-down menu.*

Is using scenes in Flash the only way to build a sequence? Absolutely not. Locate and open the file **05_TheDuel_GraphicSymbols.fla** inside the **Examples** folder in **Chapter_05**. Select **Control > Test Movie** to see the animation. It is visually the same story as in the previous example. The difference is in how the animation was built.

Instead of using separate scenes in Flash, each shot was nested inside a graphic symbol. The graphic symbols are strung together on the main Timeline in chronological order. Scrub the playback head back and forth to see the nested animation play. This technique is good for quick 30-second animated shorts, web banners, or online commercials.

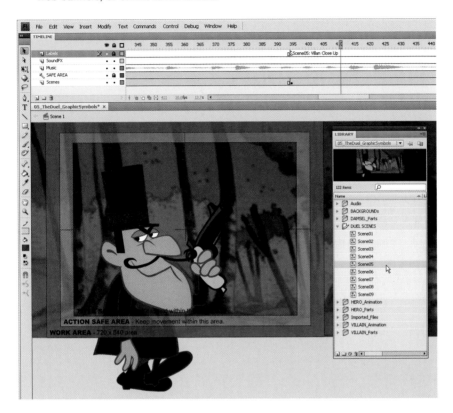

05_TheDuel_Graphic Symbols

Figure 5.18: *Flash animators often place an entire animation inside a graphic symbol's Timeline.*

Both methods are perfectly acceptable to use when building more complex animated films in Flash. The only disadvantage is a potentially large file size, since all of the assets are included in the one file. If file size is a concern, try breaking up your sequence into smaller, separate Flash FLA files. ActionScript can be used to play each published SWF file in chorological order. Chapter 9 covers interactivity in more detail. Even though Flash can store multiple scenes in one large movie, having smaller individual files provides easier editing capabilities, especially when exporting to After Effects. It also reduces the risk of file corruption that could occur using extremely long Timelines.

TheDuel_Scene_01   TheDuel_Scene_02   TheDuel_Scene_03   TheDuel_Scene_04

Figure 5.19: *Sometimes it is better to break scenes from a large Flash animation into separate FLA files and then load the published SWF files dynamically.*

No matter how you choose to build your animation in Flash, you must maintain continuity when sequencing shots together. Movement should flow smoothly and seamlessly from one shot to another. A good editor can assemble a scene without the audience noticing the individual shots. To them the scene is one continuous sequence that takes place in one certain space at a certain time.

Cutting and Continuity

A **cut** is one shot that allows you to easily change the length and/or order of the scene. Cutaways serve to enhance the story. Any shot can act as a cutaway, as long as it relates to and reinforces the main action. The goal in editing a scene is that you want the audience to presume that time and space has been uninterrupted. So how do you cut and still preserve continuity?

Figure 5.20 shows a female character speaking to a crowd. Rather than have the audience sit through her entire speech, another shot is inserted to show the crowd's reaction. With the cutaway of the spectators established, you can now cut back to the speaker at any point in her speech and in effect, condense time.

Figure 5.20: *The cutaway reaction shot (right) can help condense the story's time.*

This type of cutaway shot is commonly used in television interviews to show the reporter listening to the interviewee. A cut doesn't always have to show a reaction shot. Review the example of the boy painting the fence from the beginning of this chapter.

Each cut reinforces the progression in the action. The shots do not show every detail in painting a fence. That would take too long and the audience would become bored. The editing and cutting compress time into smaller shots that assist in moving the action along at a faster pace.

Chapter 5: Don't Lose Me

Relational Cutting

Another editing technique is called **relational cutting**. This type of cut brings together two shots that have no direct connection. If you cut from a long shot showing an airplane in flight to a medium shot of a pilot sitting in a cockpit, you have established for the audience a relationship between the two shots. Relational cutting works well between relatively static shots.

Cutting on the Action

As previously mentioned, the rhythm of a scene can also be affected by the movement within each shot. A good way to achieve a smooth transition between shots is to cut on the action. Audiences will naturally follow movement on the screen. If a movement begins in one shot and ends in the next, the viewer's eye will follow along without becoming disoriented.

For example, Figure 5.21 shows a man picking up a cup of coffee to drink. The scene consists of two camera shots. The first shot is a medium shot showing the action of the man lifting the cup. The second shot is a close-up showing the cup being raised to man's mouth. Even though the camera distance changed, the physical movement of lifting the cup is continuous. The man's movement in the second shot begins where it ended in the first shot. In editing, this is called a **match cut**.

Figure 5.21: *A match cut maintains continuity in movement from shot to shot.*

A match cut helps maintain continuity by carrying the viewer's eye smoothly from one shot to the next. Almost any kind of movement from opening a door to sitting down can be effectively shown using a match cut. In fact, it does not need to involve a large motion. A slight turn of the head or a small hand gesture will work. Match cuts can also be used to tell the story metaphorically.

A famous match cut is in Stanley Kubrick's *2001: A Space Odyssey* (1968). In the beginning of the film, a primitive ape throws a bone into the air after using it as a weapon. When the bone reaches its highest point the shot cuts to a similarly-shaped spaceship which also turns out to be a weapon of the future. This cut compositionally matches the shapes and movement between shots and creates a metaphorical connection between primitive and advanced tools of destruction.

Clean Entrances and Exits

If a character is featured in two successive shots in different locations, the cut needs to have a clean entrance and exit. If you just cut between the two shots, the change in backgrounds will be noticeable and confusing. The audience didn't see how the character got there.

06_CleanEntranceExit

Locate and open the file **06_CleanEntranceExit.swf** inside the **Examples** folder in the **Chapter_05** folder on the accompanying CD-ROM. This simple animation shows the cyclist exit the frame in the second shot. It holds the empty frame for a second or two. Then shows the second background location empty before the cyclist enters the frame. By not seeing the character on screen for a second or two, the audience will accept that he had time to travel to the different location in the following shot.

Figure 5.22: *Have your characters make a clean entrance and exit.*

If you ever watch a play, you will notice that the actors make a clean entrance and exit on the stage. They don't suddenly appear out of thin air. Apply this technique to your animation. Clean entrances and exits work well for shots where someone is moving from one place to another, picking something up, or putting something down. It eliminates awkward shifts in time and allows the audience to focus on the action without being surprised or disoriented.

Jump Cuts

A **jump cut** is an abrupt transition from one shot to another. This type of cut is used sparingly to build suspense. One type of jump cut is called a cut-in and is used to focus the audience's attention immediately on the action. The cut-in shot narrows the audience's view point in the scene. This is accomplished by using a close-up shot of something already within the frame. A good film example occurs in Alfred Hitchcock's *The Birds* (1963). In the film, Hitchcock slowly reveals the body of a dead farmer, and then shocks the audience by cutting in with three quick jump cuts to show that the corpse's eyes were gouged out.

The horrific triple cut first shows a long shot of the farmer's bloodied body, then a medium shot cuts in tighter to frame the body from the waist up, and finally a horrific close-up shot reveals the missing eyes. Rather than using a cut away or a zoom in, Hitchcock choose to use jump cuts to visually push the audience closer and add shock value to the scene.

Crosscutting

So far we have looked at cutting techniques for action that is occurring within the same space. This is called continuity editing. **Crosscutting**, also called parallel editing, cuts back and forth between events happening in different locations. A common example of crosscutting is a phone conversation. Two characters are shown on their phone in their location. The back and forth editing implies that the two events are occurring simultaneously.

Figure 5.23: *Crosscutting cuts back and forth between different locations.*

A classic film example of crosscutting happens in the *Perils of Pauline*, a silent film episodic serial from 1914. In the film, the villain ties the heroine to the railroad tracks as a train approaches. The audience's attention is switched back and forth to show the oncoming train, the woman struggling to free herself, and the hero coming to her rescue (Figure 5.23).

This editing technique works well for action films because it builds on the tension in the scene. The audience is on the edge of their seats in anticipation. Will the hero make it in time to rescue Pauline?

Crosscutting can be effectively used to contrast the action occurring in the story. In Francis Ford Coppola's film *The Godfather* (1972), the baptism of Michael Corleone's (played by actor Al Pacino) godchild in church is crosscut with scenes of Corleone's enemies being murdered by his hired men. This memorable sequence uses the editing to symbolically reflect Michael Corleone's double life he leads as head of the mafia family.

Transitioning Scenes

In addition to cuts, there are other methods you can use to transition from one scene or shot to another. A **fade** is a common transition used in early filmmaking at the start and end of every sequence. A fade increases or decreases the overall value of the scene into one color. For example, a fade to black typically indicates the end of the scene.

One scene can fade out as another scene fades in. This is called a **dissolve** and is used frequently to indicate the passage of time. For example, let's create a medium shot of a little girl standing along the side of the road. Then the shot dissolves to an extreme long shot to imply that she has been waiting for a long time (Figure 5.24).

Dissolves are also used effectively in film to show a character age or turn into a monster right before the viewer's eyes. Watch any classic monster movie from the mid to late 1940s. In *Abbott and Costello Meet Frankenstein* (1948), actor Lon Chaney Jr. is shown transforming into the Wolfman using clever makeup and camera dissolves. The dissolve transformation on screen only took seconds, while Chaney's makeup took almost ten hours.

Figure 5.24: *Dissolves convey the passage of time.*

A **wipe** transition is visually apparent to the audience and clearly marks the change. One scene wipes across the frame and replaces the previous scene. Wipes can move in any direction and open from one side to the other, or they can start in the center and move out, or the edge of the frame and move in. Contemporary film examples include George Lucas' *Star Wars* films which incorporate a sweeping use of wipes that pay homage to the pulp sci-fi serials of the 1930s and '40s.

Figure 5.25: *Wipes can move in any direction to reveal the next shot.*

The Looney Tunes and Merrie Melodies cartoon series employed an **iris wipe** to signify the end of the story. This type of wipe consists of a growing or shrinking circle that reveals the next shot in the scene. The iris wipe can center on the focal point or be used to highlight an inside joke for the audience. For example, the iris wipe can shrink down to the character winking at the audience. This type of action is referred to as "breaking the fourth wall." The character is recognizing the audience watching.

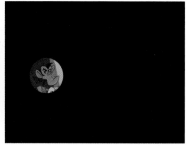

Figure 5.26: *An iris wipe can center on the focal point or be used to highlight an inside joke for the audience.*

Wipes can be cleverly hidden by the movement on the screen. In the movie *Jaws* (1975), director Steven Spielberg shows the sheriff (played by actor Roy Scheider) sitting on the beach. Another actor walks directly in front of the camera obscuring the audience's view. When the actor walks by, the audience sees a new camera position (Figure 5.27). The editor uses the movement on screen as an invisible wipe without the audience noticing.

Figure 5.27: *An invisible wipe incorporates a character's movement in the frame as a transitional element.*

Montages

A **montage** is a series of related shots. Most television commercials and music videos contain montages. For a montage to work effectively, each shot in the sequence needs to be different in composition and show a different subject. Otherwise, the end result will look like a bad cut between two similar shots of the same thing.

Action movies from the mid to late 1980s always incorporated a montage of the hero preparing for battle. Watch any Arnold Schwarzenegger film such as *Commando* (1985) or the opening scenes in Joel Schumacher's *Batman Forever* (1995). Film historians often reference a famous montage from the silent, propaganda film *Battleship Potemkin* (1925). The montage portrays the massacre of civilians on the Odessa Steps showing shots of soldiers marching, a baby carriage rolling down the flight of steps, and a woman with a bloody eye screaming.

Building Transitions in Flash

Let's take a look at building the different types of transitions you just read about in Flash. The exercises that follow offer two distinct methods. In the first method the transitions are created on the Flash Timeline using masked layers and tweened animation to achieve the effect. The second approach uses ActionScript, specifically the **TransitionManager** class, to define the animation effect through code.

 Locate the **Chapter_05** *folder on the CD-ROM. Copy this folder to your hard drive. The folder contains all the files needed to complete the chapter exercises.*

Exercise 1: Fade From Black

Let's begin by building the classic fade transition used quite often in early silent movies. Creating fades in Flash is quite simple and only involves just a handful of steps.

1. Open the file **01_FadeFromBlack.fla** in the **Chapter_05** folder you copied to your hard drive. It contains all of the artwork you need to complete this exercise. There are two layers in the Timeline labeled **fade** and **artwork**. Each object on the Stage is a graphic symbol instance.

01_FadeFromBlack

2. Click on the empty cell in frame **10** on the **fade** layer.

    ▸ Select **Insert > Timeline > Keyframe** or press the keyboard shortcut **F6** to generate a new keyframe.

3. Click on the empty cell in frame **24** on the **fade** layer and create a keyframe.

4. Click on the empty cell in frame **60** on the **artwork** layer.

    ▸ Select **Insert > Timeline > Frame** or press the keyboard shortcut of **F5**.

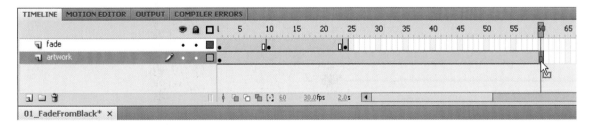

Figure 5.28: *Set up the keyframes for each layer.*

5. Select the keyframe on frame **24** of the **fade** layer. Click on the instance on the Stage. Go to the Properties panel.

    ▸ Select **Alpha** as the Style from the **Color Effect** options.
    ▸ Adjust the **Alpha** setting to **0%**. Visually, the graphic instance disappears on the Stage revealing the **artwork** layer.

6. Add a tween to the **fade** layer by right-clicking on the gray area in between the two keyframes from frame 10 to frame 24 and selecting **Create Classic Tween**.

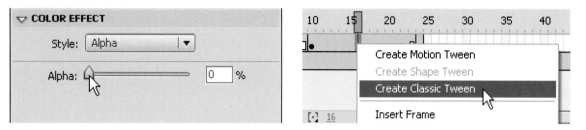

Figure 5.29: *Change the alpha color effect for the graphic symbol and apply a tween.*

7. Save your file. Select **Control > Test Movie** to see the animation. The black rectangular shape slowly fades away to reveal the art. To see a completed version of this exercise, open **01_ FadeFromBlack _Complete.fla** in the **Completed** folder inside the **Chapter_05** folder.

Figure 5.30: *Save and test your movie to see the final results.*

Exercise 2: Dissolve

Creating a dissolve in Flash is very similar to the first exercise. Instead of tweening the alpha property of a black rectangle, you use another symbol instance. Let's take a quick look.

02_Dissolve

1. Open the file **02_Dissolve.fla** in the **Chapter_05** folder you copied to your hard drive. It contains all of the artwork you need to complete this exercise. There are two layers in the Timeline labeled **shot1** and **shot2**. Each object on the Stage is a graphic symbol instance.

2. Click on the empty cell in frame **10** on the **shot 1** layer.

   ▸ Select **Insert > Timeline > Keyframe** or press the keyboard shortcut **F6** to generate a new keyframe.

3. Click on the empty cell in frame **24** on the **shot 1** layer and create another keyframe.

4. Click on the empty cell in frame **60** on the **shot 2** layer.

   ▸ Select **Insert > Timeline > Frame** or press the keyboard shortcut of **F5**.

5. Select the keyframe on frame **24** of the **shot 1** layer. Click on the instance on the Stage. Go to the Properties panel.

   ▸ Select **Alpha** as the Style from the **Color Effect** options.

   ▸ Adjust the **Alpha** setting to **0%**. Visually, the graphic instance disappears on the Stage revealing the **shot 2** layer.

6. Add a tween to the **shot 1** layer by right-clicking on the gray area in between the two keyframes from frame 10 to frame 24 and selecting **Create Classic Tween**.

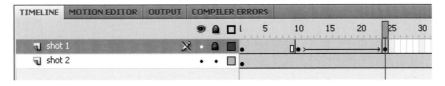

Figure 5.31: *Change the alpha color effect for the graphic symbol and apply a tween.*

7. Save your file. Select **Control > Test Movie** to see the animation. The first image slowly fades away to reveal the art. To see a completed version of this exercise, open **02_ Dissolve _Complete.fla** in the **Completed** folder inside the **Chapter_05** folder.

Exercise 3: Wipes

To create a wipe transition in Flash, you use an animated masked layer. To create a mask, you specify that a layer is a **Mask** layer, and draw a filled shape on that layer. The mask layer reveals the area of linked layers beneath the filled shape.

03_Wipe

1. Open the file **03_Wipe.fla** in the **Chapter_05** folder you copied to your hard drive. It contains all of the artwork you need to complete this exercise. There are three layers in the Timeline labeled **mask**, **shot2** and **shot1**. Each object on the Stage is a graphic symbol instance.

2. Notice that the graphic instance of the mask symbol is positioned off the left hand side of the Stage. Click on the empty cell in frame **20** on the **mask** layer.

   ▸ Select **Insert > Timeline > Keyframe** or press **F6**.

3. Click on the empty cell in frame **60** on the mask layer and create another keyframe. On frame 60:

   ▸ Click and drag the mask symbol instance on the Stage.
   ▸ Center it over the visible artwork.

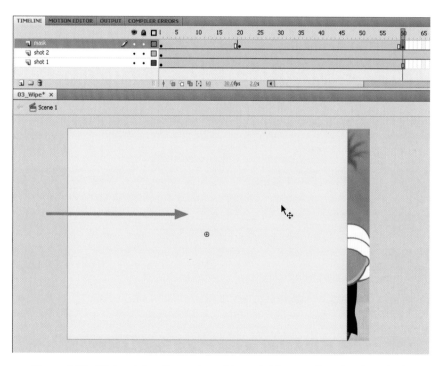

Figure 5.32: *Click and drag the mask graphic symbol to cover the artwork on the Stage.*

4. Add a tween to the **mask** layer by right-clicking on the gray area in between the two keyframes from frame 20 to frame 60 and selecting **Create Classic Tween**.

5. Right-click on the **mask** layer name and select **Mask** from the popup menu. Notice that the **shot2** layer in the Timeline has indented to show that it is a nested layer to the **mask** layer (Figure 5.33).

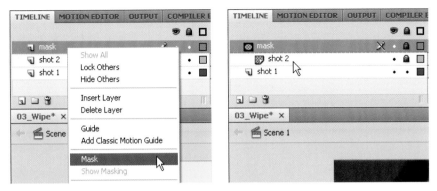

Figure 5.33: *Create a mask layer to finish the wipe transition.*

6. Save your file. Select **Control > Test Movie** to see the animation. To see a completed version of this exercise, open **03_ Wipe _Complete.fla** in the **Completed** folder inside the **Chapter_05** folder.

Figure 5.34: *Save and test your movie to see the final results.*

Exercise 4: Using the TransitionManager Class

The **TransitionManager** class provides ten transitions that can be used either as an "in" or an "out" transition. These transitions are Blinds, Fade, Fly, Iris, Photo, Pixel Dissolve, Rotate, Squeeze, Wipe, and Zoom. Each transition type can be customized to tailor the effect to the specific needs of your project.

04_ TransitionManager

1. Open the file **04_ TransitionManager.fla** in the **Chapter_05** folder you copied to your hard drive. It contains all of the artwork you need to complete this exercise. There is one movie clip instance on the Stage that has an instance name of **myScene_mc**. Since you will be referencing this instance through code, the symbol type has to be a movie clip, not a graphic symbol.

Figure 5.35: *The movie clip has an instance name that can be referenced through code.*

2. Create a new layer by clicking on the **New Layer** icon at the base of the Timeline panel. This layer will hold the ActionScript code. Double-click on the layer name and rename it **actions**. Lock the layer.

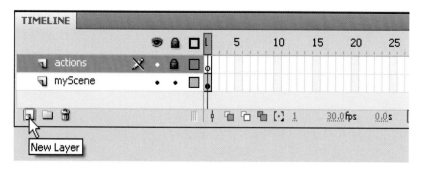

Figure 5.36: *Create a new layer to hold the ActionScript.*

3. Open the Actions panel (**Window > Actions**). The first thing you need to do is import the TransitionManager Class into your current Flash movie. Type in the following code:

```
// import Flash class packages
import fl.transitions.*;
import fl.transitions.easing.*;
```

4. Next create an instance of the TransitionManager Class and set the target movie clip to it. Add to the code you entered in the previous step:

```
// set the target movie clip
var myTransition:TransitionManager = new TransitionManager(myScene_mc);
```

5. To execute a transition use the **.startTransition()** method. This method does not require setting a target movie clip because it was already specified when you instantiated the class in the previous step. Add the following code:

```
// define and start the transistion
myTransition.startTransition({type:Fly, direction:Transition.IN, duration:3,
        easing:Strong.easeOut})
```

6. Save your file. Select **Control > Test Movie** to see the movie clip instance fly in from the left.

TransitionManager Class Deconstructed

The three common shared parameters in the TransitionManager Class are **Direction**, **Duration**, and **Easing**. The Direction parameter has two possible values: **Transition.IN** and **Transition.OUT**. The naming conventions are pretty self explanatory. The Duration is the time period required for the transition to complete in seconds. The Easing parameter dictates the movement of the transition animation.

There are five Easing classes:

- ▸ **None**—No easing is used, the animation moves at a constant speed.
- ▸ **Regular**—The animation will gradually increase or decrease in speed.
- ▸ **Strong**—A more emphasized gradual increase or decrease in the animation speed.
- ▸ **Back**—The animation will move past the final target and then go back (similar to a bounce effect).
- ▸ **Elastic**—This is a mixture of strong and back easing together.

Each of these easing types are further customized by using its easing at the start of the animation (**easeIn**), at the end of the animation (**easeOut**), or both at the start and end of the animation (**easeInOut**). Experiment by changing the code to see a different transition. For example replace the last line of code with:

```
// define and start the transistion
myTransition.startTransition({type:Fly, direction:Transition.OUT,
    duration:3, easing:Elastic.easeInOut})
```

Each transition has its own set of parameters that allow for even further customization. Let's take a look at a couple starting with the **Blinds** transition. In addition to Direction, Duration, and Easing, you can also specify the number of strips to use in the transition and whether to use vertical (**dimension:1**) or horizontal (**dimension:0**) strips. Replace the last line of your code with:

```
// define and start the transistion
myTransition.startTransition({type:Blinds, direction:Transition.OUT,
    duration:3, easing:Regular.easeOut, numStrips:50, dimension:1});
```

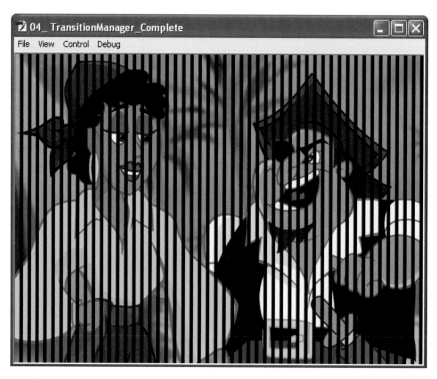

Figure 5.37: *Save and test your movie to see the final results.*

Chapter 5: Don't Lose Me

The Iris transition has two additional parameters that specify the direction from which the mask shows up and whether to use a circle or square as the shape of the mask. The shape parameter can be **Iris.CIRCLE** or **Iris.SQUARE**. The Iris' startPoint accepts any number between 1 and 9:

- ▸ **1** = Top Left
- ▸ **2** = Top Center
- ▸ **3** = Top Right
- ▸ **4** = Left Center
- ▸ **5** = Center
- ▸ **6** = Right Center
- ▸ **7** = Bottom Left
- ▸ **8** = Bottom Center
- ▸ **9** = Bottom Right

Replace the last line of your code with the following:

```
// define and start the transistion
myTransition.startTransition({type:Iris, direction:Transition.OUT,
    duration:3, easing:Regular.easeOut, startPoint:5, shape:Iris.CIRCLE});
```

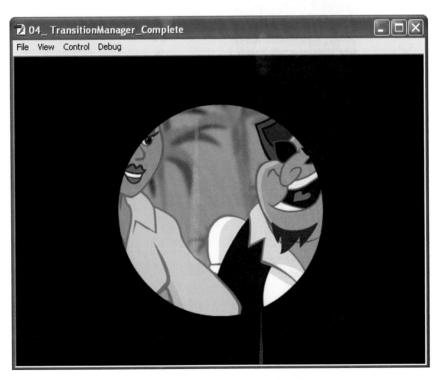

Figure 5.38: *Save and test your movie to see the final results.*

Summary

This completes the chapter on editing and maintaining continuity. Film editors achieve a cinematic illusion by editing a movie together that manipulates both time and space without the audience realizing it. The goal is to establish continuity from shot to shot. Continuity can be achieved by understanding screen direction, applying the 180-degree rule, and the proper use of cuts.

Some key points to remember include:

- Screen direction refers to the direction of movement, or the direction a character is facing within the frame.
- You can choose from a variety of camera shots and angles as long as you stay on one side of the 180-degree line.
- Neutral shots are head-on shots of a subject, with no evident screen direction.
- A good way to achieve a smooth transition between shots is to cut on the action.
- A match cut helps maintain continuity by carrying the viewer's eye smoothly from one shot to the next.
- A jump cut is an abrupt transition from one shot to another.
- Crosscutting cuts back and forth between events happening in different locations.
- A fade increases or decreases the overall value of the scene into one color.
- A dissolve fades one scene out as another scene fades in.
- A wipe transition is visually apparent to the audience and clearly marks the change.

In Flash, you can organize your entire animation into separate scenes. Nesting animation inside graphic symbols is another good technique used for quick 30-second animated shorts, web banners, or online commercials. For more complex animated movies, think about breaking up your sequence into smaller, separate Flash FLA files.

You must maintain continuity when sequencing the shots together. The next chapter deconstructs how to simulate camera movements in Flash. In addition, the chapter revisits your artistic direction by discussing some effective layout and background design tips you can incorporate into your cinematic story.

CHAPTER 6

....

Move the Camera

Movement is an integral component in film and animation. Cinematographers carefully consider when and how to move the camera to help tell the story. Every pan, tilt, dolly, track, and zoom needs to be well thought out. This chapter focuses on simulating these camera moves in Flash.

Chapter 3 briefly introduced several types of camera movements such as pans, tilts, zooms, and tracking shots. This chapter will explore how to achieve these in Flash. A general rule to follow for any type of camera movement is to always begin and end with a good composition. Before discussing each camera movement in detail, let's study a crucial compositional element that is always present in every shot and every camera move–the background.

Creating New Worlds

Backgrounds are the environment in which your story takes place. Equally important to the characters you design is the world in which they will live. Your backgrounds, characters, and props all need to graphically look as if they came from the same world. All of these elements help establish the artistic look of your story.

So what type of visual styles can you choose from? Backgrounds can be realistic, highly stylized, detailed, simple, or in some cases no background at all. No matter which style you select, remember that your characters need to relate to their environment (Figure 6.1).

Figure 6.1: *Which background design is a good graphical match?*

Similar to how you artistically cast your characters, use your imagination to scout out locations for your story. Read over your script and try to visualize what the character's surroundings might look like. Situations in the narrative provide clues as to what you have to draw and include in each scene. Ask yourself what is going on in the scene and what is your character doing. A well-designed background complements the characters, their actions and completes the frame. The key is to only design what is occurring in the shot and what will be viewed by the audience.

In Chapter 3 you read about composition and how important it is to focus the audience's attention on what is important in a shot. This can be achieved graphically in the background image. Design your backgrounds using implied directional lines to point at the center of interest. Think about the visible strokes as well. Most Flash designers use heavier stroke weights to outline their characters. This helps separate them from the background design.

Figure 6.2: *Use implied directional lines to point at the center of interest. Heavier stroke weights separate the character from the environment.*

If your scenery consists of a couple of trees and rocks, compose it to be aesthetically pleasing to the eye and instruct the eye where to look. Repetitious shapes positioned evenly throughout the background make the design boring. The eye has no place to focus on and the scene has very little depth.

To avoid a flat backgorund, apply the visual depth cues you read about in the previous chapters. First, vary the shapes and sizes of the background elements. Overlap objects and position each element sporadically to create a greater sense of depth and interest to the design. Be careful not to make the background too active or visually "noisy." Figure 6.3 illustrates how to redesign and compose a background scene to simulate more three-dimenstional depth in it.

Figure 6.3: *Avoid repetitious shapes spaced evenly in your background (top image). Use scale, overlapping elements, and random positioning for a greater sense of depth.*

When designing your background, allow for some breathing space for the eye to rest in. This doesn't have to be as blatant as a big open sky; it could be a small patch of grass seen from a high-angle shot, or a large boulder sitting in the foreground. Areas of texture placed near large areas of flat color also provide enough contrast to attract the eye.

The amount of detail can make or break a scene. Backgrounds should contain enough detail to clearly establish the location without distracting from the characters or their actions. Figure 6.4 illustrates different levels of detail in context to the camera's relative position. Generally, the closer or tighter the camera shot, the less detail present in a background.

In a long shot, there is enough detail to complement the character. In a close-up shot, the background is kept simple and uncluttered so as not to distract the audience from what the character is doing. In some instances, a background can sometimes be nothing more than a solid area of color.

Figure 6.4: *The closer the camera shot, the less detail present in the background.*

Backgrounds made up of solid areas of color can convey different moods and emotions. Figure 6.5 shows an extremely upset woman framed in a close-up shot. The color red in the background frames the character's emotional state and the zig-zag pattern accents her anger. In constrast, the background color of orange in the right image helps convey the woman's surprise and joy.

Figure 6.5: *Solid areas of color and patterns convey different moods and emotions.*

Colors can be expressed in terms of temperature and affect depth perception in a composition. Cool colors such as blue, green, and violet tend to recede into the background when placed next to warm colors such as red, orange, and yellow. The viewer's eye instinctively goes to the brightest area in an image.

You can also use color to create the illusion of depth by applying different tonal values to the objects to suggest lighting or direction. Figure 6.6 shows a cityscape that uses different sets of values. The image contains a foreground, middleground, and background. Notice how the different color values of light and dark imply a sense of three-dimensional depth to the image.

Figure 6.6: *Different values of light and dark create an illusion of depth in an image.*

Chapter 6: Move the Camera

The most important concept to remember when designing a background is that it should always enhance the action and never distract from it. Always allow for enough contrast. Backgrounds are typically shaded using muted colors so that the characters will stand out. Designing with a relatively monochromatic colors scheme tends to work best. Brighter colors can be used sparingly to frame an action or add a visual dramatic punch to a shot.

Designing Backgrounds in Flash

Optimization is the key to pretty much everything in Flash, especially if you are designing for the web. In Chapter 2, you used reusable symbols to build a character. Symbols help reduce the overall file size and computer processing. The same method works well for backgrounds.

Study your scene to figure out ways to reuse different symbols. Transforming the symbol's size or orientation gives you the flexibility to create backgrounds that look more complex than they really are. In Figure 6.7, all the trees are instances of the same movie clip symbol in the Library. Through scaling, skewing and flipping they look different. Moving all of these elements across the Stage will not greatly impact the processing time since the computer sees each instance as the same symbol.

Figure 6.7: *Figure out creative ways to reuse symbols in your background design.*

What about pixel-based backgrounds? Vector art has a crisp, clean, mechanical look that may not be suitable for your story. Bitmap images can create a softer look for your background and in some cases improve your movie's playback performance. How can that be; aren't vector images smaller than bitmap images? The answer is yes, and no.

Vector images are drawn using mathematical formulas to provide scalable graphics in a compact size. However, rendering an anti-aliased vector shape can take more processing power than rendering a bitmap image. Remember, a bitmap is pixel-based data. Although this data tends to be much larger in file size, once it is downloaded, it can be drawn quickly.

Figure 6.8: *Complex vector shapes can use more processing power than a bitmap image.*

If a vector background contains many points, it can be larger than an equivalent bitmap version. Think about this as you design your backgrounds. Even though Flash inherently creates vector artwork, a bitmap animation can, in some cases, lead to a performance increase without a significant file size increase.

When animating the backgrounds, the camera movement needs to have a sense of purpose in your visual storytelling. The movement should only be used to contribute to the audience's understanding of what they are seeing. If it doesn't help tell the story, the camera move becomes a distracting element by calling attention to itself.

There's a tendency with beginning Flash animators to overuse pans, zooms, and tracking shots in their projects. The constant motion works to your disadvantage when trying to keep the audience focused and entertained. Let's deconstruct each camera movement to see when to use them and how to build them in your Flash animation.

Panning the Camera

A pan (P) shot rotates the camera horizontally from left to right or right to left, similar to moving your head from side to side. Pans are used for establishing shots, where the camera pans across the horizon of a landscape. A pan can also give the feeling of searching for something within a shot.

Unfortunately, you can't just grab a camera in Flash and pan with it. There is no camera. To achieve a panning effect you need to design a background that is larger than the Stage's width and then tween the artwork's position moving across the Stage.

Locate the **Chapter_06** *folder on the CD-ROM. Copy this folder to your hard drive. The folder contains all the files needed to complete the chapter exercises.*

Figure 6.9: *A pan shot rotates the camera horizontally from left to right or right to left.*

Locate and open the file **01_HorizontalPan.fla** inside the **Examples** folder in the **Chapter_06** folder. Once the file has opened in Flash, select **Control > Test Movie**. The "camera" pans across the scene of a country road from left to right. Let's deconstruct the basic setup of the FLA file.

01_HorizontalPan

The image was built in Photoshop and saved as a JPEG file. Its width is larger than the Stage's dimensions. After the bitmap file was imported and converted into a graphic symbol, an instance of the background was placed at the starting position for the pan on frame 1. A new keyframe was added on frame 160 and the artwork was repositioned at the ending position of the pan. Since the artwork is larger than the Stage, it often helps to set the panned layer to an outline. That way, you can see the Stage. Finally a tween was applied by right-clicking in between both keyframes and selecting **Create Classic Tween** from the context menu (Figure 6.10).

Figure 6.10: *To achieve a pan shot in Flash use a tween to animate the artwork's horizontal position.*

02_LeadingMove

A pan shot appears rather flat and lacking depth even with movement. An effective way to enhance a long pan is to follow a smaller object such as a person walking. Locate and open the file **02_LeadingMove.swf** inside the **Examples** folder in **Chapter_06**. For this example, the pan across the cottages is much more interesting with a person walking by, leading the action.

Leading the Action

When the "camera" leads the action, allow for space between the character in motion and the edge of the frame. If there is less space in front of the character than behind it, the composition looks confined and awkward. The character appears to be running away or as if being followed. Provide more space in front of the character to visually define the area the character is walking into.

Figure 6.11: *Allow for more space in front of the character.*

Chapter 6: Move the Camera

Distorting Perspective

Think about changing perspective to create an interesting pan shot or tilt shot (vertical pan). Locate and open the file **03_DistortedPan.swf** inside the **Examples** folder in **Chapter_06**. In this example the background is designed to allow a character to walk toward the camera, pass behind it, and then walk away from it (Figure 6.12).

03_DistortedPan

Figure 6.12: *The artwork is distorted in the middle as the camera turns.*

In reality, the hallway is rectangular in shape. However, in order to achieve the camera pan from one side to the other, the artwork is distorted in the middle as the camera turns. By creating a "fish-eyed" view in the artwork, you create the illusion of the camera turning in space. This is achieved using the **Distort** and **Warp** transform tools in Photoshop. Figure 6.13 illustrates how to do this.

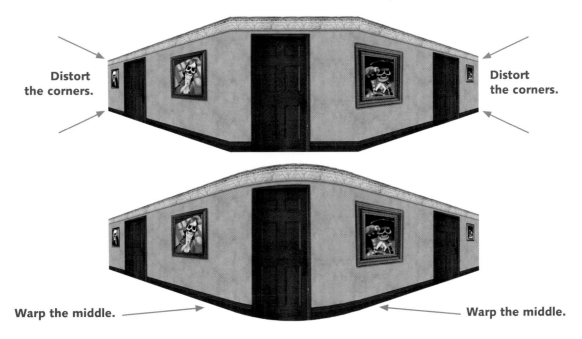

Distort the corners.

Distort the corners.

Warp the middle.

Warp the middle.

Figure 6.13: *In Photoshop, distort and warp the middle of the image.*

Similar to the first camera pan Flash example, the exported JPEG file was then imported and converted into a graphic symbol. A tween was applied to acheive the panning movement. The character was added on a different layer and scaled to achieve the illusion of walking toward and away from the camera.

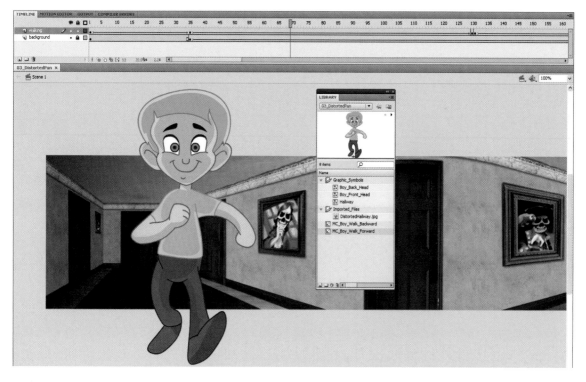

Figure 6.14: *To achieve a pan shot in Flash use a tween to animate the artwork's horizontal position.*

04_DistortedTilt

This type of perspective distortion can also graphically depict the action of looking up or down. A vertical camera pan is called a tilt. Locate and open the file **04_DistortedTilt.swf** inside the **Examples** folder in **Chapter_06**. The image was distorted in Photoshop similar to the previous example. The **Warp** Tool was used to stretch the middle section of the building (Figure 6.15 left image). The exported JPEG file was imported into Flash and converted into a graphic symbol. A tween was applied to acheive the tilt camera movement.

There are three vanishing points used in this example. Figure 6.15 illustrates each vanishing point. The top image is Point A, a bird's-eye view. The viewpoint is looking down so the edges of the skyscraper thin towards the first vanishing point. As the tween moves the "camera" up, the skyscraper widens in the middle which is at eye-level, the second vanishing point. Continue moving up to Point B (bottom image) where the edges of the skyscraper narrow again but this time in the opposite direction toward the third and final vanishing point.

Chapter 6: Move the Camera

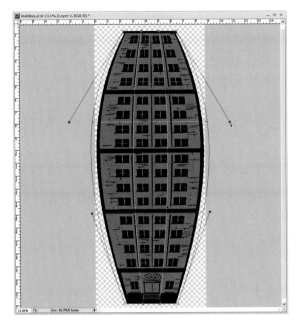

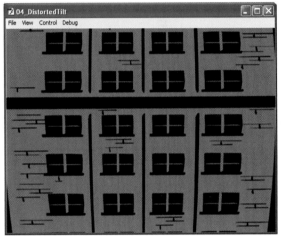

Figure 6.15: *In Photoshop, the Warp Tool was used to distort the middle of the image (above). There are three vanishing points used to create this tilt camera movement (right images).*

In a **zip pan**, the camera moves quickly from one location to another creating a blurred effect. This is commonly used as a transitional device between scenes. A zip pan can give dramatic emphasis to the subject you pan to. Locate and open the file **05_ZipPan.swf** inside the **Examples** folder in **Chapter_06**.

This scene reflects a subjective shot where you see the character's point of view. The zip pan emphasizes the boy's fear as he looks back and forth down the haunted hallway. Figure 6.16 shows the background that was used.

Even though you can blur movie clips in Flash, avoid it when animating. The blur filter requires more processing power than a bitmap image. For this example the actual blur was created in Photoshop using the **Motion Blur** filter and the bitmap panoramic image was imported into Flash and animated using a tween.

Figure 6.16: *A zip pan can give dramatic emphasis to the subject you pan to.*

Strobing Effect

If you pan too fast, vertical lines, like a picket fence, trees, or telephone poles, will create a strobe effect that flickers on screen with trailing ghosted images. This is an effect you must avoid at all costs when designing your background. To avoid the nasty flashing sensation on the viewer's eye, use diagonal lines instead of vertical lines. Do not place elements of the same size at regular intervals. Vary their size, shape and distance (Figure 6.17).

Figure 6.17: *To avoid the nasty flashing sensation on the viewer's eye, use diagonal lines instead of vertical lines.*

Zooming

Zooming is an optical effect that magnifies the image. Perspective is not affected because the foreground and background are magnified equally. You can zoom in on an object to focus attention on a particular character, action, or object in a scene, or you can zoom out to show the audience the entire picture.

In general, a zoom-in directs the audience's attention to whatever it is you are zooming in on. So zoom in on something interesting or that provides important information to push the narrative. A zoom-out tells the audience where the character is. For example, you can start on a close-up of a superhero's face, then zoom out to reveal his location high atop a skyscraper (Figure 6.18).

Figure 6.18: *Zoom in to focus attention and zoom out to show the audience where they are.*

In Flash, a zoom in on an object is achieved by scaling all of the layer's art on the Stage at the same speed. Locate and open the file **06_ZoomIn.swf** inside the **Examples** folder in **Chapter_06**. To zoom out, you would tween them decreasing in size to show the overall picture.

06_ZoomIn

Since zooms lack any sense of depth, use them to help the audience focus on flat static objects in the composition such as a painting on the wall or a letter laying on a table. Zooms should never be used to close in on a person where depth perception is important. Most cinematographers choose to use a dolly or tracking shot over a zoom.

Figure 6.19: *In Flash, a zoom in on an object is achieved by scaling all of the layer's art on the Stage at the same speed.*

Tracking Camera Movements

Cameras can travel from one place to another within a single shot. This is called a dolly, or tracking shot. The camera tracks or follows along with the subject. In some tracking shots, both the camera and the character move. For example, the camera can follow a character from behind or travel alongside them as they move across the shot.

A tracking shot can also be applied when the subject matter stays in one place and the camera moves in relation to it. The camera can move forward, called a truck in, or backward, called a truck out. This type of tracking movement adds depth to the shot. Let's take a look at how to simulate this in Flash using the 3D Translation Tool.

Exercise 1: Using the 3D Translation Tool to Create a Truck In

01_TruckIn

1. Open the file **01_TruckIn.fla** in the **Chapter_06** folder. The Timeline contains four layers: **sky**, **background**, **middleground**, and **foreground**. The artwork on each layer is an instance of a movie clip. The imagery was created in Photoshop and saved as a PNG file to retain the alpha channel. All images were created twice the size of the Stage size. Why?

Figure 6.20: *The artwork was created larger than the Flash Stage's dimensions.*

The artwork needs to be scaled to simulate a camera trucking in. Bitmap images are resolution-dependent. This means that the pixels will become more noticeable as the image dimensions are increased. To correct this, the artwork was created at the largest size possible. Scaling down a bitmap image doesn't create pixellation as scaling it up does.

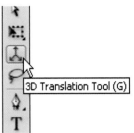

3D Translation Tool (G)

2. Select the 3D Translation Tool (**G**). Unlock the **sky** layer and single-click on the **sky** movie clip instance.

3. To change the Z position of the movie clip, go to the Properties panel and change the **3D Z Position** to **528**. This scales the image down.

Figure 6.21: *Use the 3D Translation Tool to change the depth of the sky movie clip.*

4. Repeat the following steps for the other three layers. Unlock each layer and change the **3D Z Position** for each layer to **505**.

Figure 6.22: *Use the 3D Translation Tool to change the remaining layers' depths to 505.*

5. Select the keyframe for the **background**, **middleground**, and **foreground** layers. Right-click on a highlighted keyframe and select **Create Motion Tween**.

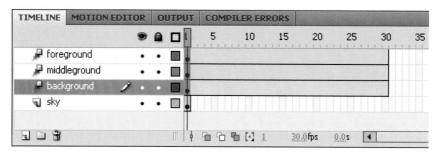

Figure 6.23: *Add a motion tween to the three layers.*

6. Scrub through the Timeline to frame **30**. Click on the foreground image on the Stage. Go to the Properties panel and change the **3D Z Position** to **-150**. A new keyframe is automatically generated on frame **30** of the **foreground** layer.

7. Select the Selection Tool (**V**). Click and drag the foreground art down below the bottom of the Stage. A motion guide appears to show the animation path. Lock the **foreground** layer.

Figure 6.24: *Change the z-depth and position for the foreground artwork.*

8. Click on the middleground image on the Stage. Go to the Properties panel and change the **3D Z Position** to **100**. A new keyframe is automatically generated on frame **30** of the **middleground** layer.

9. Click and drag the middleground art down slightly on the Stage. A motion guide appears to show the animation path. Lock the **middleground** layer.

Chapter 6: Move the Camera

Figure 6.25: *Change the z-depth and position for the middleground artwork.*

10. Click on the background image on the Stage. Go to the Properties panel and change the **3D Z Position** to **200**. Click and drag the background art down slightly on the Stage. Lock the **background** layer.

Figure 6.26: *Change the z-depth and position for the background artwork.*

11. Click on the empty cell in frame **30** on the **sky** layer. Select **Insert > Timeline > Frame (F5)** to extend the movie clip to match the duration of the other layers. You do not need to animate this layer. Why?

   In Chapter 4, we discussed how our stereoscopic vision creates two separate images that our mind merges into a single three-dimensional image. The resulting image allows us to perceive depth and estimate distance. A distant object, such as the moon in the sky, is so far away that our eyes produce essentially the same image, making depth imperceptible. That is why the sky with the moon is not scaled.

12. Save and test the movie. To see a completed version, locate and open **01_TruckIn_Complete.fla** in the **Completed** folder inside the **Chapter_06** folder.

Figure 6.27: Save and test your movie to see the final results.

Parallax Scrolling

Remember the last time you were riding in a car looking out at the passing landscape. The car was moving at a consistent speed, but different parts of the landscape appeared to be moving at different speeds. Objects farthest away, such as rolling hills, appear smaller and move slower when compared to objects in the foreground that race past the car. How does this happen?

Chapter 6: Move the Camera

The illusion is caused by two factors. One is your viewing position or vantage point, and the other is the relative distance the objects are from you. Take a look at the following example (Figure 6.28). Imagine you are in a helicopter looking straight down on three people crossing a street. Each person moves the same distance in the same amount of time. From your viewpoint above, you witness a consistent speed and distance traveled.

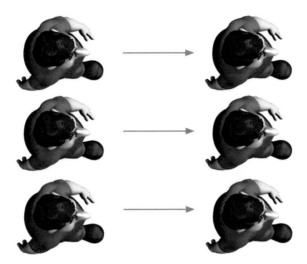

Figure 6.28: *From the top view, the three men travel at a consistent speed.*

Now imagine yourself sitting in a car watching the same three people cross the street. Your vantage point has changed. The speed and distance traveled appear to differ for each person (Figure 6.29). Why?

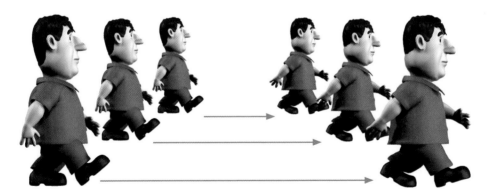

Figure 6.29: *Changing your vantage point changes the appearance of speed and distance traveled for each man.*

It all relates to our perception of depth. The person farthest away is not actually moving slower or traveling less ground. When we changed our vantage point from looking straight down to eye level, we see more of the space surrounding each person. Each person moves relative to the space they occupy. Objects closer to us will appear to travel farther and move more quickly than objects farther away.

Exercise 2: Parallax Scrolling in Flash

How do artists achieve depth in their paintings? They paint objects in the foreground, middle ground, and background. Think of each ground as a separate layer in Flash (Figure 6.30). To achieve parallax scrolling, each layer must move at a different speed.

The Walt Disney Studios perfected this technique for its animated films by inventing a **multiplane camera**. This camera used stacked planes of glass each painted with different background elements. The movements for each plane were photographed frame-by-frame. The illusion of depth was achieved by moving each plane of glass at different speeds.

Figure 6.30: *Each figure ground is a separate layer in Flash.*

In this exercise, you will also build a seamless scrolling background. This was commonly used in Hanna-Barbera cartoons such as *Scooby-Doo* as a time- and cost-saving measure for limited animation. If you ever watch an episode where the characters are driving down a road, you will notice that the background elements repeat themselves as they animate by.

Before you start, let's discuss how you would go about designing the artwork for this type of cinematic effect. The artwork's width must be at least twice the width of the Flash Stage. As discussed in Chapter 3, get into the habit of figuring out the Stage size you will use first.

1. Open **02_ParallaxScroll.fla** in the **Chapter_06** folder. This Flash movie contains the artwork you need to complete this exercise. The Timeline contains four layers: **sky and ground**, **background**, **middleground**, and **foreground**.

    The **foreground** layer contains the cyclist animation. He will remain in this position on the Stage. The illusion of movement and depth will be achieved through the tweening of the pine trees.

2. Let's start with the **background** layer. Before we do this, hide all the layers in the Timeline except the **background** layer. This will allow you to see the Stage when creating the scrolling artwork. It is good practice to get in the habit of hiding or locking layers that you are not working on. This will prevent any accidental changes that could take time to correct later on.

3. The pine tree is vector art created in Flash using the Pen Tool. It has been converted into a movie clip. Click and drag the tree instance to the left edge of the Stage. Center the top of the tree to the left edge of the Stage (Figure 6.31).

02_ParallaxScroll

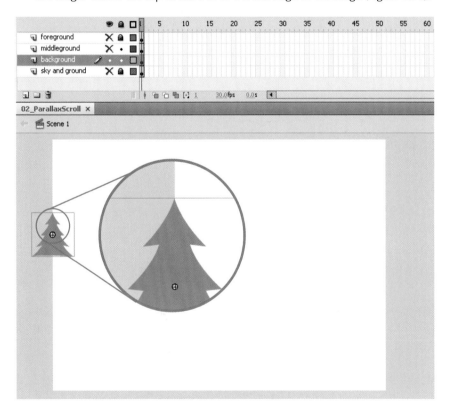

Figure 6.31: *Drag the tree to the left edge of the Stage.*

4. While the tree is still selected, choose **Edit > Copy**. Then choose **Edit > Paste in Place**. This creates a duplicate copy of the tree in the same position, on top of the original.

5. Click and drag the pasted tree to the right edge of the Stage. Hold down the **Shift** key while dragging the tree. This will constrain its vertical movement as you drag. Center the top of the tree to the right edge of the Stage. At this point you should have two trees on the Stage. Both trees are at the same vertical position (Figure 6.32). Why do this?

Figure 6.32: *Both ends must match for the parallax scrolling to work.*

In order for the parallax scrolling to appear as continuous movement, both ends of the scrolling graphic must match. You accomplished this by duplicating the tree in the same position and dragging it to both ends of the Stage.

6. Two trees are boring. We want to create a forest of trees. Since a tree is still copied to the computer's clipboard, paste in several more trees. Fill in the space between each end tree. Position these trees wherever you want (Figure 6.33).

Figure 6.33: *Paste several copies of the trees and position them on the Stage.*

You completed one requirement for the parallax scroll to work—both ends must match. The second requirement is that the scrolling graphic must be at least twice the width of the Stage in order to create the illusion of continuous movement. Currently our row of trees is the same size as the Stage width.

Chapter 6: Move the Camera

7. Select all your trees and choose **Edit > Copy**. Then select **Edit > Paste in Place**. You have duplicated the forest and pasted it exactly on top of the original trees.

8. While the pasted trees are still selected, click and drag them to the left. Hold down the **Shift** key to constrain vertical movement. Align the tree that was on the right edge of the Stage to the one on the left edge. You have now doubled the width of your forest and still maintained matching ends (Figure 6.34).

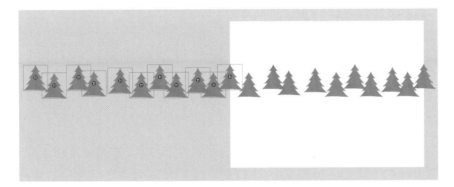

Figure 6.34: *Double the width of the forest.*

9. There is one tree too many. Select the tree in the middle of the forest and delete it. You are now left with the original tree that you moved in Step 3.

10. Group all the trees together. Select all the trees and convert them into a graphic symbol (**Modify > Convert to Symbol**). Name it **forest Back** and make sure the type is set to **Graphic** (Figure 6.35). This will make it easier to animate later.

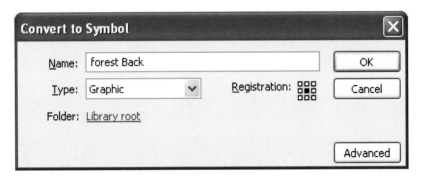

Figure 6.35: *Convert all the trees to a graphic symbol.*

11. Nest the graphic symbol in a movie clip (**Modify > Convert to Symbol**). Name it **MC_scrollingBack** and make sure the type is set to "Movie clip." Why? A movie clip's Timeline plays independently from the root Timeline. To simulate a parallax scroll, each layer will contain a motion-tweened animation that varies in lengths of time. We tween the graphic symbol inside the movie clip. The movie clip gives us the ability to layer several animations together on one frame.

12. Double-click on the movie clip that you just created. This opens its Timeline. Here you will create a motion tween using the nested graphic symbol. Click on the empty cell at frame **60**. Choose **Insert > Timeline > Keyframe (F6)**.

13. Make sure the time marker is still at frame **60**. Select the row of trees on the Stage. Click and drag the trees to the right. Hold down the **Shift** key while dragging to constrain the vertical movement. Align the tree on the left end of the graphic symbol to the left edge of the Stage (Figure 6.36).

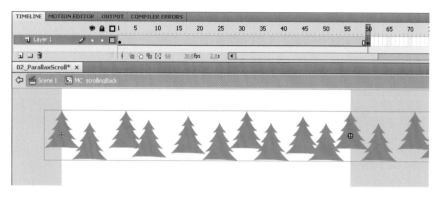

Figure 6.36: *Reposition the graphic symbol on frame 60.*

14. Right-click in between the two keyframes and select **Create Classic Tween**. Flash will generate all the in-between frames creating the scrolling movement.

15. Choose **Control > Test Movie**. The background row of trees animates in a looping scroll. There is a slight pause due to the fact that the first frame and the last frame contain roughly the same image. Close the tested movie.

16. To correct the slight pause, create a new keyframe at frame **59**. This keyframe records the movement of the graphic symbol at that point in time. Select the last keyframe and choose **Edit > Timeline > Remove Frames** (Figure 6.37). Save and test the movie again. Now the slight pause in the animation is eliminated.

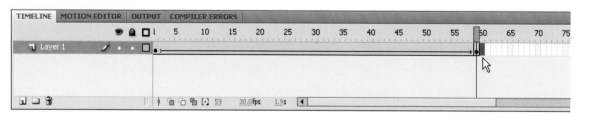

Figure 6.37: *Create a new keyframe on frame 59 and remove the keyframe at 60.*

17. Close the movie clip's Timeline by clicking on **Scene 1** in the bottom-left corner of the Timeline. On the root Timeline, hide the **background** layer and turn on the **middleground** layer. This layer contains a larger pine tree.

Chapter 6: Move the Camera

18. This larger tree is an instance of the same symbol used in the background. Symbols help reduce the final file size of your document. Figure 6.38 illustrates how the tree was altered. The symbol was scaled 200% in the Transform panel.

The color was darkened to reflect atmospheric perspective. Due to lighting conditions, objects closer to us will appear darker than objects further away. Technically, this was accomplished by selecting the movie clip instance and changing the Brightness value in the Properties panel from **100%** to **–30%**.

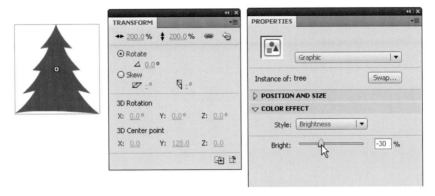

Figure 6.38: *The tree symbol properties for the middle ground.*

19. Let's see how much you have learned. The animation technique is the same as before. The only difference is the number of frames used for the scrolling movement. Instead of using 60 frames to complete its cycle, use 40 frames. Reducing the number of frames will speed up the animation.

This will reinforce the parallax motion. Objects closer to the viewer's perspective will appear to move faster than objects further away. Don't forget to correct for the slight pause in the animation. Refer to step 16 to see how to correct this.

Figure 6.39: *Both ends must match for the parallax scrolling to work. Double the width of the forest to create a continuous scroll.*

20. When you are done, save and test the movie. To see a completed version, locate and open **02_ParallaxScroll_Complete.fla** in the **Completed** folder.

Figure 6.40: *Save and test your movie to see the final results.*

Simulating Cinematic Effects in Flash

Let's wrap up this chapter by showcasing a couple more types of camera movements used by cinematographers. Let's start with a crane shot. A **crane shot** moves through space in any direction. This is achieved by mounting the camera on a crane which acts basically like a big mechanical arm.

Cinematographers often use crane shots for long or extreme long shots. In the film *Gone with the Wind* (1939), there is a famous crane shot that hovers over thousands of wounded Confederate soldiers in Atlanta. This shot effectively shows the casualties of war.

Since crane shots move through 3D space, they naturally work best within a three-dimensional environment. What about Flash? It works in 2D space. Don't despair. The 3D Rotation and Translation tools in Flash allow you to simulate crane shots that add a sense of aerial movement in a scene.

To see an example, locate and open **07_CraneShot.swf** in the **Examples** folder in **Chapter_06**. In this animation the "camera" appears to rise through space towards an apartment window. The interior scene dissolves in slowly. This is an example of a relational cut that bridges the two shots together.

Figure 6.41: *A crane shot can be simulated using the 3D tools in Flash.*

The apartment building is a movie clip that contains two nested movie clips in it. Each instance holds artwork for the front and side of the building. Using the 3D Rotation Tool, each nested movie clip was rotated to create the perspective view of the building. Only two sides are needed since you will not see the back.

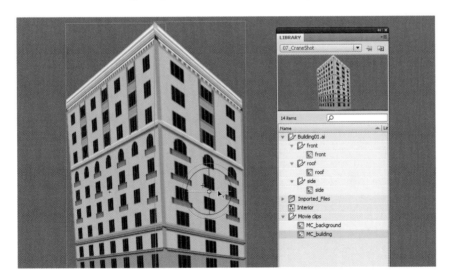

Figure 6.42: *The building is made up of two movie clips that are rotated in 3D space.*

This building movie clip becomes a 3D model container. Since there is only one perspective angle and vanishing point in a Flash movie, any 3D translation made to this movie clip's instance will automatically update its children inside. The parent building movie clip was added to the main Timeline along with a cityscape image. Together, both movie clips were animated over time using the 3D Rotation and Translation Tool to achieve the crane shot. The interior scene is another graphic symbol and fades on top of the **building** and **background** layer.

Figure 6.43: Motion tweens record the 3D translation of the building and background.

Creating a Dolly Zoom or "Vertigo" Shot in Flash

A **dolly** shot is similar to tracking whereby the camera moves in or out of 3D space. Dolly-ins are often used to slowly draw the audience closer to the main character in a scene. This movement makes the character appear more important. If the cinematographer zooms and dollys at the same time, the resulting shot creates a weird, unsettling effect.

Alfred Hitchcock introduced this cinematic effect and it is even referred to as the "Vertigo" shot. In the 1958 film of the same name, actor Jimmy Stewart's character suffers from a fear of heights. To show this character's point of view to the audience, Hitchcock created this camera movement that mimics a feeling of falling or being dizzy.

Steven Spielberg used the effect for a scene in *Jaws* (1975) where Sheriff Brody witnesses a shark attack happen before his eyes. What happens in a dolly zoom is a cameraman zooms the lens in on the center of interest while simultaneously dollying the camera out. The resulting effect creates a sense of growing unease.

To see a Flash example, locate and open **08_ZollyShot.swf** in the **Examples** folder in **Chapter_06**. In this Flash movie, the background layers move along the z-axis while the man remains stationary. This simulates the dolly zoom shot.

Figure 6.44: *A dolly zoom shot can be simulated using the 3D tools in Flash.*

The previous two examples illustrate that you can keyframe a movie clip's 3D position and rotation to simulate some effective camera movements. What about the perspective angle and vanishing point? Can you change their values over time as well? Yes, with a little help from ActionScript.

Locate and open **09_ZollyCodedNightmare.swf** in the **Examples** folder in **Chapter_06**. This camera movement creates a nightmarish effect. A similar effect was used in the movie *Poltergeist* (1982). At the end of the flim, actress JoBeth Williams runs down a seemingly endless hallway to rescue her children.

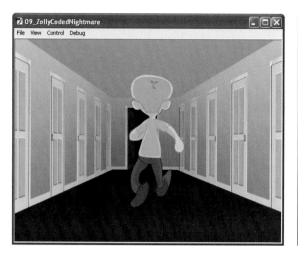 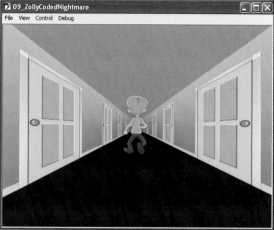

Figure 6.45: *A dolly zoom shot can be simulated using ActionScript in Flash.*

In this file the perspective projection is changed through code to create the distortion in the walls, floor, and ceiling. The character's movie clip is not affected because its 3D properties are not changed. The boy simply scales in size. The ActionScript that creates this dolly zoom is as follows.

```
var cameraLens:Number = 15;
var scaleFactor:Number = 1;

addEventListener(Event.ENTER_FRAME, createVertigo);

function createVertigo(e:Event):void {
 if(cameraLens < 155){
     cameraLens++;
 }
 root.transform.perspectiveProjection.fieldOfView = cameraLens;

 if(scaleFactor > 0){
     scaleFactor = scaleFactor - .005;
 }
 runner_mc.scaleX = runner_mc.scaleY = scaleFactor;
}
```

Summary

This chapter explored how to achieve camera movements in Flash. A general rule to follow for any type of camera movement is to always begin and end with a good composition. The most important concept to remember when designing a background is that it should always enhance the action and never distract from it. In addition to movement, lighting is equally important to cinematographers; and it is the subject of the next chapter.

CHAPTER 7

....

Light My World

Lighting is essential to cinematographers. Light can enhance a scene in a variety of ways to help tell the story and heighten its dramatic and emotional impact. Understanding how lighting affects depth, emotion, mood, and composition is the topic of this chapter.

Defining the Light

There are many elements cinematographers must take into consideration when lighting a scene. They need to be aware of how the light's intensity illuminates the actors or environment around them, how the light's direction bounces off objects, and where the highlights and shadows appear as a result of the light's position. Lights can also be the main focal point in the frame and directly affect the action occurring.

Just like cameras, there are no lights in Flash. As you storyboard your shots for your Flash movie, think of light as an element in your scene just like the virtual camera. Positioning light sources is just as important in visual storytelling as the position of the camera. Lighting, like camera shots, can make or break a scene. So where do you begin? Let start with defining light and where it comes from.

Light is a form of energy. It is made up of electromagnetic radiation. This radiation includes a wide spectrum that includes radio waves, microwaves, ultraviolet waves, X-rays, and visible light. Our eyes act as receivers for the visible light waves.

Visible light comes in the form of electromagnetic waves that we see as colors of the rainbow. Each color has a different wavelength. Red has the longest wavelength and violet has the shortest wavelength. When all the waves are seen together, they make white light (Figure 7.1).

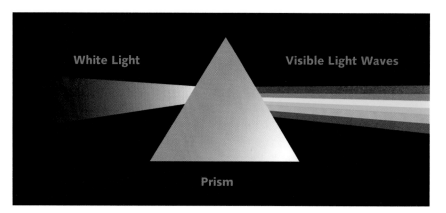

Figure 7.1: *When all visible light waves are seen together, they make white light.*

The sun is a natural source for visible light waves. Our eyes see the reflection of this sunlight off the objects around us. The color of an object that we see is the color of light reflected. All other colors are absorbed. A light bulb is another source of visible light waves. Where a light bulb and the sun differ is in their light intensity.

Intensity is the amount of light that falls upon a subject from a lighting source. It is also referred to as the level of brightness in a scene. Intensity of light plays an important role in establishing your story's location, the time of day, and the overall mood. For example, an outdoor baseball game would have a higher light intensity than a quiet, romantic dinner for two.

Another characteristic of light is its quality. The quality of light falls into two categories, hard or soft. A **hard light** is strong, bright, and directional. The singular light source is relatively smaller than the subject, like a spot light. The subject it illuminates tends to cast harsh, crisp shadows that reinforce the direction of the light source.

The opposite of hard lighting is **soft lighting** (Figure 7.2). In this situation, the light is diffused. Think of the quality of light on a cloudy day versus that of a bright, clear day. The light that falls on the subject can come from multiple sources or one large light source close to the subject. The illumination is not as directional as a hard light and the cast shadows have softer edges.

Figure 7.2: *A hard light (left image) casts harsh shadows while a soft light is not as directional and the cast shadows have softer edges (right image).*

So what are shadows? A **shadow** visually shows an interruption in the flow of light rays by an object. This obstruction produces an absence of light in the form of that shape upon another surface. Shadows fall into two categories, attached and cast shadows.

Attached shadows define an object's shape and texture. In Figure 7.3, the ball shows a slow falloff of light in the shadow area thereby illustrating its spherical shape. **Cast shadows** help define the spatial environment within a frame. A cast shadow can be attached to an object or separate. Cast shadows help define the proximity of the ball to the floor along with the light direction.

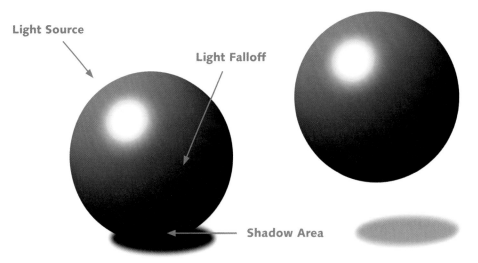

Figure 7.3: *Cast shadows can be attached to the object or separate.*

The direction and angle of a light source can greatly influence how the focal point of the shot is seen. **Frontal lighting** comes from a light source that is in the same position as the camera. The illumination pulls out the most detail in a subject, while reducing attached and cast shadows. Since the light source is directly in front of the subject, the shadows are hidden by the subject.

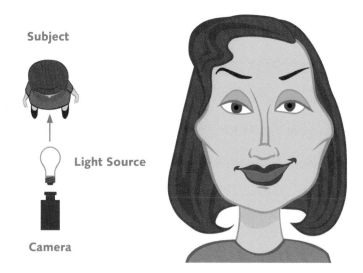

Figure 7.4: *Front-lighting reduces shadows and creates a very flat object.*

Side-lighting comes from a light source that is positioned at a right angle to the camera. This type of lighting enhances the depth of a three dimensional subject. Detail is reduced while shadow areas appear and visually define the surface of the face (Figure 7.5). Textures areas can be enhanced using this type of lighting.

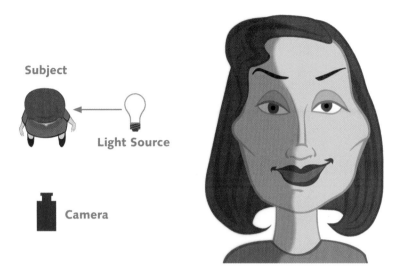

Figure 7.5: *Side-lighting enhances shadows and depth of a three-dimensional object.*

Rim lighting comes from a light source that is positioned opposite the camera, typically behind the subject. The illumination produces a silhouette of the subject. A "rim" of light appears around the shape with little to no detail. This type of lighting is typically used to separate a subject from a dark background.

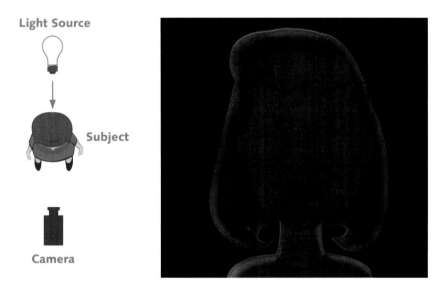

Figure 7.6: *Rim-lighting separates the subject from a dark background.*

Changing the angle of the light source influences the mood and perception of the character that is illuminated. In **low angle lighting** the light is angled below the camera. Light from below the chin can give a mysterious and sinister look to the character. **High angle lighting** can produce a dreary feeling when the subject looks downward or spiritual when the subject looks upward. In this case, the light source is angled above the camera (Figure 7.7).

Figure 7.7: *The angle of the light source can influence how the character is perceived.*

Lighting used in movies comes from either natural light, artificial light, or a combination of the two. To achieve the classic Hollywood lighting scheme, cinematographers employ a **three-point lighting** system. As you probably guessed, there are three types of lights used. These include the key light, fill light, and rim light (also referred to as a back light). Let's take a look at each light in more detail.

Lighting a Scene

In three-point lighting, the primary light source comes from the **key light**. The cinematographer typically starts with the key light when lighting a scene. It is a single source of light that is bright enough to assure proper overall exposure. The key light represents the dominant light source in the scene, such as the sun, a window, or indoor ceiling light.

A key light is positioned at a forty-five degree angle above and to one side of the camera. Since this light is the most dominant and usually shines down on the subject, it generates highlights and casts shadows, especially on three-dimensional surfaces such as a human face. To reduce the contrast between light and dark, cinematographers add a fill and rim light to the scene.

A **fill light** is a weaker light source that helps soften and extend the lighting created by the key light. It is generally positioned at an angle opposite that of the key light. For example, if the key light is on the left, the fill light should be on the right (Figure 7.8).

The fill light lightens the shadow areas, bringing out the detail in the subject and making it more visible to our eyes. Fill lights give the appearance of ambient light. Typically they act as secondary light sources that can come from lamps, or reflected light in the scene.

The last light positioned is the **rim light**. The rim light (also called back light) highlights the edges of the object. This visually separates the object from the background. The rim light (or back light) shines down on the subject from behind and helps give depth to the image (Figure 7.8).

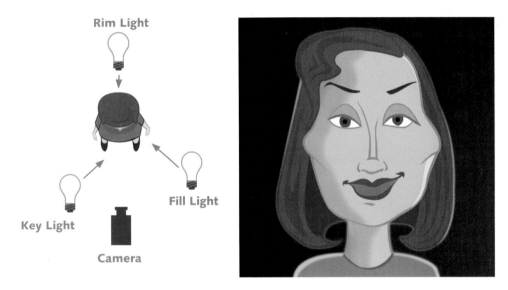

Figure 7.8: *Three-point lighting is the standard used in Hollywood movies.*

Setting the Mood

A cinematographer's job is to control the light and shadows throughout the film. Learning how to control light will influence what type of emotional impact your shots will present to the audience. The two major styles that help to establish an atmosphere or mood are high-key lighting and low-key lighting.

High-key lighting creates a scene that is bright with little contrast between the light and dark areas. This type of lighting can simulate daytime in movies and is used for upbeat, light-hearted stories. Comedies, news shows, and television sitcoms are all good examples that incorporate high-key lighting.

Low-key lighting creates a dramatic, moody scene that is dominated by dark tones. This type of lighting has a strong contrast between light and dark areas. It can simulate nighttime in movies and is used in film noir style dramas, horror, fantasy, and suspense films. Figure 7.9 illustrates the two lighting styles.

Figure 7.9: *High-key (left image) and low-key lighting (right image) are two lighting techniques used by cinematographers for establishing mood and atmosphere.*

Each of these lighting styles has a unique aesthetic value. When choosing a style, you must always consider the story. Reread your story you have chosen to animate or make interactive. Ask yourself, "How will lighting clarify each scene and impact the audience on an emotional level?" In visual storytelling, lighting needs to direct the viewer's eye.

Lighting helps organize a scene by identifying the areas of interest. One way to achieve this is through contrast. By contrasting a character from its surroundings, you create emphasis, or a focal point for the user to look at. This technique can transform a complex scene with many details into one that is easy to read and understand.

In Figure 7.10, notice how the shaft of light and cast shadow draws your attention to the woman. The dramatic lighting clearly identifies the subject of this shot. Also notice the effective use of rim lighting, which separates the woman from the room and allows her to stand out even more.

This form of dramatic lighting started in German Expressionist cinema of the 1920s and '30s. Three influential films are *The Cabinet of Dr. Caligari* (1920), directed by Dr. Robert Wiene; *Nosferatu* (1922), directed by F.W. Murnau; and *Metropolis* (1927), directed by Fritz Lang. The use of light and shadows not only define the frame but suggest the emotional state of the characters.

Figure 7.10: *Lighting needs to direct the eye to the area of interest in a shot.*

The use of shadows can also enhance the mood of a scene. Remember, hard lights create crisp shadows. These shadows can suggest a cold, sterile environment as seen in Figure 7.11. The shadow also evokes the scientist's loneliness locked away all by himself in the lab. All he has is his shadow.

Figure 7.11: *Shadows enhance the mood of a scene and also suggest the environment.*

Lighting can also define depth within a shot. As you read in Chapter 4, our atmosphere scatters light, which affects our depth perception. Figure 7.12 simulates this occurrence. The foreground, middleground, and background change in lighting and coloring to suggest three dimensions.

Figure 7.12: *Lighting can also suggest depth in a scene.*

As a designer and animator, you need to keep in mind that lighting is subjective. There are no true measurements that clearly define light. What is important to remember is that light sets a mood and evokes emotion from the audience. The choices you make in lighting help define and reinforce your story's narrative.

Simulating Lighting Effects in Flash

Let's apply what you just read about to Flash. As previously mentioned, there are no lights in Flash. You have to use the drawing tools and filters to simulate lighting effects. The following exercises focus on different static and animated lighting techniques discussed in the beginning of this chapter.

 *Locate the **Chapter_07** folder on the CD-ROM. Copy this folder to your hard drive. The folder contains all the files needed to complete the chapter exercises.*

Exercise 1: Hard Light Character Shading

1. Open the file **01_HardLightShading.fla** in the **Chapter_07** folder you copied to your hard drive. The detective's head on the Stage was traced from a scanned drawing. The imported scan was placed on its own layer in the Flash Timeline. The layer was locked to prevent it from accidentally moving. The scan was then retraced using the Pencil Tool and filled in with basic colors.

01_HardLightShading

Figure 7.13: *The traced artwork is comprised of several layers in the Timeline.*

Adding shading to our detective will make him appear more three-dimensional. The Brush in Flash is an excellent tool to create shading. Before using the Brush, first pick an appropriate color. Choosing what color to paint is simple. Start with the actual Fill Color used on the shapes. Let's start the surface shading with the detective's head.

2. Select the Eyedropper Tool (**I**) from the Tools panel. Make sure the Fill Color is also selected in the Tools panel. Move the cursor over the detective's head and click. You have just stored that skin color as the Fill Color (Figure 7.14).

Figure 7.14: *Select the Fill Color.*

Shading illustrates the falloff of light's luminosity on an object. Decrease a color's brightness slightly and you have a color for shading. The Color panel allows colors to be mixed and altered.

By default, the color mixer uses RGB (red, green, and blue) color values. Another setting is HSB (hue, saturation, and brightness). Since the brightness needs to change, this is a better setting to use.

3. To change from RGB to HSB, click on the menu icon at the top-right edge of the Color panel. Select **HSB** from the drop-down menu (Figure 7.15). The Color panel will update with the HSB color values.

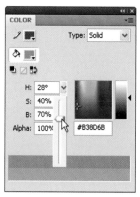

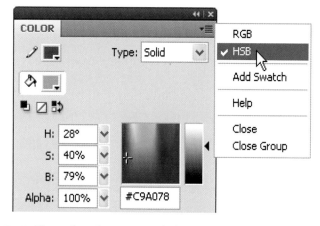

Figure 7.15: *Change the color mixing mode from RGB to HSB.*

4. Decrease the **Brightness** value (**B**) from **79%** to **70%**. This creates a new Fill Color to paint with. The new, darker color will provide the surface shading.

Chapter 7: Light My World

5. The Brush Tool paints shapes with the Fill Color. Select the Brush tool. Notice that there are options associated with this tool. These options are located at the bottom of the Tools panel. They include brush mode, size, and shape.

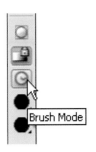

Select the **Brush Mode** drop-down menu. There are several painting options to choose from. Select **Paint Inside** from the list. This will allow you to paint brush strokes directly inside a single filled shape.

6. Make sure the **head** layer is selected in the Timeline. This is the filled shape you need to paint on. For this exercise, the light source is coming from the right side. To simulate the roundness of our detective's head, the shading would appear on the left.

7. With the Brush Tool selected, move the cursor over the head. Position it on the left side. It is important that the point of the cursor is on the flesh-tone fill (Figure 7.16). Click and drag to start painting the surface shading.

Figure 7.16: *Position the brush over the left side of the detective's face.*

8. Don't worry about keeping the brush strokes within the lines. The Paint Inside mode that you selected in Step 5 applies the strokes only in the area that you started to paint on (head). When you are done painting, release the mouse. The shading will only remain inside the head shape (Figure 7.17).

Figure 7.17: *Paint the shading over the detective's face. The Paint Inside brush mode keeps your brush strokes within the face shape.*

9. Use the Selection Tool (**V**) or the Subselection Tool (**A**) to adjust the shading's shape and number of points (Figure 7.18).

Figure 7.18: *Adjust the shading's shape using the selection tools.*

10. Let's see how much you have learned. Repeat steps 2 through 9 to shade the rest of the detective. First select a **Fill Color** using the filled shapes in the character. Decrease or increase the color's brightness using the Color panel. Increasing the brightness can be used to paint highlights on the hat and right side of the face. Make sure the correct layer is selected in the Timeline. Use the Brush Tool to paint the surface shading.

To see the completed exercise, open **01_HardLightShading_Complete.fla** in the **Completed** folder within **Chapter_07** (Figure 7.19). Traditional animators use similar shading techniques to make cartoon characters appear more three-dimensional. It is a combination of darkening or lightening a Fill Color and brushing it onto a shape.

Figure 7.19: *Shading complete.*

The Brush Tool applies this color to your object. The Paint Inside option paints brush strokes only within a single filled area. This type of surface shading produces a hard edge look similar to a hard light. There is another technique that uses gradient fills to create soft light shading. Let's take a look.

Exercise 2: Soft Light Character Shading

Gradients can create convincing lighting effects in Flash. They also provide a composition with a more realistic three-dimensional look and feel. In this exercise you will use gradients to create the illusion of depth and soft lighting.

1. Open the file **02_SoftLightShading.fla** in the **Chapter_07** folder you copied to your hard drive. The file contains all of the artwork you need to complete this exercise. The Timeline contains five layers. The **vampire** folder layer contains nested layers that make up the character (Figure 7.20).

02_SoftLightShading

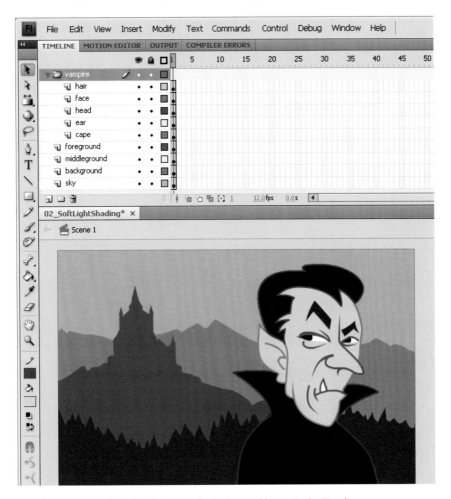

Figure 7.20: *The artwork is comprised of several layers in the Timeline.*

2. Select the vampire's cape on the Stage. Go to the Tools panel and click on the Fill Color swatch. This opens the **Color Swatches** pop-up panel. Select a grayscale linear gradient fill swatch at the bottom of the panel (Figure 7.21). The color in the cape will change to a linear gradient that blends white and black together.

Figure 7.21: *Apply a linear gradient to the vampire's cape.*

3. Go to the Color panel. Double-click on the white (left) color pointer. Select the dark blue color swatch along the bottom row (Figure 7.22). Adjust the **Brightness** value (**B**) to **30%**.

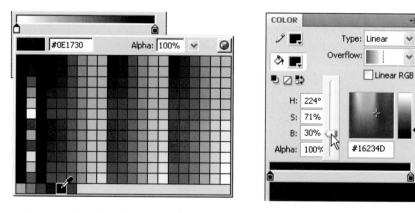

Figure 7.22: *Adjust the color gradient in the Color panel.*

4. Select the Gradient Transform Tool (**F**) in the Tools panel. Click on the rotate handle and drag to the right to rotate the linear gradient slightly. Click on the scale handle and close up the span between the blended colors. Click and drag the move handle to reposition the gradient in the cape (Figure 7.23).

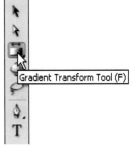

Figure 7.23: *Use the Gradient Transform Tool to adjust the linear gradient fill.*

5. Next, we will focus on shading the vampire's head. Select the Eyedropper Tool (I) from the Tools panel. Make sure the Fill Color is also selected in the Tools panel. Move the cursor over the vampire's head and click to store that skin color as the Fill Color.

6. Decrease the **Brightness** value (**B**) from **100%** to **62%**. This creates a new Fill Color to paint with. The new, darker color will provide the surface shading.

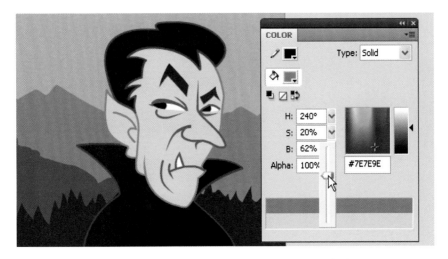

Figure 7.24: *Lower the Brightness value to darken the color for shading.*

7. Click on the **New Layer** icon. Rename the layer **shadow**. Position the new layer in between the **head** and **face** layers in the Timeline (Figure 7.25).

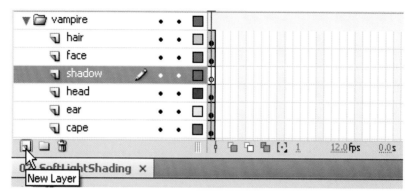

Figure 7.25: *Create a new layer to hold the shading.*

8. With the Brush Tool selected from the Tools panel, move the cursor over the head. Click and drag to start painting the surface shading (Figure 7.26). When you are done painting, release the mouse.

Figure 7.26: *Paint in the shading using the Brush tool.*

9. Adding the Blur filter to the shading will produce the soft lighting effect. First, the shading needs to be converted into a symbol. Click on the shadow. Select **Modify > Convert to Symbol**. The Symbol Properties dialog box appears. Type in **shadow** for the name. Make sure the type is set to **Movie clip**. Click **OK**.

10. Go to the Filters area in the Properties panel and add the Blur filter to the shadow movie clip instance. Increase the Blur X and Blur Y factors to **10**. This produces the soft lighting effect (Figure 7.27).

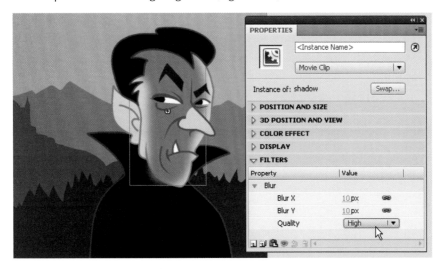

Figure 7.27: *Create a movie clip out of the shading and add a Blur filter to it.*

Some of the soft shading spills out of the head shape and onto the cape. A Mask layer will correct this. A Mask layer defines a visible area that reveals a nested layer below. For this exercise, the **shadow** layer created in Step 6 will be the nested layer. The visible area that will restrict the soft shading only to the head will be the head Fill Color itself.

11. Select the Selection Tool (**V**) from the tools palette. Single-click on the filled shape in the **head** layer and copy it (**Edit > Copy**). Do not select the stroke surrounding the head shape. Only the fill is needed.

Create a new layer above the **shadow** layer. Rename it **Mask**. Paste the filled shape in place (**Edit > Paste in Place**). This keeps the registration of the pasted shape consistent to the head Fill Color shape.

12. Make sure that the **Mask** shadow layer is selected in the Timeline. Right-click and select **Mask** from the popup menu. The mask uses the head Fill Color to reveal the soft shading layer below. Notice that the **shadow** layer indents to show that it is a nested layer (Figure 7.28). The areas of shading that spilled out of the head are now hidden.

Figure 7.28: *Create a mask layer to constrain the soft shading to the face.*

13. Select the vampire's hair on the Stage. Go to the Tools panel and click on the Fill Color swatch. Select a red gradient fill swatch at the bottom of the panel (Figure 7.29). The color in the hair will change to a circular gradient that blends red and black together.

Figure 7.29: *Apply a radial gradient to the vampire's hair.*

14. Go to the Color panel. Double-click on the red (left) color pointer. Select the pale violet color swatch along the bottom row. Double-click on the black (right) color pointer. Select the dark blue color swatch you used for the vampire's cape (Figure 7.30).

Figure 7.30: *Adjust the color gradient in the Color panel.*

15. Select the Gradient Transform Tool (**F**) in the Tools panel. Click on the scale handle and close up the span between the blended colors. Click and drag the move handle to reposition the gradient (Figure 7.31). This creates the soft highlights in the vampire's hair.

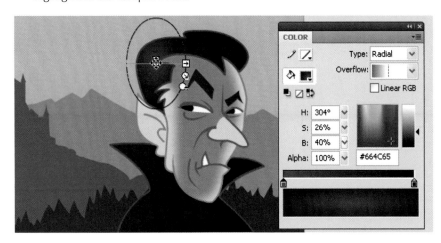
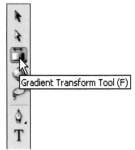

Figure 7.31: *Use the Gradient Transform Tool to adjust the radial gradient fill.*

16. Let's see how much you have learned. Create linear gradient fills for the landscape. Review Chapter 4 to apply aerial perspective to the shot. Convert the **middleground** and **background** layers into movie clips and apply a soft blur to create the illusion of depth. To see the completed exercise, open **02_SoftLightShading_Complete.fla** in the **Completed** folder (Figure 7.32).

Figure 7.32: *Shading complete.*

Exercise 3: Casting Shadows

This exercise explores the possibility of using the drop shadow filter to simulate a cast shadow from a light source. Typically drop shadows are used for buttons or text. Experiment with these filters and tools. With a few simple steps you can simulate basic lighting effects and three-dimensional space.

1. Open the file **03_CastShadows.fla** in the **Chapter_07** folder. This Flash movie contains the artwork you need to complete this exercise. Here we have a soldier on the Stage. The artwork is an instance of the movie clip.

2. Double-click on the soldier to open its Timeline. There are two layers labeled **shadow** and **soldier**. Select the soldier on the **shadow** layer.

03_CastShadows

Figure 7.33: *Select the soldier movie clip nested inside.*

3. Make sure the soldier is still selected. Go to the Properties panel and add a new filter to the instance. In the Filters section, click on the **Add Filter** icon at the bottom of the Properties panel. Select **Drop Shadow** from the popup menu. Instantly a drop shadow appears underneath the soldier.

The drop shadow adds the illusion of depth but currently it is not the desired effect we need for this exercise. The shadow needs to visually establish a ground for our soldier to march on. It will also assist in simulating a directional light source.

4. We only want to see the drop shadow so check the box **Hide Object**. Adjust the Strength from **100%** to **60%**. These settings will help make the shadow more convincing in illustrating depth (Figure 7.34).

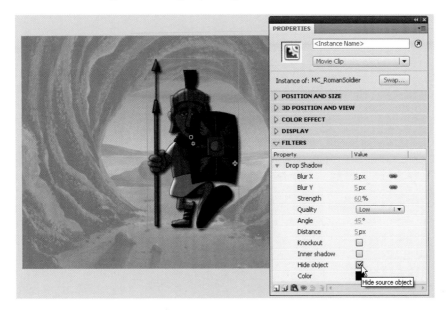

Figure 7.34: *Add a drop shadow to the soldier.*

5. Go to **Modify > Transform > Flip Vertical**. This will flip the drop shadow so that it acts more like a cast shadow coming from the soldier.

6. Skewing the drop shadow horizontally will add perspective. The Skew Tool is found in the Transform panel. Open the Transform panel (**Window > Transform**). Change the Skew value to **150** degrees in the Skew Horizontal text box. Click and drag the shadow to align with the soldier's feet.

Figure 7.35: *Skew the drop shadow to add three-dimensional perspective.*

7. Select the Free Transform Tool (**Q**) from the Tools panel. Position the cursor over the top-middle handle. Click and drag down to scale the drop shadow vertically. Position the drop shadow at the base of the soldier's feet.

8. Remember that the Timeline layers have a stacking order. The drop shadow is stacked on top of the original soldier art. Click and drag the **shadow** layer and position it underneath the **soldier** layer.

9. Select **Control > Test Movie**. Notice that the movie clip of the marching soldier animates and that the shadow also mimics the movements. Save your file.

Figure 7.36: *Save and test your movie to see the results.*

10. The soldier is marching in place. Create an animation that gives the illusion of the soldier walking into the cave. Use a Classic Tween to scale the soldier up and reposition him on the Stage. To see a completed version, open **03_CastShadows_Complete.fla** in the **Completed** folder in **Chapter_07**.

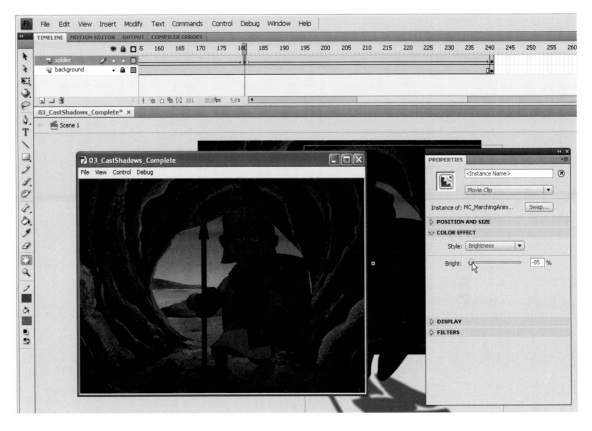

Figure 7.37: *Animate the soldier walking into the cave.*

In the completed version, the soldier animates walking into the cave. To simulate the falloff of light, the **Brightness** color effect was tweened to slowly darken the movie clip over time. The soldier was scaled to give the illusion that he is walking towards the screen.

Simulating a Rim-Light Effect in Flash

The previous example showed how easy it is to create a cast shadow by simply duplicating a movie clip and applying a drop shadow filter. You can also achieve rim lighting using a similar technique. Remember, rim lighting comes from a light source that is positioned behind the subject. The illumination produces a silhouette of the subject with a "rim" of light around the shape.

Let's take a look at one possible technique to produce a rim light in Flash. Locate and open **01_RimLight.fla** in the **Examples** folder in **Chapter_07**. Once the file has opened in Flash, select **Control > Test Movie**. The superhero strikes a pose in front of the moonlit sky. A rim of white light highlights her silhouette, separating her from the background. Let's deconstruct the setup of the FLA file.

01_RimLight

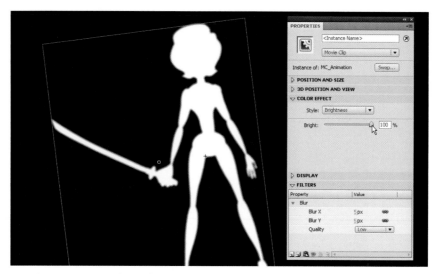

Figure 7.38: Use the Brightness color effect to create the rim-light effect.

A duplicate copy of the superhero animation was created and placed on a separate layer in the Timeline. The copy's **Brightness** value was set to **100%** in the Properties panel. This produces a white silhouette of the character with no detail. A blur filter was added to simulate soft lighting. The original movie clip was darkened. By slightly offsetting the duplicate movie clip from the original movie clip, you create the rim-light effect.

Figure 7.39: The lens flare on the blade is a simple shape with a radial gradient fill.

Chapter 7: Light My World

Animated Lighting Effects Using Masks

Masks are great tools to use for lighting effects. In the second exercise, you incorporated a mask to constrain the soft shading to the vampire's face. That mask was a still image. Masks can also animate to create unique effects. Locate and open **02_TorchLight.fla** in the **Examples** folder in **Chapter_07**. Once the file has opened in Flash, select **Control > Test Movie**.

02_TorchLight

Figure 7.40: *An animated mask is used to create the lighting effect.*

A duplicate copy of the pirate animation was created and placed on a separate layer in the Timeline. A **Tint** value was applied to the copy in the Properties panel to give the pirate an orange glow. The copy was then attached to a mask layer in the Timeline. The mask artwork is a movie clip that contains a frame-by-frame animation of the flickering highlight (Figure 7.41).

Figure 7.41: *The animated mask is a frame-by-frame animation nested in a movie clip.*

This mask layer defines a visible area that reveals a nested layer below. For this example, the **Pirate Copy** layer is the nested layer. The visible area that will reveal only the edges of the orange tinted pirate will be the mask's movie clip.

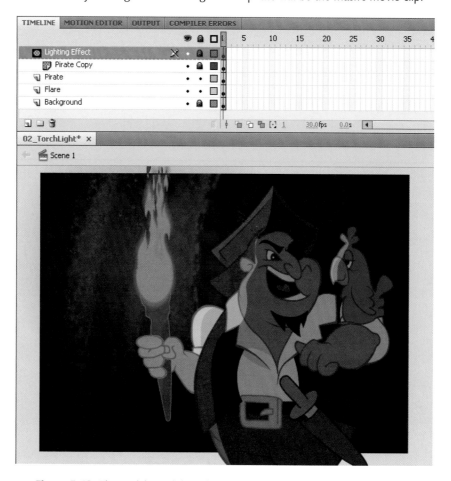

Figure 7.42: *The mask layer defines the visible area for the orange tinted pirate.*

Summary

This completes the chapter on lighting. Light sets a mood and evokes emotion from the audience. The choices you make in lighting help define and reinforce your story's narrative. When developing your animated or interactive story, you need to be aware of how the light's intensity illuminates your characters or environment around them, how the light's direction bounces off objects, and where the highlights and shadows appear as a result of the light's position.

....

CHAPTER 8

Speak to Me

Let's not forget about audio. In limited animation, sound is a crucial component in the storytelling process. Sounds can be dialog, music, and sound effects. This chapter focuses on incorporating audio into your Flash movie and character animation techniques to bring the words being spoken to life.

Recording Audio

Let's take a detour for a moment and enter the world of digital audio. Up to this point in the book, you have been using Flash to visually show a story without incorporating a lot of audio. Sound greatly enhances the user experience whether you are watching an animation or interacting with elements in a Flash movie. It is important to understand a few key principles about audio to achieve great results when integrating it into Flash.

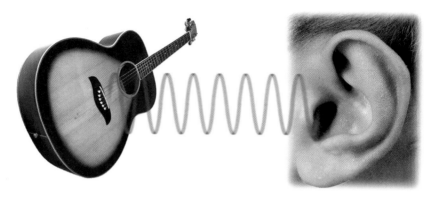

Figure 8.1: *Vibrating objects generate waves of compressed air that we hear as sound.*

What is sound? Vibrating objects, such as guitar strings or vocal cords, generate waves of rapidly varying air pressure. Sound waves occur as repeating cycles of pressure move out and away from the vibrating object. When these vibrations reach our ears, we hear sound. The **frequency**, or pitch, refers to the number of cycles (waves) per second. The **amplitude**, or intensity, of sound is the size (height of the wave) of the variations. When you see audio waveforms in software applications, they illustrate these pressure waves.

Figure 8.2: *Audio waveforms are visually represented in Flash and After Effects.*

Electronic representations of sound waves can be recorded in either **digital** or **analog** formats. Analog recordings use audio tape, which is a very thin strip of plastic, coated with magnetic particles. A microphone converts the sound pressures into electric impulses. The electric impulses align with the magnetic particles to create a pattern on the tape that represents the sound.

Computers record audio as a series of zeroes and ones. Digital audio breaks the original waveform up into individual samples. This is referred to as digitizing or audio sampling. The **sampling rate** defines how often a sample is taken during the recording process.

When audio is recorded at a higher sampling rate, the digital waveform perfectly mimics the original analog waveform. Low sampling rates often distort the original sound because they do not capture enough of the sound frequency. The frequency of a sound is measured in Hertz (Hz), which means cycles per second. A kilohertz (kHz) is a thousand cycles per second. Table 8.1 lists some common sampling rates used in digital audio.

Table 8.1: *Common digital audio sampling rates*

Sampling Rate	Usage
8,000 Hz	Low quality with low file size used for the web.
11,025 Hz	Good for narration only. Do not use for music.
22,050 Hz	Adequate quality and file size used in older multimedia.
44,100 Hz	Audio CD quality, used for video and music.
48,000 Hz	DVD quality, used for video and music.

The bit depth of each audio sample is equally as important as the sampling rate. In digital audio, bit depth describes the amount of data contained in each sample, measured in bits. You can compare audio bit depth to image bit depth. The lower the number, the less detail captured, resulting in poorer quality sound. Common examples of bit depth include CD audio, which is recorded at 16 bits, and DVD-Audio that records up to 24-bit audio.

Once the audio has been sampled, it can be saved out into a number of file formats. Flash can import three of the popular audio file formats. The imported audio works like all the other symbols in the Library panel. An audio file is added to the Timeline typically on its own layer. You can have multiple layers of audio to mix the sounds together. Here are the three common audio file formats that can be imported into Flash:

▶ **AIFF** (Audio Interchange File Format) is a standard audio format for the Mac.

▶ **WAV** (Waveform Audio Format) is a standard audio format on a Windows-based computer.

▶ **MP3** (Motion Picture Expert Group) is the file format of choice for Flash movies. It uses a compression algorithm to remove certain parts of sound that are outside the hearing range of most people. As a result, the audio still sounds great to us with a small file size.

In order to record audio, you need a good microphone. One of the best and affordable microphones is the *Logitech USB Desktop Microphone*. It averages about $20 US. The installation is as easy as plugging it into your USB port. You can create your own in-house recording studio using a computer, this microphone and its software.

Hearing Voices... Recording Dialog

Animation focuses a lot of attention on character movement to convey emotion and drive the narrative forward. There are certain times, however, when the best and most efficient way for a character to express its thoughts and actions is through speaking. Dialog can be just as effective in defining your character's personality, giving it heart and making it more believable to the audience.

Finding the right voice talent is crucial in bringing your character to life. The top animation studios match voices with the drawn characters. In Chapter 2, you read about the different design methods to incorporate when "casting" your story's characters. Each unique personality needs to have a voice to match.

Figure 8.2: *Finding the right voice talent for each character is crucial.*

Provide your voice talent with the script and character sketches before the actual dialog recording session. Explain to them the character's motivation in each scene and its overall character arc in the story. During the recording session, match the voice to the action in the scene. What does that mean?

Chapter 8: Speak to Me

For example, if the character is performing something that is very physical, that strain should be reflected in the delivery of the line. If a character is excited or nervous, the pacing and tempo of the words should be fast with a feeling of anxiety. The more insight you can provide your voice talent, the more emotional the character's performance will be on screen. Emotion is the key element.

Unfortunately Flash doesn't have a filter or component to create a character's voice. Dialog is typically recorded before the animation production begins. During the recording, ask the voice talent for multiple takes. Don't always settle on the first read. Once you have recorded the character's dialog, the next step is lip synchronization, or "lip-sync," to match up the visuals to the words.

Lip-Syncing Dialog

Lip synchronization is the technique of moving an animated character's mouth in such a way that it appears to speak in "sync" with the audio. In traditional animation, dialog is split up into its phonetic components using an **exposure** or **dope sheet**. An exposure sheet is basically a printed table divided into five sections separated by horizontal lines that represent one frame of film and vertical lines that separate each of the five sections.

An animator uses the columns to write down notes on how the action should be animated, camera movements, and dialog that may be happening in the scene. The sound is split up phonetically and marked down in the frame that it appears in the film. This type of organization and planning helps the animator by providing them with a blue print for the animated story. Exposure sheets are still used today, even by computer animators.

If you think about it, the Flash Timeline could be seen as a computer-based version of an exposure sheet. It contains layers to hold art and cells that delineate the passage of time. Notes can be added through the use of frame labels. The only difference is that the Flash Timeline runs horizontally across its workspace rather than vertically, as in an exposure sheet (Figure 8.4).

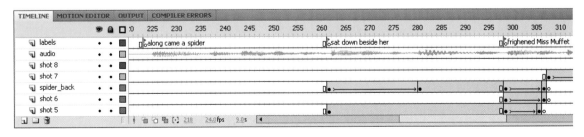

Figure 8.4: *The Flash Timeline helps you plan out animated scenes in your movie.*

The art of lip synchronization revolves around the visualization of sounds, or phonetics. An animator does not animate each letter of a spoken word but rather to the sounds being made. For example, if a character says, "hello," the word consists of five letters but it only requires three mouth shapes to animate: the "ha", "ell," and "o" sound. How many mouth shapes do you need?

Well, if you want to simplify the process, you only need two mouth shapes to lip-sync: an open and closed mouth (Figure 8.5). Think of a ventriloquist's dummy. Its mouth just opens and closes. We interpret the act of speaking through the alternating mouth shapes. What creates the illusion of speech is in the timing of the movement to the ventriloquist's voice. Look at the early Flash animations produced by *Jib Jab Media*; a simple solution that was very effective.

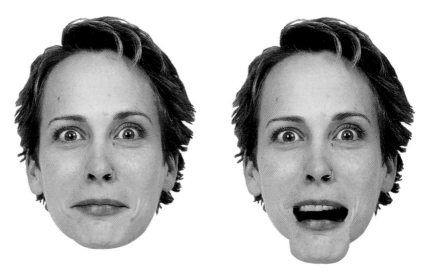

Figure 8.5: *The simplest form of lip sync only requires two mouth shapes: an open and closed mouth.*

If you want to design a more convincing lip-sync, you will need to create more mouth shapes. On an average you will need eight to ten mouths. To add actual expressions and realistic mouth-movements, study how the shape of the mouth changes with each sound. Traditional animators often place mirrors close by when they animate so that they can act out the scene and observe their actions.

Animating dialog can be a time-consuming process in Flash. Mouth shapes need to be broken down into phoneme shapes. Each mouth shape should correspond to a specific sound or range of sounds. Let's experiment with building a lip-sync in Flash. The first exercise walks you through a basic example to illustrate the steps involved in making your character speak.

Exercise 1: Creating a Lip-Sync in Flash

There is no question that animating dialog is tedious yet rewarding in the end. One technique that will help speed up your time is to create a virtual exposure sheet using the Flash workspace. As previously mentioned, an exposure sheet acts as a blueprint for the animator. Applying this concept in Flash will let you know the sequence of words and mouth shapes needed. Let's begin.

 *Locate the **Chapter_08** folder on the CD-ROM. Copy this folder to your hard drive. The folder contains all the files needed to complete the chapter exercises.*

1. Open the file **01_BasicLipSync.fla** in the **Chapter_08** folder you copied to your hard drive. The file contains all of the artwork you need to complete this exercise. Once the file has opened in Flash, select **Control > Test Movie**. The character is set up and the mouth shapes have been created, so all you need to do to complete the shot is to make the secret agent talk. (Figure 8.6).

01_BasicLipSync

Figure 8.6: *The character has been set up and is ready to speak.*

2. Select **File > Import > Import to Library.** Locate and select **AreUThere.wav** in the **Audio** folder in **Chapter_08**. Click **Open**. Go to the Library to see that the WAV file has been added. Click on the **Play** arrow in the thumbnail preview area to listen to the audio.

3. Go to the Timeline and create a new layer. Position it at the top of the layers, above the **monitor** layer. Rename it **audio**.

4. Click and drag **AreUThere.wav** from the Library panel to the Stage. The audio is added to the **audio** layer. To see the entire waveform in the Timeline, click on the empty cell on frame **60**. Select **Insert > Timeline > Frame (F5)** to extend the audio to frame 60.

5. To magnify the waveform, right-click on the **audio** layer name and select **Properties**. In the Layers Properties dialog box, change the layer height to **300%**. Click **OK** (Figure 8.7).

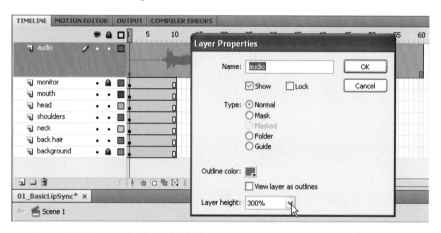

Figure 8.7: *Increase the layer height from 100 to 300% to see the waveform better.*

6. Go to the Properties panel and set the Sync property to **Stream**. This enables you to hear the sound file as you scrub back and forth in the Timeline.

7. Create a new layer directly above the **audio** layer by clicking on the **New Layer** icon at the base of the Timeline panel. Rename the layer **labels**. This layer will act as the exposure sheet to record the words spoken in the audio file.

8. Scrub through the Timeline to frame 9. This is where the dialog begins in the audio. Click on the empty cell on frame **9** of the **labels** layer. Select **Insert > Timeline > Blank Keyframe** (the keyboard shortcut is **F7**). Go to the Properties panel and enter **are** in the Name text entry box.

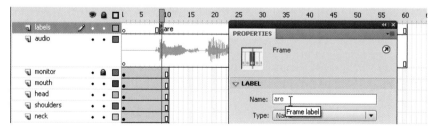

Figure 8.8: *Label the frames using the Name property in the Properties panel.*

9. Repeat this step to set labels for the remaining words spoken in the dialog. To do this, add these frame labels on the following frames:

   ▶ On frame **12** add a frame label named **you**.
   ▶ On frame **19** add a frame label named **still**.
   ▶ On frame **25** add a frame label named **there**.

10. Extend all the remaining layers that contain artwork to frame 60. Shift select the empty cell on frame **60** from layer **monitor** to layer **background** to select multiple layers. Select **Insert > Timeline > Frame (F5)**.

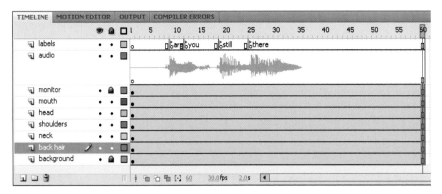

Figure 8.9: *Extend the remaining layers to frame 60.*

11. Now that you have set up the frame labels to correspond to the dialog, it is time to create the lip-sync. Before you do that, let's deconstruct how the artwork is built. The secret agent's head contains all of the facial features except the mouth. The mouth is a separate graphic symbol.

    Double-click on the mouth to open its Timeline. Scrub through the frames to see the different mouth shapes. The lower chin is also nested inside. This will animate depending on which mouth shape is shown on the main Timeline.

Figure 8.10: *All of the mouth shapes are nested inside a Graphic symbol.*

Figure 8.11 illustrates the mouth shapes built for this exercise. Each shape has been converted into a graphic symbol and then nested inside another symbol one frame after another. Using this technique, you can then control which frame is shown on the main Timeline. Let's see how that works.

"A" | "Aaah"   "E" | "Eeee"   "I" | "Eye"

"O" | "Oh"   "Q" | "U" | "Oooh"   "F" | "V" | "Fuh"

"Mmmm"   "La" | "Luh" | "Tha"   Any Consonants

Figure 8.11: *Mouth chart used for this exercise.*

12. Close the graphic symbol and return to the main Timeline. While the mouth symbol is still selected go to the Properties panel. Under the Looping section, select **Single Frame** from the Options menu. Type in **8** for the frame number. The graphic symbol displays the nested mouth shape on the eighth frame.

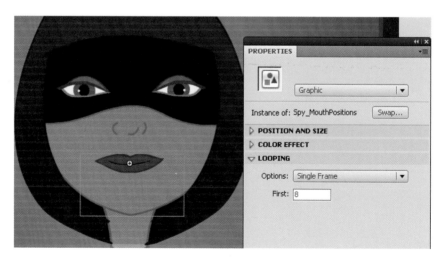

Figure 8.12: *Set the graphic symbol to display a single frame in the Properties panel.*

13. Scrub through the Timeline to frame 9. This is where the dialog begins in the audio with the word "are." Phonetically, that would be pronounced "aah - rrr." Add a keyframe (**F6**) to the **mouth** layer. Go to the Properties panel and type **2** in the Looping section to display the corresponding "Aah" mouth shape.

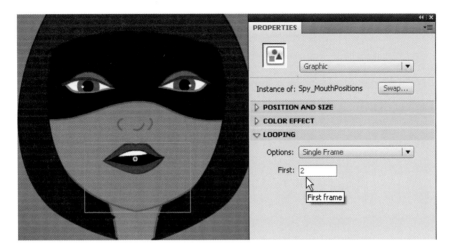

Figure 8.13: *Change the displayed frame number to correspond to the audio.*

14. Repeat the previous step to complete the lip-sync. To do this, add a keyframe on the following frames and change the graphic symbol's displayed frame:

   - On frame **12** add a keyframe and change the graphic symbol's frame to **10**.
   - On frame **14** add a keyframe and change the graphic symbol's frame to **5**.
   - On frame **17** add a keyframe and change the graphic symbol's frame to **6**.
   - On frame **19** add a keyframe and change the graphic symbol's frame to **1**.
   - On frame **21** add a keyframe and change the graphic symbol's frame to **10**.
   - On frame **23** add a keyframe and change the graphic symbol's frame to **4**.
   - On frame **25** add a keyframe and change the graphic symbol's frame to **9**.
   - On frame **28** add a keyframe and change the graphic symbol's frame to **3**.
   - On frame **31** add a keyframe and change the graphic symbol's frame to **10**.
   - On frame **36** add a keyframe and change the graphic symbol's frame to **8**.

15. Save and test your movie. Each mouth shape is only on screen for a short duration of time. Our eyes optically blend the shapes together to give the illusion that the character is talking. You can reuse the same mouth shape for different sounds; there are no real rules for lip-syncing.

16. To see a completed version, open **01_BasicLipSync_Complete.fla** in the **Completed** folder inside the **Chapter_08** folder. The animation was nested in a movie clip and repositioned in the cell-phone art. The symbol was rotated using the 3D Rotation Tool to match the perspective in the background art.

Figure 8.14: *The completed lip-sync animation is nested inside a movie clip and rotated to fit the background artwork.*

Mixing Sound Effects

Sound effects can enhance your visual storytelling without you having to show or animate a lot on screen. How is that possible? Think about sounds that can come from off-screen. For example, Figure 8.15 frames a character who is frightened by the unknown. Adding scary off-screen sound effects such as creaking doors and footsteps can heighten the visible tension in the shot.

Figure 8.15: *Off-screen sound can enhance the scene without you showing a lot.*

Exercise 2: Mixing Audio in Flash

Let's take a look at how to integrate and mix audio in Flash. A scene has already been created. In this exercise you will add several sound effects to an existing animation in Flash. The sound effects imply action such as a character walking down a hallway. In this situation, hearing the sound is more effective than seeing the action as it builds tension in the scene. It also reduces your production time since you do not have to animate a character walk cycle.

1. Open the **02_OffScreenSound.fla** file in the **Chapter_08** folder you copied to your hard drive. The file contains all of the artwork you need to complete this exercise. Once the file has opened in Flash, select **Control > Test Movie**. The woman sitting in the room is startled by the detective who opens the door. The lip-syncing has been completed; you need to mix the sound effects together.

02_OffScreenSound

Figure 8.16: *The animated scene is ready for sound effects to be added.*

Let's take a moment to walk through a typical workflow. Animated scenes in Flash start with the animatic. Using that as a template for the frame composition and timing, the artwork is created and distributed on layers in the Timeline. Next, character poses are built as per the storyboard and/or animatic.

As you read in Chapter 2, each character is built and composed of many symbols. Expressions and body movements are tweened to capture the personality of the character and the action in the scene. Lastly, the lip-sync is built by assigning instances to mouth shapes that correspond to the audio track.

In this example, the lip-syncing was achieved by using a different technique from the first exercise. In the first exercise, you nested all the mouth shapes in one graphic symbol. Using the Properties panel, you instructed which frame to display on the Stage to create the illusion of speech (Figure 8.17).

Figure 8.17: *One technique to create a lip-sync in Flash is to store all of the mouth shapes inside a Graphic symbol.*

Another technique is to swap the symbols on a frame-by-frame basis. In this example, the woman's mouth shapes are stored as separate graphic symbols in the library, not nested in one graphic symbol. Keyframes were added on the **Mouth Shapes** layer. The Properties panel allows you to easily swap selected symbols on the Stage with other symbols located in the Library (Figure 8.18).

Figure 8.18: *Another technique is to swap the mouth shape symbols frame-by-frame.*

2. Before you add the audio, let's set up the frame labels so that you can easily see the scene's structure. Select the blank keyframe on frame **1** of the **labels** layer. Go to the Properties panel and enter **drive by car** as the frame label.

3. Repeat this step to set labels for the remaining animation. To do this, add these frame labels on the following frames:

   ▸ On frame **90** add a blank keyframe with a label named **footsteps closer**.
   ▸ On frame **147** add a blank keyframe with a label named **open door**.

4. Create a new layer directly above the **dialog** layer by clicking on the **New Layer** icon at the base of the Timeline panel. Rename the layer **car SoundFX**.

5. Click and drag **DriveBy.wav** from the Library panel to the Stage. The audio is added to the **car SoundFX** layer.

6. Create a new layer directly above the **car SoundFX** layer by clicking on the **New Layer** icon. Rename the layer **walking SoundFX**.

7. Click and drag **Walking.wav** from the Library panel to the Stage. The audio is added to the **walking SoundFX** layer.

8. Create a new layer directly above the **walking SoundFX** layer by clicking on the **New Layer** icon. Rename the layer **door SoundFX**.

9. Scrub through the Timeline to frame 147. This is where the door begins to open. Click on the empty cell on frame **147** of the **door SoundFX** layer. Select **Insert > Timeline > Blank Keyframe** (the keyboard shortcut is **F7**).

10. Click and drag **OpenDoor.wav** from the Library panel to the Stage. The audio is added to the **door SoundFX** layer.

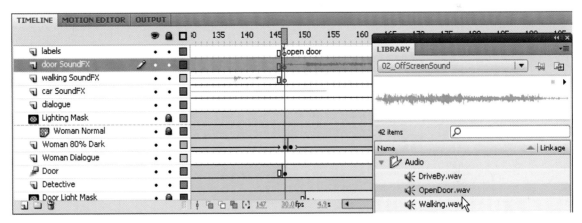

Figure 8.19: Add each sound effect to a different layer in the Timeline. Use the frame labels to sync the effect with the animation on Stage.

11. Save and test your movie. The creaking door sound effect drowns out the dialogue a little. Let's edit the volume of the audio file. In Flash, you can define the starting point of a sound or control the volume of the sound as it plays. You can also change the point at which a sound starts and stops playing.

12. Select a frame that contains the **OpenDoor.wav** sound on the **door SoundFX** layer. Go to the Properties panel and click on the **Pencil** icon next to the Effect option. This opens the Edit Envelope dialog box.

13. Scrub through to the end of the audio clip. To change the sound envelope, drag the envelope handles to change levels at different points in the sound. Envelope lines show the volume of the sound as it plays. To create additional envelope handles (up to eight total), click the envelope lines. To remove an envelope handle, drag it out of the window (Figure 8.20).

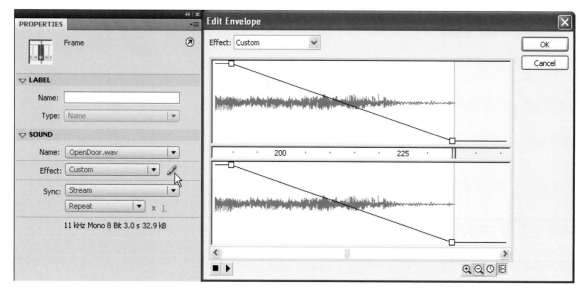

Figure 8.20: *To adjust the sound envelope, drag the envelope handles to change the volume levels at different points in the sound.*

14. To see a completed version, open **02_OffScreenSound_Complete.fla** in the **Completed** folder inside the **Chapter_08** folder. These two exercises demonstrate two different techniques for lip-syncing in Flash and how to mix sound effects to add atmosphere, making a scene more believable.

Figure 8.21: *Save and test your movie to see the final results.*

Exploring Facial Expressions

The last section of this chapter looks at character animation techniques to bring the spoken words to life. Talking heads are boring. Simple gestures speak to a character's personality and their emotional state of mind. It is always a good idea to incorporate body gestures and facial expressions as the character "talks." These expressions do not have to be over the top; in fact, they can be as subtle as raising of an eyebrow or a wink to the audience.

Figure 8.22: *Facial expressions can range from very subtle to over the top.*

In Chapter 2, you read about character design. A character's face is extremely important to its design. In addition to the dialog, the way a face displays emotion can speak volumes. Think of a villain grinning with pure delight as he ties the damsel to the train tracks. Compare that to the friendly smile of the superhero as he saves the day. Each expression helps define the character.

Figure 8.23: *Facial expressions define the character's personality, emotional state of mind, and motivation from shot to shot.*

When designing your character, sketch out a range of emotions on a single sheet of paper. This will help you to see how one emotion can animate into another. What are the basic emotions? They are joy, anger, sadness, jealousy, fear, surprise, and disgust. Figure 8.24 shows you examples of different types of emotions your character can have in your story.

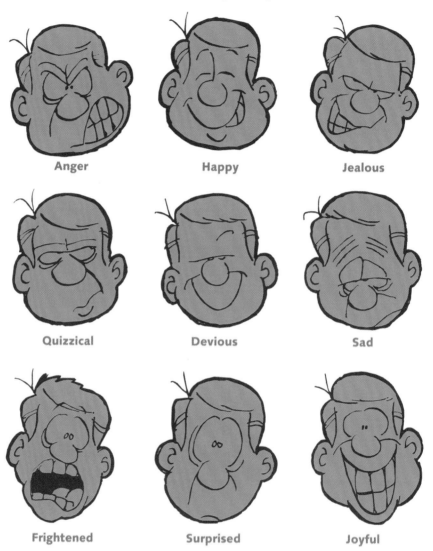

Figure 8.24: *Sketch out a range of emotions for your characters.*

Notice how the heads tilt, squash and stretch to portray each emotion. Exaggeration is applied for dramatic emphasis. These are traditional animation principles being used. As a character animator, you need to be an actor as well. Stand in front of a mirror or record yourself acting out the scenes in your story so that you can better understand the subtleties in human expression.

Exercise 3: Creating an Emotional Character in Flash

1. Open the file **03_FaceTween.fla** in the **Chapter_08** folder you copied to your hard drive. The file contains all of the artwork you need to complete this exercise. The man's face is comprised of graphic symbols except for the mouth and eyebrows. There are still shapes on the Stage (Figure 8.25).

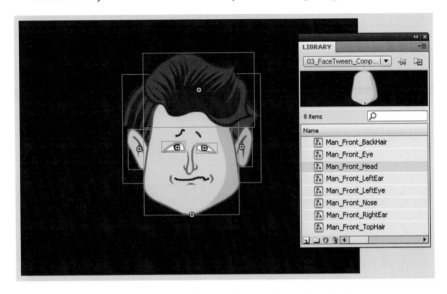

Figure 8.25: *The character is made up of shapes and graphic symbols.*

2. Extend all the layers to frame 10. Shift select the empty cell on frame **10** to select multiple layers. Select **Insert > Timeline > Keyframe (F6)**.

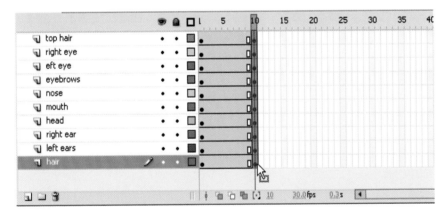

Figure 8.26: *Add a keyframe for all the layers on frame 10.*

3. Select the keyframe on frame **10** of the **mouth layer**. You are going to change the stroke's shape to create a smile for the character. Select the Selection Tool (**V**). Hover the cursor over the stroke and you will notice the cursor change and have a curved line next to it.

4. Click and drag the stroke by pressing and holding the left mouse button. Adjust the stroke to create a smile for the character. Move the character's dimples to each side of the smile (Figure 8.27).

Figure 8.27: *Adjust the mouth's stroke and position of the dimples on frame 10.*

5. Select the Free Transform Tool (**Q**). Make sure you are on frame **10**. Make subtle changes to the face. Try the following:

   ▸ Rotate the ears slightly
   ▸ Raise the eyebrows
   ▸ Stretch the head to elongate it a small percentage
   ▸ Stretch the hair, nose, and eyes

Figure 8.28: *Use the Free Transform Tool to make subtle changes to the face.*

6. Apply a Shape Tween to the **eyebrows** and **mouth** layers. Apply a Classic Tween to the remaining layers. Save and test your movie. Shape tweens are great for subtle changes to a stroke object. The tween creates a morph between both keyframes that looks more organic than a motion tween.

So far in this chapter, we nave been focusing on the mouth. As you have seen, making simple adjustments to the mouth's shape can start you on your way to animating expressive characters. One aspect that still needs to be addressed is the character's eyes and eyebrows. As the old saying goes, "The eyes are the window to the soul." When designing your character's different emotional states, don't gloss over the general eye shapes. When combined with the eyebrows, they can communicate emotion just as effectively as the mouth.

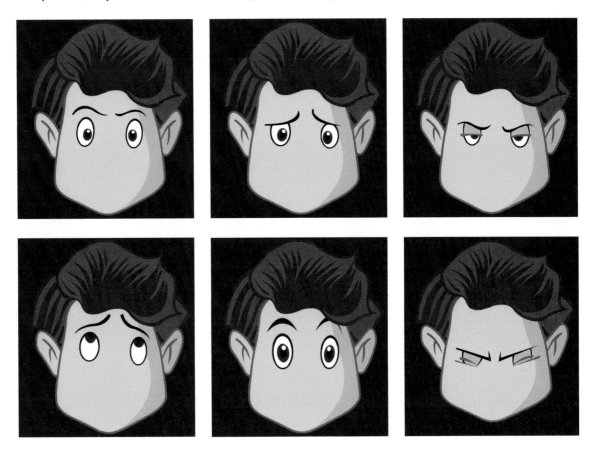

Figure 8.29: *What do the eyes tell you about the character's emotional state.*

When animating the eyes, keep in mind that our eyes dart and do not tween from side to side. They can move very quickly. In terms of Flash, we are talking about one to two frames. That doesn't mean that you can't slow the eyes down for a smoother motion, as needed perhaps for a dopey or sleepy character.

Don't over compensate and have the eyes darting all over the place, unless your character is psychotic. Eyes need time to readjust and focus. Subtle eye darts can bring the character to life. Just make sure that the eye movement reinforces the character's personality, matches the dialogue being spoken and enhances the action in the shot. So how do you do that in Flash?

Locate and open **EyeDart.fla** in the **Examples** folder in **Chapter_08**. Once the file has opened in Flash, select **Control > Test Movie**. The woman nervously looks to her right to make sure no one is following her down the alley. The eye animation is nested within a graphic symbol. Similar to the lip-sync exercise, the Properties panel is used to instruct which frame of the animation to display on the Stage. This allows you to pause and rewind the animation.

Figure 8.30: *The eye movement accents the character's emotional state.*

Let's deconstruct the eye animation. Double-click on the eyes to open the graphic symbol's Timeline. The animation consists of seven frames (Figure 8.31). A mask layer defines the shape of the eyes. Notice that the dart of both pupils consists of a frame-by-frame animation. This technique works best for this type of eye movement. On the fourth frame the eyes are completely shut.

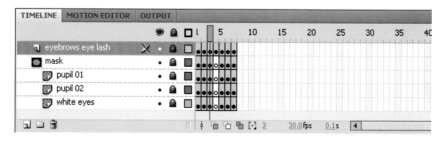

Figure 8.31: *The pupils in the eye are animated frame-by-frame.*

Posing Your Character

A character can speak to the audience in many ways, whether it is through dialog, facial expressions, or gestures. As you design and storyboard your scenes, ask yourself what is motivating the characters and what emotional message needs to be communicated in the shot. You need to get inside your character's head and see what is making it tick. Then, it is your job to express this through your visuals and animation.

The first pass through an animation is often referred to as **blocking**. Key poses are determined to establish timing and placement of characters and props in a given shot. In addition, posing the character helps reinforce its personality. In Chapter 2, you read about the line of action. This defines the character's posture and movement.

Figure 8.32: *Use strong poses in the shot. Keep in mind the line of action that runs down the spine of the character.*

Avoid vertical straight up and down torso (left image in Figure 8.32). That only makes the character look stiff, wooden, and boring. Use curves (C-shape and S-shape) to add interest to the character's spine. Don't forget about balance and weight. Heavier objects tend to move much slower than thinner ones.

Referencing Live Video for Animation

Animating a walk cycle is one of the most complex series of poses to build for a character. Every body part moves from frame to frame. To help understand a basic walk pattern, video record yourself or your friends walking or acting out the scene you are animating. You can then import that video into Flash and trace over the movements. This is called **rotoscoping**.

Exercise 4: Creating a Walk Cycle in Flash

Rotoscoping was invented by Max Fleischer, who used it to animate the character Koko the Clown in the series *Out of the Inkwell* (1915). Fleischer traced over live-action film movement in *Gulliver's Travels* (1939) and in an animated series based on the *Superman* cartoons. Walt Disney animators used this technique to study the human form and animals in motion for their featured films. You are going to do something similar in this exercise.

You are not going to actually trace the video, but use it as a guide to build a walk cyle for an existing character. All you need is a video. Locate the **Video** folder inside **Chapter_08**. This folder contains QuickTime and Flash Video (FLV) files for you to study. The digital video files were created in *Poser*, a popular 3D software package that ships with prebuilt characters and walk cyles.

1. Open the file **04_WalkCycle.fla** in the **Chapter_08** folder you copied to your hard drive. The file contains all of the artwork you need to complete this exercise. The character is comprised of graphic symbols. Each symbol's registration point has been repositioned to "hinge" the character properly. All of the body parts are nested in a movie clip on the Stage.

04_WalkCycle

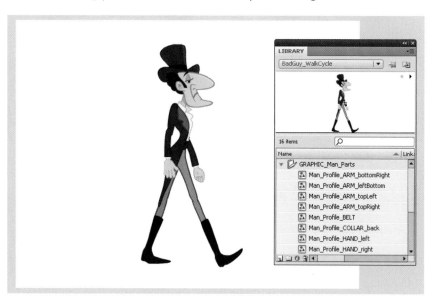

Figure 8.33: *The character is made up of graphic symbols.*

2. Double-click on the character to open the movie clip's Timeline. Select the blank keyframe on the **video** layer. When you import a video into Flash, you have a couple of options to choose from. You can either embed the video directly on the Timeline or load it externally as a separate file. Which option is the best to use? That all depends on the video and what you need it for. Table 8.2 offers some suggestions.

Chapter 8: Speak to Me

Table 8.2: *Embed the video or load it externally?*

Video / Purpose	Embed	External
5 seconds or under with no audio	X	
Used to trace frames for rotoscope animation	X	
Used for interface interactivity (buttons, preloaders)	X	
Longer than 5 seconds with audio		X
Used for instructional training		X
Used in conjunction with cue points		X

3. Select **File > Import > Import Video**. This opens the Import Video Wizard.

4. The wizard first asks you to locate the video file. Make sure On Your Computer is selected. Click **Browse**. In the Open dialog box, locate the **Walk.flv** file in the **Videos** folder inside the **Chapter_08**. Select it. Click **Open**.

5. For the deployment options, select **Embed FLV in SWF and play in timeline**. Click **Next** to continue.

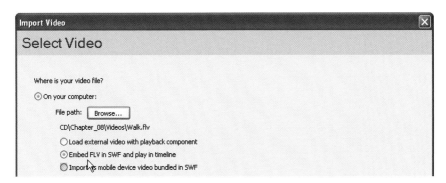

Figure 8.34: *Locate the video to import on your computer and choose to embed it on the Timeline.*

6. For the embedding options, select **Embedded Video** for the Symbol type and uncheck the Audio checkbox. The video symbol will allow you to scrub through the frames in the Timeline and see the walk cycle. Click **Next** to continue.

Figure 8.35: *Embed the video in a graphic symbol on the Timeline.*

7. Select the Free Transform Tool (**Q**) and resize the video symbol to match as close as you can to the proportions of the character (Figure 8.36).

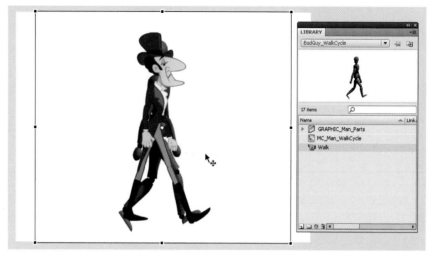

Figure 8.36: *Scale the video symbol.*

8. Now comes the fun part. Position and rotate each body part to match as closely as you can to the video walk cycle; add new keyframes as you continue.

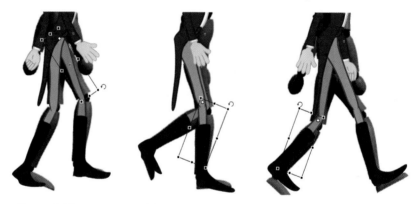

Figure 8.37: *Reposition each body part to align as close as possible to the video walk cycle.*

9. To see a completed version, open **04_WalkCycle_Complete.fla** in the **Completed** folder inside the **Chapter_08** folder.

Summary

Walking also speaks a lot about a character. Through subtle movement, there is an unlimited number of different types of walk cycles you could build, from running to dragging your feet. Try and build a video library of different types of body language. The next chapter discusses adding interactivity using ActionScript to enhance audience participation with your story and characters.

....

CHAPTER 9

Interact with Me

Audience participation can go beyond passively watching your story to interacting with it and its characters. ActionScript provides the tools to enhance the user experience. This chapter focuses on adding interactivity to your Flash movie.

Interactivity in Flash

The previous chapters explored how animation enhances your visual story. Motion and shape tweens were used in Flash to simulate camera movements and lighting techniques. This chapter explores using ActionScript to add interactivity to your Flash files. ActionScript is Flash's programming language. It allows you to create a variety of interactions from simple to complex.

ActionScript uses object-oriented programming (OOP). Objects are the types of data that Flash can store. Examples of objects include graphics, sounds, and text. Objects belong to a larger group called a class. Examples of classes include the **MovieClip** class, **Sound** class, and **Math** class. Each object and class has a unique set of properties that can be accessed, controlled, and altered through ActionScript. Table 9.1 highlights the properties associated with a movie clip.

Table 9.1: *Movie clip properties*

Property	Definition
x, y	Controls the movie clips horizontal (x) and vertical location (y).
rotation	Controls the rotation of the movie clip in degrees.
scaleX, scaleY	Controls the scale percentage; a value of 1 = 100%.
alpha	Controls the movie clip's transparency; a value of 1 = opaque.
height, width	Stores the height and width of the movie clip's bounding box.

This chapter begins with an ActionScript primer for the **MovieClip** class and its properties. The exercises will incorporate ActionScript to control a character on the Stage and create interactive camera movements. Let's get started.

The Main Event

Flash is event-driven. Events can be external or internal. External events are the ways that the user interacts with the file. Examples of external events include: clicking with the mouse, moving the mouse, and pressing a key on the keyboard. The user does not have control over internal events. Internal events can be the playback marker leaving one frame to play the next or the completion of a sound.

Flash uses an **event listener** to detect, or "listen" for specific events. Once the event is detected, an **event handler** creates a response to the action in Flash. Here is a simple event: a user clicks with the mouse on a button. This is an external event. If the button has an event listener called **CLICK** attached to it, it will detect the click. Your interactive movie responds to the user through an event handler that instructs Flash to go to another frame. Let's experiment with events to control a movie clip instance on the Stage.

Exercise 1: Mission Control

The first exercise walks you through how to access and control the movie clip properties. It also incorporates **variables** into the interaction. What are variables? They are containers that store values in your Flash movie. You can store, update, and retrieve the value of a variable.

 Locate the **Chapter_09** *folder on the CD-ROM. Copy this folder to your hard drive. The folder contains all the files needed to complete the chapter exercises.*

1. Open the file **01__Properties_Variables.fla** in the **Chapter_09** folder you copied to your hard drive. The file contains all of the artwork you need to complete this exercise. The Timeline contains three layers: **rocketship**, **buttons**, and **background** (Figure 9.1).

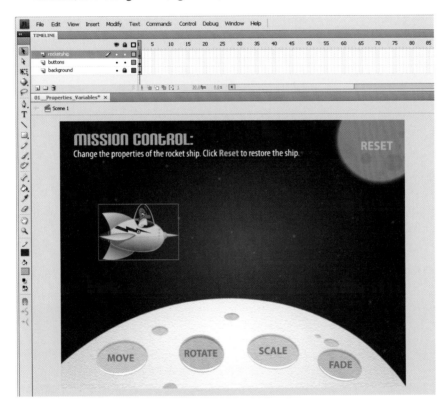

01_Properties_Variables

Figure 9.1: *You will use the buttons to control the rocket ship.*

2. Create a new layer directly above the **rocketship** layer by clicking on the **New Layer** icon at the base of the Timeline panel. Rename the layer **actions**. Lock the layer. Flash developers typically dedicate a layer to hold all the ActionScript. Before you can start coding, you need to name the movie clip and all of the buttons on the Stage. This is done in the Properties panel.

3. Select the rocket ship instance. Go to the Properties panel and enter **ship_mc** in the instance name box (Figure 9.2).

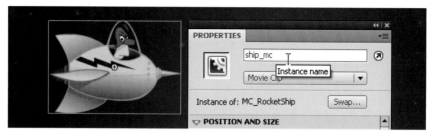

Figure 9.2: *Name your movie clip instance through the Properties panel.*

4. Repeat the process with all of the buttons on the **buttons** layer. To do this, single-click on each button to select it. Go to the Properties panel and type in an instance name. Enter the following instances names for the buttons:

   ▸ For the "move" button, give it an instance name of **move_btn**.
   ▸ For the "rotate" button, give it an instance name of **rotate_btn**.
   ▸ For the "scale" button, give it an instance name of **scale_btn**.
   ▸ For the "fade" button, give it an instance name of **fade_btn**.
   ▸ For the "reset" button, give it an instance name of **reset_btn**.

5. With your instances properly named, click on the blank keyframe on the **actions** layer. Open the Actions panel. If the Actions panel is not open, you can access it by choosing **Window > Actions**. The keyboard shortcut is **F9**.

6. Let's start with the **move_btn** button. The first thing you need to do is add an event listener to it. This listener will "listen" for an external event, a mouse click. Enter the ActionScript as shown.

```
// define event listeners
move_btn.addEventListener(MouseEvent.CLICK, onMove);
```

Let's quickly deconstruct the code. The event listener is attached to the button. This is referred to as the event object. **MouseEvent** is the event type. **CLICK** is the specific event to "listen" for. The final component, **onMove**, is the name of the event handler that will respond to the listener when it detects the user clicking on the **move** button.

7. Add the event handler to the ActionScript you just entered. An event handler is a **function**. Functions tell Flash what to do by grouping statements together. Conceptually, **statements** are like sentences. They can instruct Flash to go to another frame in the Timeline, or in this case change a movie clip's properties.

```
// define event handlers
function onMove(e:MouseEvent):void {
    ship_mc.x += 10;
}
```

8. Save and test your movie. Click on the **move** button and the rocket ship moves
    forward. The statement in the event handler tells Flash to take the horizontal lo-
    cation (**x**) of the rocket ship (**ship_mc**) and add 10 pixels to its current location
    (**+= 10**). If you type in "**−= 10**" then the ship will move backwards.

    It is important to understand how to move objects in the Flash 2D coordinate
    system. The top left corner is the origin point (0,0). The bottom right corner is
    (800, 600), the dimensions of the Stage. To move an instance forward you add
    to its current horizontal location (**x**). To move backwards, you subtract. The
    same method works for the vertical location of the instance. If you add to the
    y property, the object will move down; subtract to move the object up.

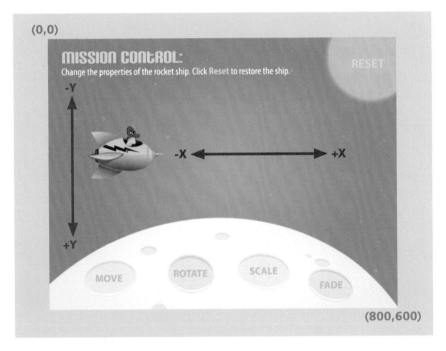

Figure 9.3: *The 2D coordinate system in Flash.*

9. Add an event listener to the "rotate" button. This will also "listen" for a mouse
    click. Enter the following code to the Actions panel.

```
rotate_btn.addEventListener(MouseEvent.CLICK, onRotate);
```

10. Add the event handler that responds to the listener. Enter the following code:

```
function onRotate(e:MouseEvent):void {
    ship_mc.rotation += 10;
}
```

11. Save and test your movie. Click on the **rotate** button and the rocket ship turns clockwise 10 degrees. The statement in the event handler tells Flash to take the current rotation of the rocket ship and rotate it 10 degrees. If you type in "-= 10" then the ship will rotate counter-clockwise.

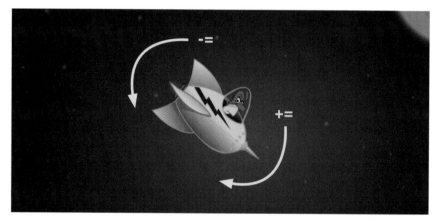

Figure 9.4: *You can rotate the instance clockwise by adding to its current rotation or counter-clockwise by subtracting from its current rotation.*

You have been using the **CLICK** event to change the instance properties. This event detects when the mouse button is pressed and released. There are several other types of Mouse Events that you can "listen" for. Table 9.2 describes them.

Table 9.2: *Mouse events*

ActionScript	Definition
MouseEvent.MOUSE_DOWN	...when the mouse button is pressed down
MouseEvent.MOUSE_UP	...when the mouse button is released
MouseEvent.CLICK	...when the mouse button is pressed and released
MouseEvent.MOUSE_OVER	...when the cursor is over the event target
MouseEvent.MOUSE_OUT	...when the cursor moves off the event target

12. Add an event listener to the "scale" button. This will "listen" for the cursor positioned over the button. Enter the following code to the Actions panel.

```
scale_btn.addEventListener(MouseEvent.MOUSE_OVER, onScale);
```

13. Add the event handler that responds to the listener. Enter the following code:

```
function onScale(e:MouseEvent):void {
    ship_mc.scaleX = ship_mc.scaleY = 2;
}
```

14. Save and test your movie. Move the cursor over the "scale" button and the rocket ship doubles in size. The statement in the event handler tells Flash to take the current horizontal and vertical scale of the rocket ship and increase it 200%. If you type in ".5" then the rocket ship will shrink to half its size (50%).

15. Add two event listeners and handlers to the "fade" button. One listener will "listen" for the cursor positioned over the button. Another listener will detect when the cursor rolls off the button. Add the following code.

```
fade_btn.addEventListener(MouseEvent.MOUSE_OVER, fadeRollOver);
fade_btn.addEventListener(MouseEvent.MOUSE_OUT, fadeRollOut);

function fadeRollOver(e:MouseEvent):void {
    ship_mc.alpha = .5;
}
function fadeRollOut(e:MouseEvent):void {
    ship_mc.alpha = 1;
}
```

16. Save and test your movie. Move the cursor over the "fade" button and the rocket ship becomes semi-transparent. The statement in the event handler tells Flash to take the alpha property of the rocket ship and decrease it 50%. Setting the alpha value back to **1**, makes the ship opaque. A value of **0** makes the rocket ship transparent.

17. How do you restore the ship back to its original condition? Use variables to store the movie clip's properties prior to adding the event listeners and handlers. To create a variable in Flash you need to define three properties: the name, data type, and value. Add the following code to the top of the Actions panel before the first listener you created in Step 6.

```
// create a custom variable to store the information
var pPosition:Number = ship_mc.x;
var pRotation:Number = ship_mc.rotation;
var pAlpha:Number = ship_mc.alpha;
var pXscale:Number = ship_mc.scaleX;
var pYscale:Number = ship_mc.scaleX;
```

To define a variable in ActionScript you first type in **var**. This is followed by a custom name for the variable that you can reference later in the code. The data type tells Flash what type of data will be stored in the variable. For this example you are storing numbers. The value is the current movie clip's properties.

18. Add an event listener and handler to the "reset" button. This will "listen" for a mouse click. Add the following code to bottom of the Actions panel.

```
reset_btn.addEventListener(MouseEvent.CLICK, onReset);

function onReset(e:MouseEvent):void {
    ship_mc.x = pPosition;
    ship_mc.rotation = pRotation;
    ship_mc.alpha = pAlpha;
    ship_mc.scaleX = pXscale;
    ship_mc.scaleY = pYscale;
}
```

19. Save and test your movie. Click on all the buttons to change the location, rotation, and scale of the rocket ship. Click on the **reset** button to restore the ship back to its original condition. The statements in the event handler tell Flash to take all of the movie clip properties and set them equal to their original value that you stored in variables in Step 17.

This completes the exercise. Understanding properties and variables lays the foundation for your ActionScript knowledge. The next exercise focuses on animation created through code, not on the Timeline.

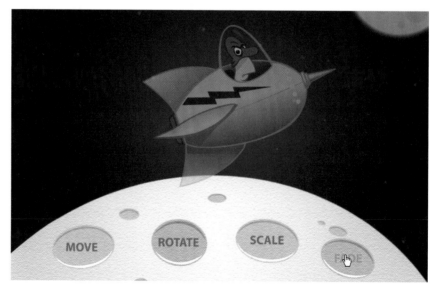

Figure 9.5: *Save and test your movie to see the final results.*

Exercise 2: ActionScript-Driven Animation

The first exercise focused on external events that the user can control. As mentioned at the beginning of chapter, internal events can be the playback marker leaving one frame to play the next. In this exercise, you will create an animation through ActionScript. In addition, you will add a **conditional statement** to check the location of the movie clip instance you are moving.

1. Open the file **02__ActionScriptAnimation.fla** in the **Chapter_09** folder you copied to your hard drive. The file contains all of the artwork you need to complete this exercise. The Timeline contains three layers: **actions**, **rocketship**, and **background** (Figure 9.6). The movie clip already has an instance name.

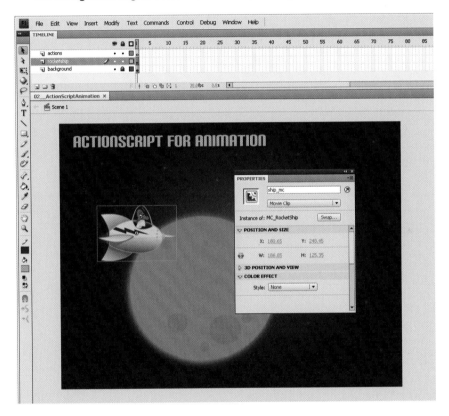

02_ActionScriptAnimation

Figure 9.6: *The movie clip has an instance name of* **ship_mc***.*

2. Click on the blank keyframe on the **actions** layer. Open the Actions panel. If the Actions panel is not open, you can access it by choosing **Window > Actions**. The keyboard shortcut is **F9**.

3. For this exercise, you will use the **Event.ENTER_FRAME** event listener. This event will constantly be detected as the playback marker leaves the first frame and returns back to frame 1. Add the following code to the Actions panel.

```
// create a custom variable to store the information
var speed:Number = 5;

// define event listeners
ship_mc.addEventListener(Event.ENTER_FRAME, moveShip);

// define event handlers
function moveShip(e:Event):void {
    // change the location and rotation properties
    e.target.x += speed;
    e.target.rotation += speed;
}
```

4. Save and test your movie. The rocket ship spirals out of control and moves off the right edge of the screen. The statements in the event handler tell Flash to take the event target's (**ship_mc**) **x** and **rotation** properties and set them equal to their current value plus the value you stored in the variable named **speed**.

   The continuous motion is achieved through the event listener. **ENTER_FRAME** is an internal event that is constantly being detected throughout the playback of the SWF file. Each time this event is detected, the **moveShip** function is called. This function updates the rocket ship's location and rotation on the Stage.

Figure 9.7: *The internal ENTER_FRAME event creates the animation on the Stage.*

   The rocket ship keeps animating even after it has moved off the right edge of the Stage. Let's create a conditional statement that tells Flash to bring back the rocket ship on the opposite side of the Stage (Stage left). **Conditionals** are a set of statements that only execute if some condition is true. These are commonly referred to as "IF" statements.

5. The condition you will be testing for is the ship's horizontal location. If that value is greater than the width of the Stage (800), then the rocket ship's **x** property will be reset to the left edge of the Stage (0). Add the following conditional inside the **moveShip** function.

Chapter 9: Interact with Me

```
// define event handlers
function moveShip(e:Event):void {
    // add a conditional statement to test the location of the ship
    if(e.target.x >= stage.stageWidth + e.target.width){
        e.target.x = 0 - e.target.width;
    }
    // change the location and rotation properties
    e.target.x += speed;
    e.target.rotation += speed;
}
```

6. Save and test your movie. The rocket ship continues to spiral out of control and move off the right edge of the screen. After the ship has completely vanished from the screen, it reappears on the left side of the Stage.

    The conditional statements in the event handler test to see if the rocket ship's (**e.target**) horizontal position (**x**) is greater than the Stage's width plus the width of the ship (**stage.stageWidth + e.target.width**). By adding the width of the rocket ship, you guarantee that the ship is completely off the Stage before repositioning it. To see a completed version, open **02__ActionScriptAnimation_Complete.fla** in the **Completed** folder.

 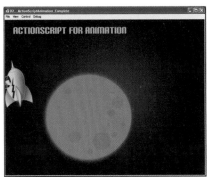

Figure 9.8: *The conditional statement resets the location of the rocket ship after it animates off the right edge of the Stage.*

Controlling Camera Movements

Now that you have a working knowledge of ActionScript and how it can control movie clips, let's apply it to the cinematic techniques discussed in previous chapters. The next three exercises focus on controlling camera movements through code. As discussed in Chapter 6, camera movements include pans, tilts, zooms, and tracking shots. A parallax scroll is a form of tracking shot used to create the illusion of depth in animation.

Exercise 3: Parallax Scrolling using ActionScript

This exercise will create a parallax scroll using bitmap artwork. The movement will be controlled through ActionScript. A completed version is provided in the **Completed** folder. Locate and play **03_ParallaxScrollControl_Complete.swf**.

Figure 9.10: *Click on the arrows to have the character walk through the scene.*

03_ParallaxScrollControl

1. Open the file **03_ParallaxScrollControl.fla** in the **Chapter_09** folder. This Flash movie contains the artwork you need to complete this exercise. The Timeline contains four layers: **background**, **middleground**, **walker**, and **actions**. The man will remain in this position on the Stage. The illusion of movement and depth will be achieved by animating the environment around him.

Before you start coding, let's deconstruct how the bitmap images were created in Photoshop. As discussed in Chapter 6, for parallax scrolling, the artwork's width must be at least twice the width of the Flash Stage. To prepare the bitmap images to scroll properly, each layer's starting width was at least 550 pixels. The middleground graphic was a little bit larger. The image was duplicated and added to the right end of the graphic. This doubles the size of the artwork (Figure 9.11). The Clone Stamp Tool was used to blend the seams and make both edges match.

The sky and clouds artwork was saved as a JPEG file. The middle ground was saved as a PNG file. PNG files retain the transparency of the alpha channel. After being imported into Flash, the artwork was converted into a movie clip and positioned on the appropriate layer in the Timeline.

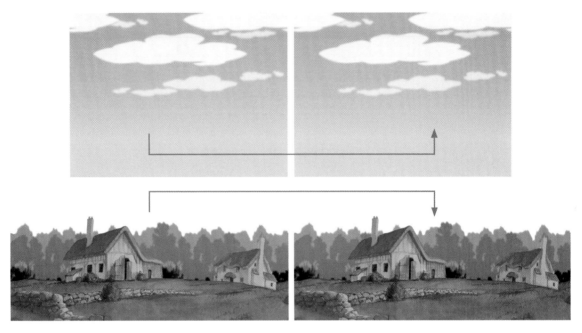

Figure 9.11: *Create a seamless scroll in Photoshop.*

Each layer of the background was given an instance name of **background_mc** and **middleground_mc**. The character is a movie clip with an instance name of **walker_mc**. Double-click on the man to open the movie clip's Timeline.

The first frame contains the static pose of the gentleman. Frames 2 through 18 contain the walk cycle poses. An **actions** layer stops the Timeline from playing on the first frame. The actions on frame 18 loop the playback marker back to the frame labeled **loop**. This will create a looping walk cycle while the user clicks and holds down the mouse button on either the left and right arrows on the main Timeline (Figure 9.12).

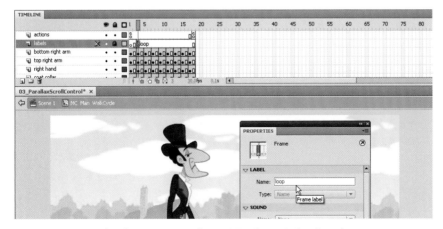

Figure 9.12: *The character movie clip contains the nested walk cycle.*

2. Now that we have discussed the artwork, it is time to code the parallax scroll. Click on the blank keyframe on the **actions** layer. Open the Actions panel. If the Actions panel is not open, choose **Window > Actions**.

3. First, you need to define two variables that will store which direction to scroll the artwork. Two event listeners need to be attached to the next and back arrow buttons that have instance names of **backward_btn** and **forward_btn**. The listeners will detect a **MOUSE_DOWN** and **MOUSE_UP** external event. Add the following code in the Actions panel.

```
// define boolean variables to start and stop the parallax scroll
var moveLeft:Boolean = false;
var moveRight:Boolean = false;

// add event listeners to the buttons for mouse down event
forward_btn.addEventListener(MouseEvent.MOUSE_DOWN, moveLayers);
backward_btn.addEventListener(MouseEvent.MOUSE_DOWN, moveLayers);

// add event listeners to the buttons for mouse up event
forward_btn.addEventListener(MouseEvent.MOUSE_UP, stopLayers);
backward_btn.addEventListener(MouseEvent.MOUSE_UP, stopLayers);
```

4. Notice that both the **forward_btn** and the **backward_btn** call the same event handlers for the different event types. This will help consolidate the amount of code needed. A simple conditional statement can be written in the event handlers to check to see which button is calling the function.

Add the event handlers that responds to the listeners. Add the following code:

```
// create event handler to respond to the listeners
function moveLayers(e:MouseEvent):void {
    // check to see which button has been clicked
    if (e.target.name == "forward_btn"){
      // set boolean variable to true
      moveLeft = true;
    } else {
      moveRight = true;
    }
    // play the man movie clip's timeline (start walking)
    walker_mc.play();
}

function stopLayers(e:MouseEvent):void {
    moveLeft = false;
    moveRight = false;
    walker_mc.gotoAndStop(1);
}
```

Let's deconstruct the ActionScript. The **moveLayers** function first checks to see which button has called it using a conditional "IF" statement. If the instance name of the event target calling the function is equal to (==) the name **forward_btn**, then the variable **moveLeft** is set to true. If that condition is false, then the variable **moveRight** is set to true.

5. Save and test your movie. If you click on the next or back arrows only the character walks in place. The next step is to use the values of **moveLeft** and **moveRight** to animate the background layers. To do this, you will need to add an **ENTER_FRAME** listener to the Stage similar to what you did in the second exercise. Add the following code in the Actions panel.

```
// add event listener to the stage to create the parallax scroll
stage.addEventListener(Event.ENTER_FRAME, timeToScroll);

// create a event handler that moves the layers
function timeToScroll(e:Event):void {
    // move the layers only if moveLeft or moveRight is true
    if(moveLeft){
        parallax(middleground_mc, 5);
        parallax(background_mc, 2);
        walker_mc.scaleX = 1;
    } else if (moveRight){
        parallax(middleground_mc, -5);
        parallax(background_mc, -2);
        walker_mc.scaleX = -1;
    }
}
```

The code calls a custom function called **parallax** every time the Timeline enters the frame. It also passes two parameters into the function (**middleground_mc, 5**). Parameters are additional bits of information that a function may need in order to execute the code correctly. For this example, this refers to the instance name of the movie clip calling the function. The number 5 refers to the speed at which the instance will move.

This script also changes the walker movie clip to walk in the correct direction. Setting the scaleX property to **–1** flips the movie clip horizontally. Setting it to **1** puts it back to the original dimensions.

6. The last thing you need to do is add the parallax function to actually move the background layers. The code prevents each layer from moving off the screen depending on which direction the artwork is moving. It checks to see how far the instance has moved to the right or left. If it has moved too far, Flash shifts it back over to create a seamless loop. Add the following code.

```
function parallax(layer:MovieClip, speed:Number):void {
    // conditional to check the location of the background layers
    if (layer.x <= 0){
        layer.x = layer.x + layer.width/2;
    }else if (layer.x >= layer.width/2){
        layer.x = layer.x - layer.width/2;
    }
    // change the horizontal position of the layers
    layer.x -= speed;
}
```

The **parallax** function has two parameters associated with it: layer and speed. When the function is called from the **timetoScroll** event handler, the instance name stored in this is passed into the function's parameter layer. The numeric value (**5**) is passed into the function's parameter speed.

The **parallax** function uses the information passed into its parameters to move the correct instance at the defined speed. This type of programming makes the code reusable and allows you to revise or update it more efficiently.

7. This completes the exercise. Save and test your movie. The ActionScript builds on the first two examples to create a seamless scrolling animation. By changing the **speed** value for each background layer, you achieve a parallax scroll. The next exercise focuses on creating an interactive tracking movement.

Exercise 4: Depth Illusion Under User Control

In cinematography, a camera can move forward, called a truck in, or backward, called a truck out. This type of tracking movement adds depth to the shot. In Chapter 6 you built an animation on the Timeline that simulated this effect using the 3D Translation Tool. Let's put that camera movement under user control using ActionScript.

04_Walkthrough

1. Open the file **04_Walkthrough.fla** in the **Chapter_09** folder. This Flash movie contains the artwork you need to complete this exercise. The Timeline contains three layers: **3D Space MC**, **buttons**, and **actions**.

2. The background artwork is a movie clip with an instance name of **world_mc**. Double-click on the artwork to open its Timeline. The layered animation simulates a truck-in camera movement (Figure 9.13). In this exercise, you are going to write ActionScript that controls the playback on this movie clip. Depending on which arrow the user clicks on, the movie will play forward or reverse. This technique can be further expanded on to create a simulated 3D environment that a user could walk through and interact with.

Figure 9.13: *The movie clip contains a tweened animation simulating a camera truck-in.*

3. Close the movie clip and return to the main Timeline. Click on the blank keyframe on the **actions** layer. Open the Actions panel. If the Actions panel is not open, choose **Window > Actions**.

4. Similar to the previous exercise, you need to define two variables that will store which direction to move the artwork and the total number of frames inside the movie clip. The variable **moveIt** will be used to control the playback of the movie clip. Two event listeners need to be attached to the two arrow buttons that have instance names of **arrowIn_btn** and **arrowOut_btn**. The listeners will detect a **MOUSE_DOWN** and **MOUSE_UP** external event. Add the following code in the Actions panel.

```
// set up variable that will move the timeline forward or back
var moveIt:Number;
// record the total number of frames in the 3D scene's movie clip
var totalNumFrames:Number = world_mc.totalFrames;

// stop the world's timeline from animating
world_mc.stop();

// add event listeners for the arrow buttons
arrowIn_btn.addEventListener(MouseEvent.MOUSE_DOWN, zoomIn);
arrowOut_btn.addEventListener(MouseEvent.MOUSE_DOWN, zoomOut);

arrowIn_btn.addEventListener(MouseEvent.MOUSE_UP, stopZoom);
arrowOut_btn.addEventListener(MouseEvent.MOUSE_UP, stopZoom);
```

5. The variable **totalNumFrames** stores the total number of frames (**totalFrames**) used in the **world_mc** movie clip instance on the Stage. Storing that information is essential in determining whether the animation has finished or not.

   Notice that both the **arrowIn_btn** and the **arrowOut_btn** call the same event handlers for the different event types. Just like in the parallax scroll exercise, a conditional statement can be written in the event handlers to check to see which button is calling the function. Add the event handlers that responds to the listeners. Add the following code:

```
// add event handlers
function zoomIn(e:MouseEvent):void {
    moveIt = 1;
}
function zoomOut(e:MouseEvent):void {
    moveIt = -1;
}
function stopZoom(e:MouseEvent):void {
    moveIt = 0;
}
```

6. The event handlers are pretty simple. The functions change the value of the variable **moveIt**. The next part of the ActionScript will use this information to animate the movie clip. If the value of **moveIt** is equal to **1**, the movie clip will play back normally. If the value is **–1**, the movie clip will play in reverse. If the value of **moveIt** is equal to **0**, the movie clip stops on the current frame being displayed. Basically, you are building simple playback controls using the arrows.

   Add the following code in the Actions panel:

```
// add event listener for zooming animation
world_mc.addEventListener(Event.ENTER_FRAME, truck);

function truck(e:Event):void {
    // get the current frame
    var thisFrame:uint = world_mc.currentFrame;
    // update to the next frame
    thisFrame += moveIt;

    // test the ends of the movie clip
    if (thisFrame > totalNumFrames) { thisFrame = totalNumFrames; }
    if (thisFrame < 1) { thisFrame = 1; }

    // display the new frame on the stage
    world_mc.gotoAndStop(thisFrame);
}
```

7. Save and test your movie. Click on the arrows to walk into or out of the 3D scene (Figure 9.14). The **truck** function uses two more properties associated with movie clips, **totalFrames** and **currentFrame**. The **currentFrame** property stores the current frame being displayed on the Stage. When both properties are used together, you can control the playback of any movie clip on the Stage.

Figure 9.14: *Save and test your movie to see the final results.*

Exercise 5: Simulating a Panorama

Panoramic images create a full 360-degree image. If done photographically the photographer stands in the middle of some environment of interest and takes a number of partially overlapping photos around a full 360 degrees. There are numerous software applications that allow you to stitch the individual shots together into one single panoramic image that displays the whole scene.

1. Open the file **05_360LookAround.fla** in the **Chapter_09** folder. This Flash movie contains the artwork you need to complete this exercise. The Timeline contains four layers: **background**, **character**, **buttons**, and **actions**.

05_360LookAround

2. The woman is a movie clip with an instance name of **character_mc**. Double-click on the character movie clip to open its Timeline. The artwork is a frame-by-frame animation of the woman's head and shoulders turning 360 degrees. There are 29 frames, not 30. The first frame and frame 30 would be the same.

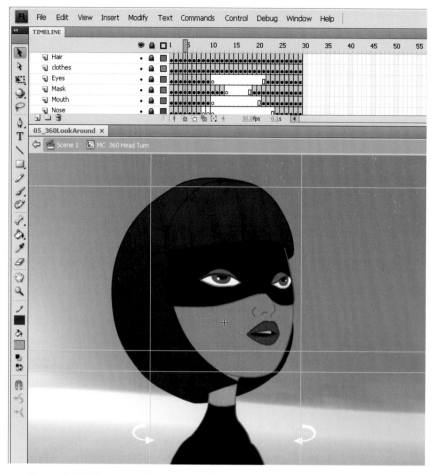

Figure 9.15: *The movie clip contains a frame-by-frame animation.*

3. Close the movie clip and return to the main Timeline. Double-click on the background that has an instance name of **world_mc**. This image was rendered from Bryce, a 3D software program. The image created is a **cylindrical panorama**. This means that the left side of the image aligns with the right side of the image. The robot was added in Photoshop (Figure 9.16).

Figure 9.16: *The left side of the cylindrical panorama aligns with the right side.*

After being imported into Flash, the panoramic image was converted into a movie clip and animated to pan across the Stage. Notice that the number of frames it takes to complete the pan is 29, the same number of frames it takes to turn the character around 360 degrees. This is important in order to synchronize the panning movement with the head turn (Figure 9.17).

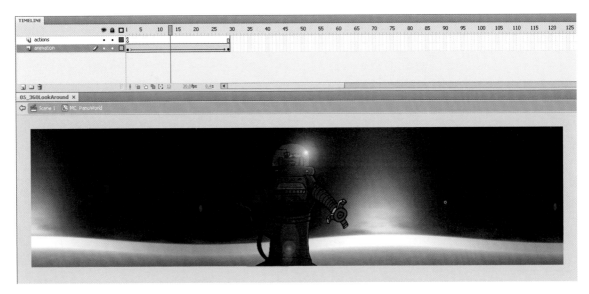

Figure 9.17: *The movie clip contains a tweened animation that is the same number of frames as the head turn animation.*

4. Close the movie clip and return to the main Timeline. Click on the blank keyframe on the **actions** layer. Open the Actions panel. If the Actions panel is not open, choose **Window > Actions**.

5. The first part of the ActionScript is nearly identical to the previous exercise. Two event listeners need to be attached to the two arrow buttons that have instance names of **cw_btn** and **ccw_btn**. Add the following code in the Actions panel.

```
// set the direction of frame movement in the clip
var moveIt:Number = 0;
// set the number of frames in the object movie clip
var totalNumFrames:Number = character_mc.totalFrames;

// add listeners for clockwise and counter-clockwise arrows
cw_btn.addEventListener(MouseEvent.MOUSE_DOWN, setClockWise);
cw_btn.addEventListener(MouseEvent.MOUSE_UP, stopRotation);
ccw_btn.addEventListener(MouseEvent.MOUSE_DOWN, setCounterClockWise);
ccw_btn.addEventListener(MouseEvent.MOUSE_UP, stopRotation);
```

Controlling Camera Movements

6. The event handlers follow the same concept as the previous exercise. If the value of **moveIt** is equal to **1**, the movie clip will play back normally. If the value is **–1**, the movie clip will play in reverse. If the value of **moveIt** is equal to **0**, the movie clip stops on the current frame being displayed. Add the following code.

```
// set up eventHandlers
function setClockWise(e:MouseEvent){
    moveIt = -1;
}
function setCounterClockWise(e:MouseEvent){
    moveIt = 1;
}
function stopRotation(e:MouseEvent){
    moveIt = 0;
}
```

7. To animate the two movie clips, you need an **ENTER_FRAME** event listener. Add the following code to the Actions panel.

```
// rotate the character and world
character_mc.addEventListener(Event.ENTER_FRAME, spinObject);

// create the event handler for the ENTER_FRAME listener
function spinObject(e:Event):void {
    // get the current frame
    var thisFrame:Number = character_mc.currentFrame;
    // update to the next frame
    thisFrame += moveIt;
    // test the ends of the movie clip
    if (thisFrame > totalNumFrames) { thisFrame = 1; }
    if (thisFrame < 1) { thisFrame = totalNumFrames; }
    // display the correct frame for the character and world
    character_mc.gotoAndStop(thisFrame);
    world_mc.gotoAndStop(thisFrame);
}
```

8. Save and test your movie. Click on the arrows to pan 360 degrees around the scene. The **spinObject** function uses the **currentFrame** property. Based on the value of **moveIt**, you control the playback of both movie clips on the Stage. By changing the current frame for the **character_mc** and the **world_mc** at the same time, your synchronize the animation (Figure 9.18).

These exercises incorporate both external and internal events. Some key points to remember are that external events are driven by the user. An internal event occurs every time the files enters a frame (**ENTER_FRAME**). Even though there is only one frame in the Timeline, Flash constantly leaves and re-enters it.

Figure 9.18: *Save and test your movie to see the final results.*

Directing the Characters

So far, you have been interacting with the Flash movies using the mouse. The next exercise focuses on another external event: keypress. Flash can detect a keypress for any key on the keyboard. Here you will use the arrow keys to direct your character on where to go on the Stage.

1. Open the file **06_SceneChanger.fla** in the **Chapter_09** folder. This Flash movie contains the artwork you need to complete this exercise. The Timeline contains three layers: **background**, **man**, and **actions**. The man is the villain from *The Duel* animation discussed in Chapter 5. It is a movie clip that contains the character's walk cycle and it has an instance name of **walker_mc**.

2. Double-click on the background movie clip to open its Timeline. The movie clip contains five frames with different backgrounds and has an instance name of **backdrop_mc**. These could represent the different locations in your story.

06_SceneChanger

Figure 9.19: *The movie clip contains a series of background images.*

3. Close the movie clip and return to the main Timeline. Click on the blank keyframe on the **actions** layer. Open the Actions panel. If the Actions panel is not open, choose **Window > Actions**.

4. The first part of the ActionScript defines the variables that are needed. With a keypress interaction, you need to create variables to assist Flash in determining which arrow is pressed. For this exercise, you will use the left and right arrow keys. After the variables are defined, event listeners are added to the Stage to detect the **KEY_DOWN** and **KEY_UP** event types. An **ENTER_FRAME** event listener is also added to physically move the villain across the Stage. Add the following code in the Actions panel.

```
// initialize arrow variables
var leftArrow:Boolean = false;
var rightArrow:Boolean = false;

// define which frame the background is on
var currentBackdrop:Number = 1;
// set the number of frames in the background movie clip
var totalNumFrames:Number = backdrop_mc.totalFrames;

// stop the walking man from animating
walking_mc.stop();

// set the speed for moving the movie clip
var speed:Number = 3;

// add event listeners
stage.addEventListener(KeyboardEvent.KEY_DOWN, keyPressedDown);
stage.addEventListener(KeyboardEvent.KEY_UP, keyPressedUp);
stage.addEventListener(Event.ENTER_FRAME, moveMan);
```

5. Next add the event handlers for the **KeyboardEvent** listeners. Each key is assigned a specific **keyCode** in Flash. The left arrow key has a **keyCode** of **37**. The right arrow key has a **keyCode** of **39**. If either one of these keys is pressed the corresponding variable becomes true and the villain plays his walk cycle.

```
// set arrow variables to true
function keyPressedDown(e:KeyboardEvent) {
    if (e.keyCode == 37) {
        leftArrow = true;
    } else if (e.keyCode == 39) {
        rightArrow = true;
    }
    // start playing animated walk cycle
    walking_mc.play();
}
```

```
// set arrow variables to false
function keyPressedUp(e:KeyboardEvent) {
    if (e.keyCode == 37) {
        leftArrow = false;
    } else if (e.keyCode == 39) {
        rightArrow = false;
    }
    walking_mc.gotoAndStop(1);
}
```

Just the opposite happens when either key is released. The variables become false and the character's movie clip goes to the first frame and stops.

6. Let's add the event handler that directs the character's movement on the Stage. The code is similar to the parallax scroll exercise in terms of moving and flipping the character horizontally using the **scaleX** property. Once the character has left either side of the Stage, the value of **currentBackdrop** is either increased or decreased by one. This variable's value corresponds to the frame numbers inside **backdrop_mc**. Add the following code to the Actions panel.

```
// move every frame
function moveMan(e:Event) {
    // if the left arrow ley is pressed
    if (leftArrow) {
        walking_mc.x -= speed;
        walking_mc.scaleX = -1;
    }
    // if the right arrow key is pressed
    if (rightArrow) {
        walking_mc.x += speed;
        walking_mc.scaleX = 1;
    }
    // check man's location on the Stage
    if (walking_mc.x >= stage.stageWidth + walking_mc.width){
        walking_mc.x = 0 - walking_mc.width;
        // add 1 to the value of currentBackdrop
        currentBackdrop++;
        // call function to change the scenery
        changeBackground();
    }else if (walking_mc.x <= 0 - walking_mc.width){
        walking_mc.x = stage.stageWidth + walking_mc.width;
        // subtract 1 from the value of currentBackdrop
        currentBackdrop--;
        // call function to change the scenery
        changeBackground();
    }
}
```

7. The last part of the ActionScript is the custom function that changes the scenery on the Stage. Conditional statements test to see if the **backdrop_mc** is on the first or last frame. This will create a continuous loop through all five frames.

```
// custom function to change the scenery
function changeBackground(){
    // check to see if the movie clip is on the last frame
    if(currentBackdrop > totalNumFrames){
        currentBackdrop = 1
    // check to see if the movie clip is on the first frame
    }else if(currentBackdrop < 1){
        currentBackdrop = totalNumFrames
    }
    // jump to the correct frame
    backdrop_mc.gotoAndStop(currentBackdrop);
}
```

8. Save and test your movie. Press either the left or right arrow keys on your keyboard to move the villain from scene to scene (Figure 9.20). Notice that the character makes a clean entrance and exit for each background. In Chapter 5, you read that clean entrances and exits work well for shots where someone is moving from one place to another. By not seeing the character on-screen for a second or two, the audience will accept that he had time to travel to the different location in the following shot.

Figure 9.20: *Save and test your movie to see the final results.*

Enhancing a Story Using ActionScript

This chapter focused on several techniques for adding interactivity to your Flash movie. The exercises didn't necessarily tell a story, but were more intended to demonstrate how to apply the ActionScript to achieve a specific camera movement or ways to control the characters on the Stage. Let's wrap up the chapter by looking at how you can integrate the different exercises from this chapter into a Flash movie to enhance a story. Locate and play **Dolores_Umbrella.swf** in the **Examples** folder inside **Chapter_09**.

This interactive story was designed and developed by Karli Tucker, a graduate student in the Computer Graphics Design MFA program at the Rochester Institute of Technology. The story invites the user to participate in helping Dolores Weatherbee use her umbrella for three different adventures. In the end, she shows her granddaughter, Edith, the importance of carrying an umbrella with you at all times.

Figure 9.21: *This interactive story invites you to introduce yourself to the main character, Dolores Weatherbee.*

The artwork was illustrated, inked, and painted using water colors. Each part was scanned into the computer and assembled in Flash. This creates a unique visual style that matches the artist's vision. Since the intended delivery method was for CD-ROM or downloaded to the user's hard drive, the file size was not an issue using the bitmap images.

The main part of the story involves Dolores walking down a street and running into three different scenarios that she solves using her umbrella. The parallax movement uses the same code from Exercise 3. Each scenario has a button that loads in external SWF files into the main scene when clicked.

Figure 9.22: *Help Dolores use her umbrella to solve some urban problems.*

As mentioned in Chapter 5, if file size is a concern, try breaking up your story sequence into smaller, separate Flash FLA files. ActionScript can be used to play each published SWF file in chronological order. To do that you need to create a **Loader** class. This allows you to import an external SWF, JPEG, or PNG file using a **URLRequest** to define the path to the file. A coding example is shown below.

```
// create an empty mc container to load animation into
var contentBox:MovieClip = new MovieClip();
addChild(contentBox);

// create a loader for the external content
var myLoader:Loader = new Loader();
var myFile:URLRequest;

// example of how to load in the external swf file into Flash
myFile = new URLRequest("fileName.swf");
myLoader.load(myFile);
contentBox.addChild(myLoader);
```

You can also load in external Flash Video (FLV) files to build your story. Locate and play **Eganwo.swf** in the **Examples** folder inside **Chapter_09**. This digital graphic novel was designed and developed by Brian Kowalzyk, a graduate student in the Computer Graphics Design MFA program at the Rochester Institute of Technology.

Pronounced "ee-gan-woo," this is the first issue set in an apocalyptic world. Each spread of the graphic novel loads in external FLV files. When the cursor rolls over each panel, limited animation plays to enhance the narrative and user experience. The user navigation allows you to jump to any section of the graphic novel at any time.

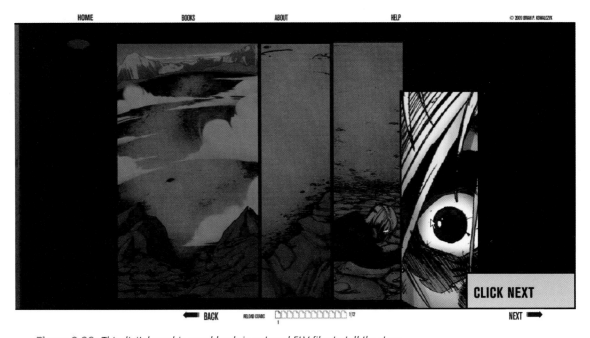

Figure 9.23: *This digital graphic novel loads in external FLV files to tell the story.*

The artwork was drawn by hand, inked, and scanned into Photoshop where it was colored. Special attention was used to keep the visual look as hand-drawn as possible. The animations were built in Adobe After Effects rather than Flash. The compositions were rendered out as separate FLV files.

Each video was loaded into Flash using the Import Video Wizard. The deployment was set to progressive download instead of embedding on the Timeline. A Flash ProgressBar UI component was also used to provide user feedback as the video progressively downloads from the web. Two event listeners were added to the FLVPlayback. One monitored the number of bytes loaded into the movie. The second listener detected when the video had completely loaded into Flash. A coding example is shown on the following page.

```
// import Flash packages
import fl.video.*;
import fl.controls.ProgressBarMode;

// set variables
var flvScene = display;

/ add Event Listeners and load the video
flvScene.addEventListener(VideoProgressEvent.PROGRESS, onLoading);
flvScene.addEventListener(VideoEvent.READY, videoReady);
```

Figure 9.24: *The user has multiple ways to read and interact with the story.*

Summary

This chapter focused on ActionScript and the **MovieClip** class and its properties. The exercises incorporated ActionScript to create interactive camera movements and controllable characters. Now that you have finished reading the chapter, you should be able to:

- ▶ Describe objects, classes, properties, and methods
- ▶ Construct ActionScript code for specific events
- ▶ Create interactive movement in Flash
- ▶ Reproduce camera movements using ActionScript

The next, and final, chapter focuses on optimizing and publishing your Flash movies for the web and video.

CHAPTER 10

Optimize and Publish

Your Flash movies can be published for the web, exported to video to be burned onto a DVD, or imported into video compositing software such as Adobe After Effects for further enhancement. This chapter offers some tips to optimize and publish your Flash movies for the web and video.

Optimizing Graphics

Performance is key when publishing Flash movies to the web. Vector images are drawn using mathematical formulas to provide scalable graphics in a compact size. However, rendering an anti-aliased vector shape can eat up a lot of processing power if you do not design your artwork wisely.

To optimize your vector art, try and reduce the number of strokes and points used. Use the Optimize Curves dialog box (**Modify > Shape > Optimize**) to reduce the number of vectors in a drawing (Figure 10.1). This reduces file size, but if you compress too much the quality of your artwork will suffer.

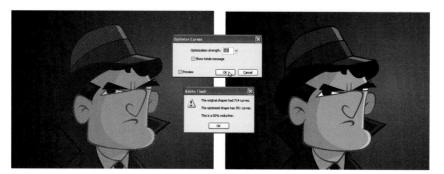

Figure 10.1: *Use the Optimize Curves dialog box to reduce the number of vectors in your artwork.*

A more tedious approach would be to use the Subselection Tool (**A**) to manually remove and adjust your vectors. Either way, optimizing the curves reduces your file size and improves the SWF file performance. As a designer, you need to determine how much quality you are willing to sacrifice for better performance.

Gradients look nice, but can slow down performance due to the fact that a gradient uses many colors and the calculations to display it can be processor intensive. Flat shading may be the best way to go to achieve a 3D look. Also use transparency and filters sparingly in your web-based Flash movies. That doesn't mean you can't use them, just use them wisely when needed.

When using bitmap images, always use 72-dpi resolution. Anything higher is not optimal for the web. Use only JPEG and PNG files saved from Adobe Photoshop or Fireworks. Use the Save for Web & Devices feature in Photoshop to preview how much compression you can apply without sacrificing quality.

As mentioned in Chapter 2, for textures that are busy with detail, you can compress quite a bit without noticing the artifacts. Also equally important is to avoid scaling bitmaps larger than their original dimensions. Design each bitmap in Photoshop at 100% the size it will be in Flash. Scaling bitmaps reduces the quality of the image and is processor intensive.

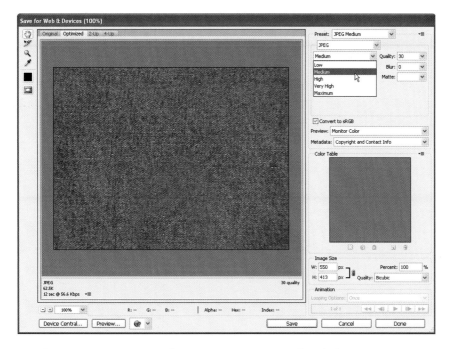

Figure 10.2: *Experiment with compression settings to reduce the bitmap image to the smallest size possible while still maintaining image quality.*

Preloading in Flash

There is nothing more frustrating for a user than going to a website and waiting for the SWF to load. One way to keep the user from moving on is to visually show them how long the files is going to take to load. This is achieved using a preloader. The ActionScript for this resides typically on the first frame of your FLA file. Let's take a look at an example.

 Locate the **Chapter_10** *folder on the CD-ROM. Copy this folder to your hard drive. The folder contains all the files needed to complete the chapter exercises.*

Locate and open **01_Preloader.fla** in the **Examples** folder in **Chapter_10**. Click on the keyframe on frame 1 of the **actions** layer. Open the Actions panel. If the Actions panel is not open, choose **Window > Actions**. The concept of a Flash preloader is rather simple. You tell Flash using ActionScript to compare the amount of data loaded with the total data in the movie.

The code adds an event listener to the main Timeline's **loaderInfo** property. This "listens" for the progress of that event. Basically, you are telling Flash to detect how much data has loaded. Whenever something is being loaded, the function **showStatus** is called to update the progress bar on the Stage. See the code example on the following page.

```
// stop the timeline until the file has loaded completely
stop();

// add eventlistener to the root timeline
root.loaderInfo.addEventListener(ProgressEvent.PROGRESS, showStatus);
root.loaderInfo.addEventListener(Event.COMPLETE, finished);

// create event handlers
function showStatus(e:Event):void {
    // create a variable that stores how much date has loaded
    var showPercent:Number = e.target.bytesLoaded/e.target.bytesTotal;
    // update the preloader bar by scaling it
    bar_mc.scaleX = showPercent;
}
function finished(e:Event):void {
    play();
};
```

The function **showStatus** first defines a variable called **showPercent** and data
types it as a **Number**. Its value is the amount of bytes loaded. On the next line
the horizontal scale of **bar_mc** is set equal to the value stored in **showPercent**.
It is important to note that the registration point for this movie clip is at the
middle, left edge of the graphic (Figure 10.3).

Figure 10.3: *The registration point for the preloader bar is at the left edge.*

A second event listener is added to the main Timeline's **loaderInfo** property.
This detects when the file has completely loaded. It calls the function **finished**.
This function plays the rest of the Flash movie. The goal of a preloader is to
load quickly, so keep it simple. Save any complex animation for your story.

Using the QuickTime Exporter

The QuickTime Exporter in Flash allows you to save your movies as a QuickTime,
Windows AVI, or an image sequence. There are two methods in which you can
export your Flash file. The first method renders on a frame-by-frame basis all
content placed directly on the Flash Timeline. The second option allows you to
export dynamic content over a period of time. This includes ActionScript-driven
animation that uses movie clips. Let's explore each method in detail.

This exercise provides a step-by-step tutorial on using the Flash QuickTime Exporter to save content on the Timeline to a fixed-frame video format. Movie clips are supported using this first method. The artwork can be a movie clip, a graphic symbol or vector shape.

1. Open the **02_QuickTimeExporter** folder inside the **Chapter_10** folder.

2. The scene contains an animation that is made up of several layers. The artwork is nested within a graphic symbol. The layer labeled **SAFE AREA** contains the Title Safe and Action Safe guides for NTSC D1 video. All titles and text are framed within the Title Safe area (Figure 10.4). Notice that it is a guide layer. It is visible in the Flash FLA file but will not be included in the exported movie.

 *Title Safe and Action Safe templates are provided in the **Chapter_03** folder for you to use in your projects. Simply copy the frame and paste it into your file.*

Figure 10.4: *The title is contained within the Title Safe area.*

3. Select **File > Export > Export Movie**. This opens the QuickTime Movie dialog box. Select a final destination for the rendered movie. Make sure the file format is set to QuickTime. Click **Save**.

4. The QuickTime Export Settings dialog box appears. Make sure the width and height are set to 720 and 540 respectively. The Stop Exporting area provides the two exporting methods mentioned at the beginning of this exercise. Since this Flash movie is a frame-by-frame animation, you want to stop exporting when the last frame is reached. Click on **QuickTime Export Settings**.

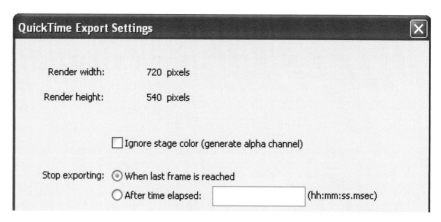

Figure 10.5: *QuickTime Export Settings provides several options to choose from.*

5. The Movie Settings dialog box allows you to adjust the video and audio settings. There is no audio in this file. Turn off the audio export by unchecking the checkbox next to Sound (Figure 10.6).

6. Click on the **Settings** button under the Video area. This opens the Standard Video Compression Settings dialog box (Figure 10.6). Here you can adjust the compression settings. Animation compression works well for Flash movies. Leave the frame rate at 30 fps. Click **OK** twice to return to the QuickTime Export Settings dialog box.

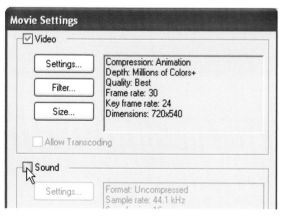

Figure 10.6: *The QuickTime Exporter allows you to control the video compression.*

7. Quit out of all other applications so only Flash is open. Click **Export**. The QuickTime Exporter captures every frame as an SWF movie in the background to create the QuickTime movie. This can take a few minutes.

   You may need to lower the frame rate to prevent frames dropping. What does this mean? If the video size and fast frame rate are too much for the QuickTime Exporter, certain frames will be dropped as it renders the movie.

8. A dialog box will appear when the QuickTime movie is complete. Click **OK**.

Chapter 10: Optimize and Publish

Exporting ActionScript-Driven Movies

Flash CS3 introduced the ability to export content over a period of time to a QuickTime file format. You define the amount of time and the QuickTime Exporter records the movement on the Stage whether it is frame-by-frame or ActionScript driven. This is a huge improvement and good news for Flash programmers who want to export their dynamically driven movies to video.

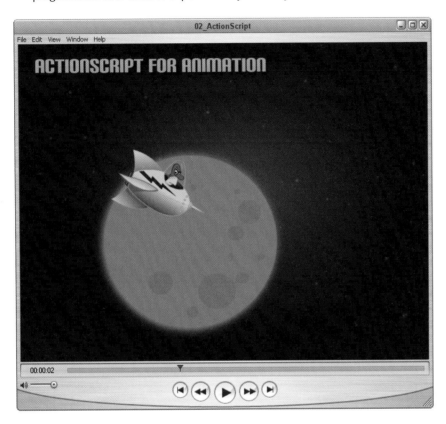

Figure 10.8: *The finished QuickTime movie file uses ActionScript-driven content.*

This final exercise provides a tutorial on exporting an ActionScript-driven animation using the QuickTime Exporter. To see an example, locate and play the **02_ActionScript.mov** in the **Completed** folder (Figure 10.8). When you finish this exercise you will be able to export movie clips controlled by ActionScript to a video format.

This example is from Chapter 9. The retro rocketship was created in Flash as a short, frame-by-frame animation stored in a movie clip. Through the use of ActionScript, the movie clip animates across the Stage.

1. Let's review the Flash code. Open **02_ActionScript.fla** inside the **Chapter_10** folder. Click on the keyframe on frame 1 of the **actions** layer. Open the Actions panel. If the Actions panel is not open, choose **Window > Actions**.

```
// create a custom variable to store the information
var speed:Number = 5;

// define event listeners
ship_mc.addEventListener(Event.ENTER_FRAME, moveShip);

// define event handlers
function moveShip(e:Event):void {
    // change the location and rotation properties
    e.target.x += speed;
    e.target.rotation += speed;
}
```

The statements in the event handler tell Flash to take the event target's (**ship_mc**) **x** and **rotation** properties and set them equal to their current value plus the value you stored in variable named **speed**.

The motion is achieved through the event listener. **ENTER_FRAME** is an internal event that is constantly being detected throughout the playback of the SWF file. Each time this event is detected, the **moveShip** function is called. This function updates the rocket ship's location and rotation on the Stage.

2. Select **Control > Test Movie** to preview the animation. The rocket ship spirals out of control and moves off the right edge of the screen. Close the SWF file. Select **File > Export > Export Movie**. This opens the QuickTime Movie dialog box. Select a final destination for the rendered movie. Make sure the file format is set to QuickTime. Click **Save**.

3. The QuickTime Export Settings dialog box appears. Make sure the width and height are set to 800 and 600 respectively.

4. In the Stop Exporting area select **After Time Elapsed** and enter **00:00:08**. Flash will record activity on the Stage for eight seconds. This method includes movie clips in the captured frames. Click on **QuickTime Export Settings**.

5. The Movie Settings dialog box allows you to adjust the video and audio settings. There is no audio in this file. Turn off the audio export by unchecking the checkbox next to Sound.

6. Click on the **Size** button under the Video area. This opens the Export Size Settings dialog box. Make sure the width and height are set to 800 and 600 respectively.

7. Click **OK** twice to return to the QuickTime Export Settings dialog box.

8. Quit out of all other applications so only Flash is running. Click **Export**. A dialog box will appear when the QuickTime movie is complete. Click **OK**.

Chapter 10: Optimize and Publish

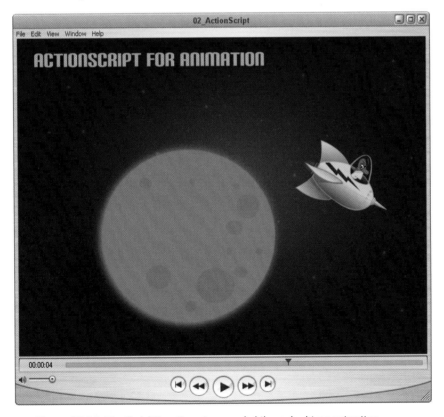

QuickTime Export Settings

Render width: 800 pixels

Render height: 600 pixels

☐ Ignore stage color (generate alpha channel)

Stop exporting: ○ When last frame is reached

◉ After time elapsed: `8` (hh:mm:ss.msec)

Store temp data: ◉ In memory (recommended for higher frame rates)

○ On disk (recommended for longer movies)

Figure 10.9: *To export ActionScript-driven content, select* **After Time Elapsed** *and enter a value. Flash will record any activity on the Stage for the time entered.*

9. Go to the folder on your hard drive where you saved the QuickTime movie. Launch the QuickTime movie in the QuickTime player. The ability to export ActionScript-driven content is a great improvement for Flash.

Figure 10.10: *The QuickTime Exporter recorded the code-driven animation.*

Summary

This completes the chapter and this book. Some key concepts from this chapter to remember include:

- Vector images are drawn using mathematical formulas to provide scalable graphics in a compact size.

- Rendering an anti-aliased vector shape can eat up a lot of processing power if you do not design your artwork wisely.

- Use the Optimize Curves dialog box (**Modify > Shape > Optimize**) to reduce the number of vectors in a drawing.

- Gradients use many colors and the calculations to display them can be processor intensive.

- Flat shading may be the best way to go to achieve a 3D look.

- When using bitmap images, always use 72-dpi resolution.

- Use only JPEG and PNG files saved from Adobe Photoshop or Fireworks.

- Use the Save for Web & Devices feature in Photoshop to preview how much compression you can apply without sacrificing quality.

- Design each bitmap in Photoshop at 100% the size it will be in Flash.

- Scaling bitmaps reduces the quality of the image and is processor intensive.

- The goal of a preloader is to load quickly, so keep it simple. Save any complex animation for your story.

- As a designer, you need to determine how much quality you are willing to sacrifice for better performance.

- To export movie clips to video, use the QuickTime Exporter.

Flash Cinematic Techniques focused on the visual structure of a story: camera placement, composition, color, motion, lighting, editing, and sound. These tools not only illustrate what's going on in a scene, but also advance the story and elevate its emotional impact for the audience. Hopefully you have been inspired to apply these techniques to your next animated or interactive Flash movie. Thank you for taking the journey.

Index

flat background, 161
flat shading, 276
Flattened Bitmap Image option, Photoshop, 50
FLV (Flash Video) files, 273
focal length, 116
focusing attention, 95, 116–118
4:3 frame aspect ratio, 60–61
frame aspect ratio, 60
frames
    defined, 69–70
    rates, 63–64
Free Transform Tool
    adjust position for bone's end points, 54
    for facial expressions, 238
    Illustrator, 47
frequency, 220
frontal lighting, 194
Fuller, Warren, 67
functions, 248

G

Garland, Judy, 10
Gerald McBoing-Boing (1951), 14
German Expressionism cinema, 198
The Godfather (1972), 146
Gone with the Wind (1939), 186
Gradient Transform Tool, 56, 206–207, 210–211
gradients, 115, 205, 276
graphic symbols
    building sequences with, 140–141
    mouth shapes, 228–232
    nesting animation in, 158
    overview, 37
graphical style, 31
graphics, optimizing, 276–277
graphics table, 42
grays, 30
green, 30, 107
guides layer, 121
Gulliver's Travels (1939), 242

H

Halloween (1978), 77, 136
hand-drawn (traditional) animation, 12
Hanna-Barbera, 15, 49, 180
hard light, 193, 201–205
HD (high-definition) television, 61, 63
Hercules (1997), 25
hero, 4–5
Hertz (Hz), 221
high angle lighting, 196
high angle shot, 75
high-definition (HD) television, 61, 63
high-key lighting, 197–198
highlights, 115
Hitchcock, Alfred, 6–7, 76
horizontal lines, 100
horror movie sequences, 138
HSB color, 202

Humpty Dumpty nursery rhyme, 2–3
Hz (Hertz), 221

I

IF statements, 254
illusion of roundness, 115
illustrating space, 79–84
Illustrator, Adobe, 45–48
implied directional lines, 161
Import Video Wizard, 273
Importer Wizard, Illustrator, 45
intensity, light, 193
interactivity
    ActionScript-driven animation, 253–255
    controlling camera movements
        depth illusion under user control, 260–263
        overview, 255
        parallax scrolling with ActionScript, 256–260
        simulating panorama, 263–267
    directing characters, 267–270
    enhancing story with ActionScript, 271–274
    main event, 246
    mission control, 247–252
    overview, 245
interlaced video, 64–65
interposition, 114
invisible wipe, 148
Iris transition, 156
iris wipe, 147

J

jawbone structure, 22
Jaws (1975), 147, 189
JibJab Media, 14, 49
"jitters", 65
jump cuts, 144–145

K

Kelly, Grace, 9
key light, 196
KeyboardEvent listeners, 268
kilohertz (kHz), 221
Kubrick, Stanley, 76

L

Lang, Fritz, 198
Layer Outline toggle, 37
layers, 19
lead room, 97
leading lines, 102
lighting
    defining light, 192–196
    effects
        lighting effects using masks, 217–218
        casting shadows, 212–215
        hard light character shading, 201–205
        overview, 200
        simulating rim light effect in Flash, 215–216
    soft light character shading, 205–211

payoffs, 9
perception of depth, 109–111
Perils of Pauline, 145
persistence of vision, 69
personalities
    exaggerating, 27–28
    expressing, 22
perspective
    angles of, 119–123
    distorting, 169–172
    overview, 111–113
Perspective Angle, 121
Phase Alternating Line (PAL) video format, 62–63
phoneme shapes, 224
photo collage character, 49
Photoshop, Adobe, 49–55
pixel aspect ratio, 62
pixel-based backgrounds, 165
pixels, 13
    overview, 32–41
    square versus non-square, 62–63
Place layers at original position option, Illustrator, 45
"plausible impossible", 4
plot, 2
PNG files, 256
point of view (POV), 134
Poltergeist (1982), 189
posing characters
    creating walk cycle in Flash, 242–244
    live video, referencing, 241
    overview, 241
positioning light, 192
POV (point of view), 134
Preloader, 277
pressure sensitive tablets, 42
pressure waves, 220
ProgressBar UI component, 273
progressive video, 64–65
Properties panel
    constraining joint rotation in, 54
    to display animation on Stage, 240
    labeling frames, 90, 226
    naming moving clip instance through, 248
    setting symbols to display single frame, 228
    swapping symbols, 232
proportions, characters, 28–29
protagonist, 4
Psycho (1960), 138–139
publishing
    exporting ActionScript-driven movies, 281–283
    optimizing graphics, 276–277
    overview, 275
    preloading in Flash, 277–278
QuickTime Exporter, 278–280
pupils, eye, 240
purple, 30

Q

QuickTime Exporter, 278–280

R

racking focus, 118, 123–125
radiation, electromagnetic, 192
Raiders of the Lost Ark (1981), 9
raster graphics, 13
Rear Window (1954), 8–9
recording audio
    dialogue, 222–223
    overview, 220–222
rectangles, 20
red, 30, 107
registration points, 47, 54
Regular Easing class, 155
Reiniger, Lotte, 31
relational cutting, 143
relative size, 113–114
repetitious shapes in backgrounds, 162
"reset" button, Properties panel, 248
resolution, 4, 6
resolution-independent artwork, 12
reversed screen direction, 131
RGB colors, 67, 202
"rigging", 52
rim-lighting
    effect for, 215–216
    overview, 195
    positioning, 197
rising tension, 4–5
root bone, 52
"rotate" button, Properties panel, 248
rotoscoping, 241
Rule of Thirds, 96–99

S

sampling rate, 221
Save for Web & Devices feature, Photoshop, 276
Save for Web feature, Photoshop, 56
scalability, 13
"scale" button, Properties panel, 248
Scene panel, 139
scenes
    defined, 69–70
    stories, 6–8
    transitioning, 146–148
Scheider, Roy, 147
Schindler's List (1993), 11, 106
Schumacher, Joel, 148
Schwarzenegger, Arnold, 148
"scratch" audio track, 88
screen text, 65
seamless scrolling background, 180
Séquential Couleur Avec Memoire video format, 62–63
Selection Tool
    to adjust curves of stroke, 36
    adjusting shading with, 203
    creating varied lines, 44
sequences, 69
Séquential Couleur Avec Memoire video format, 62–63